Homestyles

how-to projects,
room designs,
and awareness activities
that build feelings
into your home

by curt lamb

illustrations by deborah pierce

St. Martin's Press · New York

dedicated to Robin

Copyright © 1979 by Curt Lamb.
All rights reserved. For information write:
St. Martin's Press, 175 5th Avenue, New York,
N.Y., 10010.
Manufactured in the United States of America

A Jeffrey Weiss book

Graphic design by Booth Simpson Designers

Typesetting by Technical Composition

Cover Photo by Sam Sweezy, Back Cover Photo by Nick Wheeler

Library of Congress Cataloging in Publication Data

Lamb, Curt; Homestyle; 1. Interior Decoration;
I. Title; NK2110.L33; 747 '.8 '83; 78-21201;
ISBN 0-312-38899-3; ISBN 0-312-38900-0 pbk.;

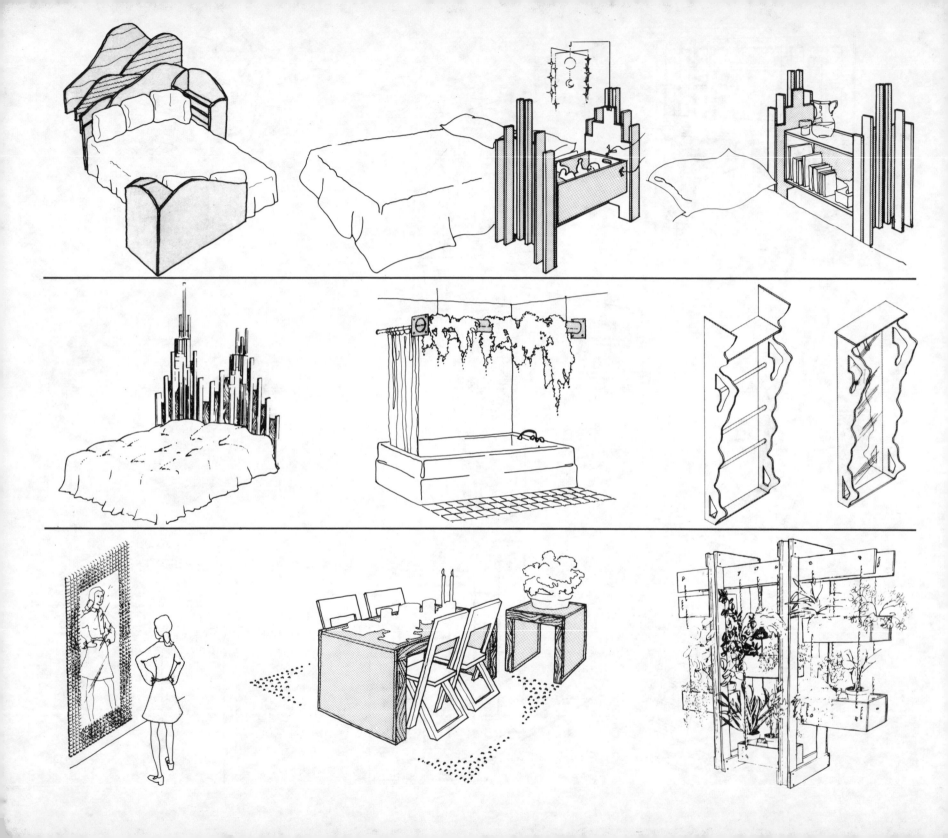

Contents

How I Came to Write This Book

The ideas for this book took shape during several years of work with a group doing architectural and urban design projects. Over time, we realized how seldom the actual users of a place were involved in the design process. We resolved to work at designing *with* people rather than *for* them.

Gradually we developed and tested a number of techniques for engaging the people who inhabit an environment, in decisions concerning it.

Whenever possible, we created a small "family" of users for each member of a design team to meet with on a regular basis. A series of activities was developed for these meetings that allowed the participants' deep-felt hopes and fears to surface. These sessions almost always generated the kind of sharing that fills your heart with warmth and your mind with ideas.

During this work, it became clear that homes are the places where people have the most real control over their environment. In the larger world, buildings seem to be getting ever bigger and more impersonal. At home, we can still make a place that expresses and supports the person we really are.

I began to wonder if people were getting the kind of assistance in fixing up their homes that we were providing users of our architectural projects. In popular books and magazines I found plenty of practical advice on home maintenance and improvement (and lots of sales pitches masquerading as practical advice). Most prominent, of course, were all those photographs of impeccably designed rooms and pages of advice about making your home just like them. The hidden message of these photos was evident, however: You can't make your home beautiful without professional help.

There were many useful books to guide the search for self-understanding and growth in areas like health, interpersonal relationships, and spiritual awareness. I resolved to create a book that would deal with creating a place to live in the same spirit.

For several years I collected ideas and inspiration from friends and colleagues. The year I spent actually writing the manuscript and preparing the drawings was filled with many wonderful events in my own home. Deborah and I moved from an apartment to a new home shared with several good friends. Together we created a new set of rooms to nurture our new lives as a family and household. Our son, Robin, was born in our new bedroom and another space was transformed into his first nest. The basement garage of our new home became a woodshop where many of the ideas presented here were tested. We built a "Social Bed" for our housemate Carolyn. Everyone began eating under a "Fellowship Light." In a beautiful study, whose windows were often piled to the sashlock with snow, Deborah and I worked on the drawings and text presented here. We hope that the results will bring you the kind of appreciation of your own place that we found in putting it together.

As you will soon see, I borrowed freely from scores of other authors and illustrators who have observed life at home. The book owes much of its spirit to the wit and vision of these people.

On a more immediate level, many friends and colleagues gave generously of their insight, support and professional skill, from the initial conception of the book to its final production. Among these, I would like to give special thanks, to Jeff Weiss, Booth Simpson, Neil Klineman, Kathryn Sumpter, Ron Alex, Harvey Brown, Peter Lorenz, Jerry Simon, Jack Howe, Virginia Reiser, Steve Carr, Carolyn Sagov, Nick Wheeler, Robert Mergedichian, Sam Sweezy, Chuck Plaisted, Richard Krauss, David and Diane Raphael, William Lam, John Holbrook, and Steve Tilly.

Several organizations extended support to the project as well: The Boston Architectural Center, Arrowstreet Inc., The Loeb Library of the Harvard Graduate School of Design, and the Environmental Design Group.

At several points along the way, my parents made available their insight as professional journalists. My sisters, Deslonde and Candy, gave helpful comments concerning the section on children's places.

Day by day involvement in the crises and celebrations of making a book happen was the assignment of my new household: Carolyn, Neil, Stanley, Marjy, Debbie, Daniel and Alex.

Homes from the Heart

1

Home is where the heart is. The computer analyst knows it. The cross-country truck driver knows it. The people wandering from room to room at a party know it. When the working day is through, when the partygoers head out into the darkened street, everyone is heading home. Even astronauts must go home.

This, we say, is the place I live. This is where I rest and sleep. This is where I gather my strength, make plans, prepare. Here is where my family will be. Here is where my heart lies.

This place, then, should be as full of meaning as our lives. It should show care. It should be complex and simple, peaceful and lively. It should accept us for who we really are, not shame us with identities conjured up by furniture advertisers.

Rooms and Feelings

Links between rooms and feelings are not always cultivated, but the potential is always there, waiting to be tapped. It is this potential that gives our homes such a profound influence on our lives. Appropriately designed living space is constantly reminding us of good moments from the past, calling up different sides of our personality, providing refuge from the world, and encouraging joyful experience of the present. Getting these interactions right is what we mean by "feeling at home" where we live.

Homes affect us in many ways. Psychiatrists often report that depression first appears as bad feelings about the environment—rooms grow oppressive, colors turn lifeless, walls close in. Happiness and positive feelings are frequently registered in good feelings about the environment as well—we notice the sun pouring in a window, or appreciate the warmth of a shower, or just feel good sitting at the kichen table.

The places we live can limit our activities. If doing carpentry means taking over the kitchen, you will probably not get beyond projects that can be accomplished between meals. Everyone needs quiet time alone, but most people are shy about insisting upon it. If your space is such that getting time alone requires constant policing of other people's presence, you will not be alone very much.

Environments can promote activities as well. Creating a place that celebrates letter writing will probably make you a better letter writer. Making your kitchen a better place to cook can improve your cooking. If you want to develop photographs, you need a darkroom.

Environments reinforce our identity. Like clothing, they are a visible expression of the way we see ourselves. Truly responsive environments offer little resistance to the artifacts of ourselves and our friends. Space is easily made for children's paintings, valued objects, craftwork, and evidences of accomplishments outside the home. A kind of gentle chaos often prevails in homes which reflect their owners' identity. Frequently the least ordered parts of our living space are the most dynamic. A well-used project area, for example, reveals work in progress, and hints at projects past and future.

As a living space responds to the unpredictable flow of activities and impulses, smaller-scale orderings take on new meaning as well. Only a true music lover will take the time to order a shelf of albums by composer or artist.

Rooms also have deep cultural and psychological associations that can enrich our lives. Some of these are rooted in our childhood experience with houses—the parents' bedroom we entered so respectfully, or the kitchen seen as an extension of the cookie jar.

Other meanings come from our history as a people. Our living rooms, for example, have roots in the Victorian parlor, described by a turn-of-the-century architect as "a comparatively small reception room used for the visitor who calls in the way of mere ceremony, or in the way of business, or on a single occasion without the immediate prospect of intimate acquaintance with the family." Other connotations emerge from the nature of interior space itself. Gaston Bachelard has chronicled many of these in his book, *The Poetics of Space* (Beacon Press). He describes the cellar, for example, as the "dark entity" of the house. "The cellar dreamer knows that the walls of the cellar are buried walls, walls with earth behind them. . . . In the attic, the day's experiences can always efface the fears of night. In the cellar, darkness prevails both day and night, and even when we are carrying a lighted candle, we see shadows dancing on the dark walls."

Most of the chapters to follow take a particular room of the house as a theme. You needn't have a lot of rooms to realize the ideas of this book, however. Living in an efficiency apartment, or even a small house, simply means you must bring a variety of feelings into each space. Focusing on the emotional meaning of a room clarifies the task of coping with cramped quarters. If you are the kind of person, for example, who is warm and relaxed in relating to people but organized and efficient when it comes to work, there would be real loss if these two personalities were homogenized into a single space that was too spartan for friendly conversation and too chaotic for work. Lighting, furniture placement, partial barriers, and other techniques can be used to zone a space for separate moods or selves.

Many forces in contemporary life keep home and heart distant. Recent trends suggest that owning a home is out of the question for increasing numbers of people. A study by the Joint Center for Urban Studies reports that the number of people who can afford a home has dropped recently by nearly half. The quality of newly constructed private residences seems to be going up, but only because three quarters of the population have given up on buying a new house at all.

The environments being constructed for the majority of us are increasingly smaller, plainer, and less evocative of any history. Of every six new homes constructed today, one is a mobile home and three more use industrialized construction and preassembly techniques.

People who live in apartments have grown to expect little support from their architecture. Most apartment rooms are interchangeable, with low ceilings, square walls, and small windows. Landlords have veto power over most efforts to personalize a rented home. In the ominous words of the standard contract, "The Lessee shall not paint, decorate or otherwise embellish and/or change and shall not make nor suffer any additions or alterations to be made in or to the leased premises without the prior written consent of the Lessor."

People who decide to purchase a home find bankers in a comparable position of power. Many bankers will underwrite only hard-core improvements like plumbing and structural repair, not gestures like installing a greenhouse window or revealing a brick wall.

Architects and interior designers are involved in less than two percent of all new home construction and renovation. When they do participate, they rarely initiate the kind of personal exploration of feelings that this book encourages. Interior designers tell each other horror stories about getting entangled in their clients' lives—like the one about the husband who tore down the bedroom partition that his wife had directed the architect to install. Out of sheer self-defense, these professionals have stopped inquiring very deeply about their clients' hopes, fears, and feelings.

Not all the forces that distance us from our homes are external. People spend more time away from home than they used to. Vacations are longer, excursions to restaurants more frequent. Women, who have traditionally taken the lead in home improvements, are working in increasing numbers. More and more people find themselves setting up house alone (the number of young adults living alone increased 134% between 1970 and 1978).

There is ever less permanence in homes. The average American family moves once every five years, a terribly brief span for associations to take root and grow. Environments, like friendships, need time to age. The people and places we remember most dearly are those that have stuck with us through good times and bad.

Using This Book

The story that unfolds as you use this book will be your story. Many of the exercises, like "Dream Catching" or "Your Parents' Party," can only be completed with your participation. Each chapter contains several pencil-and-paper exercises to help you understand the special ways you think about and use space. Surveys like "Where Is Your Living Room" and "Bedroom Efficiency Review" will help you appreciate your home as it now stands and find imaginative ways to improve it.

What follows is a bit like a scrapbook as well as a step-by-step manual. It got that way because it is natural to fix up a place in bits and pieces as you experiment with new ideas, buy a piece of furniture or some new material, and continue daydreaming about the future. Because of this format, you can open the book to almost any page to begin.

Behind this scrapbook quality, however, is an order that will help you organize your thinking about fixing up a house or apartment. Each chapter is divided into the same kinds of sections. The first section contains "fantasy explorations" and "surveys" which help you turn inward toward the discovery of feelings and ideas about yourself and the place you live. These are followed by a middle section containing "goals/solutions" and "inspirations," which begin the translation of needs and aspirations into specific recommendations for change. Finally,

a major portion of each chapter is given over to "how-to projects" and "room designs" providing step-by-step instructions for home improvements relating to themes of the chapter. The next few pages describe each of these sections in more detail and give a general introduction to the home fix-up approach we will be taking.

Inspirations

Inspirations are examples of places which might be quite different from the one you want to create but which have a particular quality you really like. We have included several pages of inspirations in most of the chapters to follow.

The best way to use inspirations is to invent your own. Suppose, for example, that you spend a lot of time cooking and want your kitchen to look more professional, less dainty. Ask yourself for an inspiration, a place that really expresses what it would mean for a kitchen to be professional. You might remember the time you toured the kitchen at your favorite restaurant and found huge stainless steel pots, tile floors, polished metal counters, utensils hanging everywhere, a mechanical stirring machine as big as a robot, enormous stoves, etc. This is definitely different from any kitchen that would fit in your house, but maybe there are ideas here that could be transformed for your own use: Why not use stainless steel cookware, or install a tile counter, or display an outsized mixer.

Inspirations don't have to be realistic to work. Often humorous or improbable ones will give you the best ideas. If you want your home to feel cozy, think about a really snug place, like a cave or log cabin. If you want your living room to be ultra-modern, find photographs of space capsules.

The particular inspirations we have included in each chapter may or may not speak directly to your own needs. They are there, however, to encourage you to reflect on the kind of crazy ideas which are often the source of true inspiration about home fix-up.

Ad Hoc Inspirations

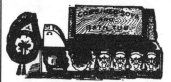

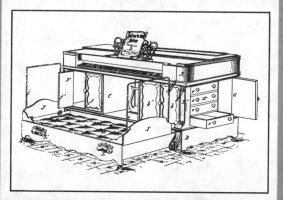

Four tributes to the home inventor: **1.** A sofa-bath tub, complete with 18 gallon tub, improved heating device, waste water attachment, and rubber apron. **2.** A bed for socializing as well as sleeping. **3.** A two-story home heating center. **4.** A piano which converts into a bedroom set.

Home Inspirations

1

2

3

4

5

Knowing which places evoke feelings of home for you will help bring this quality to your own house or apartment. Here are several entries in our collective scrapbook of home memories: **1.** An English cottage. **2.** A seaside villa in the special vocabulary of 20th century design. **3.** Cave dwellings of the kind that biblical scholars say surrounded Bethlehem and provided a manger home for western religion. **4.** A one-room log cabin. **5.** A seaside gate lodge in stone. **6.** A small castle in Wales.

6

Fantasy Explorations

Our many selves are the most important resource we bring to fixing up our space. The first part of each chapter is devoted to revealing the sides of our personality that are most involved with a particular room of the house.

In thinking about home design, many people consult only their "tasteful" self. Unfortunately, this is one of our least sympathetic selves—always making judgments and putting other people down. Style setters have always encouraged the "tasteful" approach to environment to make themselves indispensable to clients who mistrust their own judgment. But all of our selves can play the game of designing the places we live. Each of us has a private and a social self, for example. The one might be indulged by a curtained four-poster bed or reading nook, the other by creation of a special place for outdoor cookouts.

Fantasizing is a kind of adult play, a conscious shaping and enjoying of the free flow of your own imagination. It is thus an excellent technique for liberating the resources of memory and invention we have been describing.

Fantasies can be used for heightening self-awareness, improving relationships within groups, creating understanding within families, and much more. If you want to explore some of these broader dimensions of fantasy, spend an evening with a friend completing some of the fantasy exercises in Herbert Otto's book *Fantasy Encounter Games*

(Harper and Row, Publishers). Most of all, however, fantasizing is just plain fun.

For many people, fantasizing about their homes has become associated with a desperate search for status through interior design. This kind of longing brings anxiety, not pleasure. Don't get stuck fantasizing about a Persian rug. Go for broke. Imagine that you are a Persian Prince, surrounded by a desert environment of rugs and cloth.

Playing with inner-generated fantasy will help you avoid having your fantasies directed by the advertising industry. Fantasizing beyond your means can be healthy. The problem arises only when envy and pretense take over.

Bachelard tells of the English writer Ducis, who wrote a series of poems describing his fantasy country cottage —flower beds, kitchen garden, little wood, etc.—even though he lived in a city apartment. Ever since he was young, Ducis had hoped to have a small country house, so at the age of 70, he gave one to himself on his authority as a poet. By writing about these places, he made them a part of his life. Once, Ducis reports, a country fellow, taken by the poems, volunteered his services as overseer of the estate for a place to live and whatever wages might seem fair.

Some of the fantasies in this book (like "Your Parents' Party") will help you understand the importance of history and tradition in your environment. Others ("Relaxing Fantasy") explore physical sensations. Still others ("Nighttime Spirituality" or "Moods and Foods") explore themes suggested by rooms of the house.

Fantasies can help you decide how you want your home to be. If you want to know whether your kitchen should be old-fashioned or modern, invent a fantasy about each approach. If you think you want your bathroom to be more sensual, try the "Royal Bath" fantasy.

Carrying out fantasy exercises is easy, whether you're alone or with a friend. First read the brief instructions (aloud if you are with others). Because full relaxation is important to clear the mind and prepare it for internal messages, you will want to find a quiet place where you won't be interrupted. Get comfortable. Shut your eyes and relax. Concentrate for several minutes on letting the muscles of your body go limp. Inhale deeply. As you exhale, direct the breath to your legs, torso, chest, and head in succession. Turn your mind slowly to the fantasy at hand. Take as long as you wish. Put yourself directly into the experience. Let it unfold like a story. Turning your attention to details is the best way to get involved. Imagine the expressions on people's faces, the clothing you and other people are wearing, what is hung on the walls, etc. When you have completed the fantasy, slowly open your eyes. If you are with a friend, wait until you have both finished and recount your fantasies to each other.

Fantasies About Home

Roots

Your great-great-grandparents have invited you back in time to meet them. Imagine who these people might be. Enter the town in which they live, and approach their house. Have a conversation with them in which they tell you about their friends and the activities they enjoy. Let them take you on a tour of the special places and things in their home.

Home from School

You are in grade school. Classes have just let out on a Friday afternoon. Jacket in hand, you run out of the building. Imagine walking home, arriving at your house or apartment, entering, and beginning an activity there. What is the weather like? When do you catch the first glimpse of your home? Does the front door open easily?

Surveys

We have included several pencil-and-paper surveys in each chapter. These have been designed to open up new ways of thinking about rooms of the house rather than identify particular solutions. They can thus be enjoyed whether or not you are planning to spend a lot of time changing your space. In the chapter on kitchens, for example, we have included surveys called "Eating Style," and "Paper Cooking," but none that ask you to list improvement priorities or tools to buy. Priorities and tools can be postponed until you have some concrete ideas about what you want to do.

Decay/Renewal Survey

Being delighted by a place is partly being in a delightful place and partly being our delightful self. Being bored by a place is almost always being our bored self. This exercise can help you understand how changing your attitude about a place can often affect your enjoyment of it.

Three events are listed in the chart below. Each of them can be an indication of "decay" or "renewal," depending on your point of view. In the spaces provided, list positive and negative responses you might have.

Event	Reasons the event might be positive	Reasons the event might be negative
Your grandmother gives you an outsized, tufted, Victorian chair.		
You are forced to leave your house or apartment for one month.		
A carpenter friend decides he can only pay back a loan from you with six months of carpentry.		

Home Story Survey

The story of your life is written in the environments you have inhabited. My grandmother devoted a year to writing a family history for posterity. What emerged was a book filled with detailed descriptions of all the houses where she had ever lived. "In 1921," she wrote, "we moved to Washington, D.C. We had a nice screened porch on this house, and a large ice cream freezer that we made good use of. That winter there was a very heavy snowstorm causing milk to be rationed. People had to show their children to the milkman to get their quota. . . ."

It is appropriate to begin by looking back. In this survey, you create your own dwelling history by listing all the homes where you have ever lived.

YOUR AGE	0		10		20		30		40

Mark an "X" here each time that you changed homes.

Darken in a cluster of squares, one for each room of the house.

Mark an "X" here if you changed cities in the move.

Write as much of the address as you can remember here.

To complete the survey, simply mark an "X" at your age each time you changed homes. Directly below the "X" draw a tiny diagram of the house or apartment by making a cluster of squares, one for each room. Count only major rooms of the house. If there were two floors in the house,

make a little diagram for each floor. Don't worry about stairs and closets. The idea is to give an idea of how big each place was. In the space below that, mark an "X" if moving into this house or apartment meant moving to a new city or town. Finally, along the bottom, list the addresses of all your homes.

When you have finished, stand back and look at the story told by our time-line of dwellings. Are there patterns? Did your moves take you closer to nature, or farther from it? Does it seem obvious from the pattern so far what your future homes will be like?

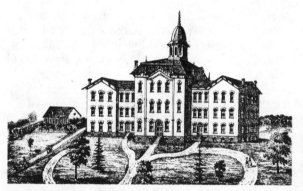

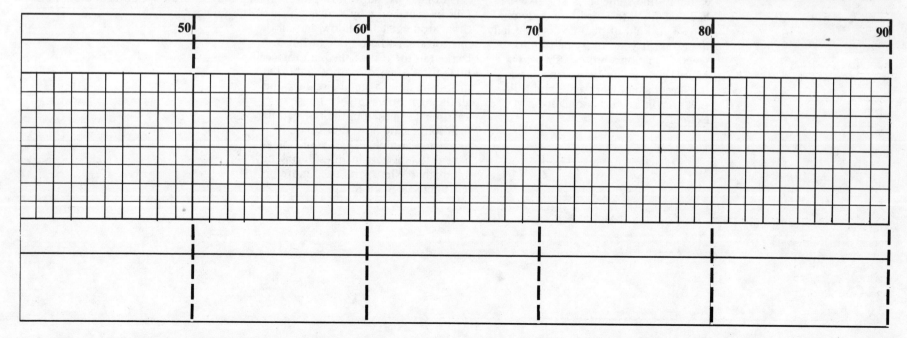

Home Plan

The main reason to draw a plan of your house or apartment is to appreciate it in a new way. Sketching up such a plan will give you a new perspective on your home as you find out how thick walls are, where closets fit into each other, how circulation spaces are laid out, etc. A plan inevitably captures a miniaturized essense of a place. You will find yourself looking at it again and again.

Plans are very useful for drawing up alternative arrangements for your space. You can make a dozen copies of your plan for this purpose, or buy some tracing paper to lay over your original drawing. A wide variety of furniture arrangements will quickly suggest themselves. Try a diagonal arrangement. Imagine where you would place new elements, like storage cabinets, a built-in sofa, or a breakfast nook.

If you want to rearrange furniture in your present home, or if you are thinking of moving to a new one, cut out pieces of cardboard to represent each piece of your furniture and move them around on your plan. You will almost certainly find some surprises, like the bed that fits into a bedroom only one way. This kind of planning is especially important if you are trying to put several functions into one space. On paper, you can invent dozens of ways to place a small workspace and a sitting area in a living room, for example.

Circulation problems emerge clearly on a plan. You might find it interesting to draw a circulation diagram of your entire home. Take a copy of your plan and draw a line on it for all the ways that you walk from room to room. If you use a particular path a lot, draw several lines. Every house, you will discover, has certain natural circulation paths. Keeping these paths clear will ease movement. In some rooms, however, you may want to block these paths to slow people down and give the room a feeling of depth.

To understand more about home lighting, try the following exercise with two copies of your plan:

On one copy, show how natural light falls in your home by drawing a small circle around each window and all the interior areas where sunlight falls. Darken in the rest of the plan to accentuate these areas of natural light. On the other, draw a small circle around all the light bulbs in your house or apartment. Darken in the rest of this plan to indicate how your house is illuminated at night. Does your home have different personalities during day and night? What parts need more or less light?

Drawing a plan of your house is relatively easy. We have included a grid to help you get started. Each square on this grid represents one foot. Most houses and apartments will fit on this sheet, but be careful to locate your drawing so it makes best use of the page. If you live in a larger place, or a two-story house, you may have to continue drawing on a second sheet.

Use a tape measure or yardstick to measure the overall dimensions of a room first. Draw this overall shape on your plan (in pencil so you can erase easily). Locate windows, doors, and radiators. Give walls their proper thickness—about 6 inches. An easy way to draw windows and doors is shown.

Draw a plan of your house or apartment on this page.
Each square on this page represents one foot.

draw walls like this. doors like this →

and windows like this →

Goals/ Solutions

The goals/solutions pages of each chapter begin the process of establishing specific goals for a space and translating these into detailed proposals for change. Each of these pages is filled with concrete solutions, sorted according to a variety of goals which help you focus on the larger purposes you have in mind. In setting goals for a place, it is useful to think of planning for feelings, activities, convenience, and safety.

Plan for Feelings

Bad feelings can compromise our efforts to improve a place. Sometimes these are easy to spot—perhaps a place feels dark, cluttered, or shabby. Sometimes a room just seems ordinary, and you find yourself avoiding it. Many things can contribute to bad feelings. Sometimes a place is associated with unpleasant experiences or people. Rooms tend to get identified with a certain period in our life, particularly the time when we last fixed them up. Over time, our own growth and that of the room go in different directions—a rug frays, colors fade, the legs of a chair wobble. A distance grows between us and the place.

The more contact we can make with our feelings concerning a place, the easier it is to set new goals for it. You will find negative feelings translating naturally into positive goals. If you feel that a room is neglected, caring for it is the logical goal. If a room feels too dark, then brightening it up is the answer.

Discover your positive feelings about a place. Too often we think of our rooms as adversaries, filled only with problems. Fixing up a place then becomes an impossible game of trying to make low ceilings seem higher or high ceilings lower. Allow your space to be itself. You will find that every room has its own unique properties.

Plan for Activities

There are many mismatches of activity and space in the typical home. Bedrooms are often underused, with children, who need more space, getting cramped quarters while their parents have a bedroom with much wasted area. Bathrooms are usually undersized; dining rooms, too big. Kitchens tend to be called on for many functions and almost always get overcrowded in the process. Most homes have too little workspace, whether for sewing, desk work, or car repair.

There is always room for improvement in matching activities to space. Don't accept traditional ideas about what should go on in a room. Think about eating in your living room, putting an office in the bedroom, or using the bathroom as a greenhouse.

Plan for Maintenance and Safety

American homes are not designed for ease of maintenance. Paint and plaster are the biggest offenders. Exterior paint, for example, does not extend the life of a house significantly and results in a costly repainting job every five years. There are steps you can take in designing a space that will make it easier to care for—choosing a floor color that does not show dirt or building a kick space under kitchen cabinets.

Safety is a real issue in home design as well. Researchers have documented over 20,000 deaths a year in home accidents. If there are children or older people in your household it is imperative that you take steps to recognize the special safety problems they face (an excellent government publication, *A Design Guide for Home Safety,* discusses these issues in detail). We have included "Efficiency Checklists" in the chapters on bathrooms, bedrooms, and kitchens to help you see how your rooms measure up in terms of safety and convenience.

Once you have a clear sense of your goals for a space, you can begin thinking about solutions. Just as goals should relate to feelings and activities, so solutions can involve changes in yourself and your activities, as well as your space.

Changing how and where you do activities can solve many environmental problems. If your bedroom feels unsatisfactory, consider changing the way you get dressed. If this is an activity you love, create a dressing alcove with full length mirrors and a place to sit down. If it's not, minimize the space dedicated to it by moving half your clothes into long-term storage and buying a bureau that will fit inside your closet.

How-to Projects

All the chapters contain step-by-step instructions for several do-it-yourself projects. Each of these projects was designed to highlight the drama of a particular room. The glowing shape of the Fellowship Light, for example, casts a quiet glow on the eaters below and a spotlight on the food being served. You will always have a special feeling about a project you have worked on yourself. Its story becomes your story—the board that wouldn't fit, the extra coat of paint, the midnight effort to wrap things up.

All year long our homes provide us unstintingly with respite and pleasure. A kind of grateful homage is thus involved when we return the gift of attention and care. There is always a spirit of hopefulness when we rent a floor polisher or start work on a piece of furniture. In patching walls and painting we finally take the time to get acquainted with a room on *its* terms. On these days, we understand that the more we care for our environment, the more it will care for us.

Almost any skill can be turned to good account in fixing up your place. If you take pictures, create a photo mural. If you can weld, make an iron bed. If you enjoy cooking, decorate walls with the tools of your trade. For those uneasy with aesthetics, there is always plumbing—defined by Norman Mailer as "the prevention of treachery in closed systems."

Most of the projects in this book involve woodworking, an excellent skill for interior design because it can create changes as small as a picture frame and as large as a house. Construction details have been kept simple to keep projects within reach of beginners. The only power tools required are a 1/4-inch drill and a saber saw, both available in sturdy models for under $25. The best way to get a handle on carpentry is to do a project with a friend who has a little more experience than you.

Several of the projects we have included use Tri-Wall, an extra-strong, corrugated cardboard, 1/2 inch thick, that comes in large sheets. This is a wonderfully versatile material for home projects. It is easily cut with a saber saw (a toothless blade eliminates sawdust) and bonds tight with white glue. With several sheets of Tri-Wall you can manufacture an endles array of storage boxes, children's furniture, lamps, and household art. The temporary quality of the material opens up a whole range of projects that don't seem serious enough for wood. The Workshop for Learning Things will supply you with an instruction manual and the name of a local Tri-Wall supplier (see Sources, p. 204).

Sewing is a wonderful skill to use in fixing up a home. Several of the projects we have included gain their personality from the fabric you select for them, and there is a virtual explosion of fabric designs to choose from these days, from photographic prints to impressionist patterns. Between curtains, upholstery, and framed fabric, almost any room can be given a new identity through selection of fabrics alone. For one third the price of a new living room chair you can recover an older one in a striking contemporary fabric. An overstuffed chair with straight lines can be slipcovered in less than a day: Pin a fabric on it inside-out, stitch the pin-basted seams, and turn the cover right-side-out.

25

Often a very small project can have a big impact on your space. "There is nothing too little for so little a creature as man," wrote Samuel Johnson. A favorite piece of jewelry can be used to set the color scheme for an entire bedroom. Display of a few photographs can bring a whole world of memories to a place. Several years ago we moved to a new city for nine months. We were able to fit all the possessions and furnishings we needed into our van. Perhaps the most important box we packed was the one filled with our "symbols"—a banner someone had sewed for our wedding, several books of photographs, a treasured piece of cloth, a wall map. . . . With these installed, anyplace could become our home.

Before you undertake a do-it-yourself project, think carefully about how long it will take. Don't underestimate the importance of shorter projects, those requiring a day or weekend to complete. The timeless way of building has always been to construct things a little at a time, adjusting as you go. The ad hoc quality that results is often more appealing than the order created by more full-time, full-speed efforts.

In planning even small projects, remember that both purchasing supplies and doing final finish work can consume up to half a day. Try to buy materials for a weekend project during the week so you can plunge in first thing Saturday morning. It is always best to start work when stores are open so you can exchange materials and pick up extra tools without setting back your progress.

Make doing a project enjoyable. If it involves new skills or interests, buy a new book on the topic. Visit a store that specializes in the appropriate equipment. Treat yourself to one new tool each time you undertake a project. Planning can be an enjoyable part of a project. If you are painting, play with big swatches of color before you decide on one (use a Color-aid swatch book, available at any art supply store). When we painted our kitchen, we made a cardboard cutout of the four walls and painted this first. This miniature paint job became a natural decoration to hang in the room when we finished the full-scale one. Make the environment for doing a project pleasant. Consider working outdoors or moving a set of stereo speakers into the workshop. Invite friends over to help out.

Room Designs

Many opportunities open up when you begin to think in terms of an entire room instead of a single project. The final section of each chapter thus contains ideas for designing rooms as a whole. Because environments are almost always experienced one room at a time, thinking in terms of rooms allows us to establish important unities within our environment. This generally emerges as a need to have things "go together" or "match." Professional decorators often prey on this impulse and spend large amounts of time and money creating obsessively coordinated furniture and decoration schemes. Underlying the search for unity, however, are basic human impulses. Unified environments create places of order and meaning in a world where chaos often seems to hold the upper hand.

There is something in the notion that beauty thrives on order. Order within a room helps highlight the beauty of special objects or places it contains. Keeping furniture and decoration to a bare minimum will accentuate the architectural qualities of a space and allow the natural world outside to become a part of the space within.

Each chapter includes several room designs—original sketches of places which express some of the themes developed in rooms of the house. Each is accompanied by detailed descriptions of important design features. Although their idiosyncracies will probably keep you from wanting to copy them exactly, these rooms should encourage you to plunge ahead with your own ideas.

2 Bedroom Spirituality

Unlatch the front door and let the cat slip in. Shut the door and bolt it tight. Take a last tour of each room in the house to turn off the lights and shut the windows. Lock the back door. Climb darkened stairs to the second floor; enter the bedroom. Open the window for some night air; lie down and look around.

It's hard to see much of the room. The bright print on the wall has turned somber. Darker areas where furniture should be, and the shrouded ceiling, are barely discernible. As the curtains rustle in front of the window, our minds begin to drift as surely as the cloth. Are bedrooms empty places, or gateways to deeper realms of experience? Does consciousness drift away here or is this its temple?

Many of life's most spiritual experiences are associated with the bedroom. Most of us were conceived and many of us brought into the world here. If we pray at home, it is probably at our bedside. Bedroom walls witness sexual intimacy and encompass a vast dream world each night. Death, though unfamiliar with the rest of the house, knows its path to the bedroom.

Bedroom events like these have spiritual dimensions which have defined religious experience for millennia. Because the post-industrial age has placed organized religion on the defensive our age has the special opportunity of recreating the spiritual dimensions of human life from personal experience. It is an exhilarating time for spiritual growth. A new globalism has now made the spiritual insights of other cultures and eras accessible to us. For some this has meant a search for contemporary relevance in older Christian and Eastern religious traditions. Others have found meaning in physical disciplines as varied as yoga, karate, and the "inner game of tennis." Instruction in many forms of meditative relaxation is now widely available. A new openness to sexual fantasy has enabled many to experience greater physical and emotional intimacy. Some are turning to serious investigation of psychic phenomena. Others have been introduced to new forms of consciousness by family physicians who see their value in mitigating the life stresses that contribute to such problems as hypertension and heart disease.

Most of these approaches to understanding turn us away from the larger institutions of society toward more personal experience. Our homes thus become the de facto temples of this new spirituality; and within our homes, bedrooms become the most appropriate places for undertaking its activities and showing evidence of its fruits.

This chapter, then, focuses on what I call "bedroom spirituality" and how it can be reflected in the nature of the place you sleep. In the next few pages are presented some first hand accounts of home-based spiritual experience. Several exercises for promoting awareness follow, including two surveys of your bedroom and how it functions. Several goals for fixing up your bedroom are matched against practical ideas for change. The chapter concludes with several projects and room designs aimed at bringing out the inner life of your bedroom.

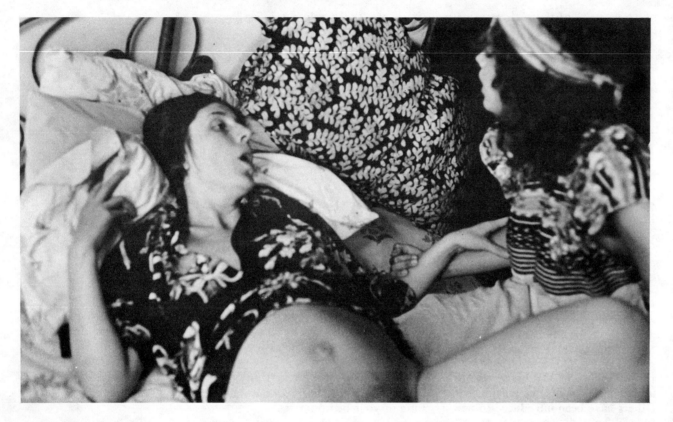

Birth

The first manifestation of bedroom spirituality is birth. Although most of our grandparents were born at home, their sons and daughters were told that home birth was old-fashioned. Computerized monitoring, access to emergency care, anesthesia, and specialists of all kinds formed part of the new argument for birth in the hospital.

Indeed, modern medical practice has greatly reduced rates of maternal mortality through understanding and control of infection. It now appears, however, that each new technique for institutional management of birth brings increased risk to the baby. Emphasis on hospital births is the primary reason that babies born in America are more likely to die than in 14 other countries of the world. Anesthetics used during labor keep the mother from working with the natural rhythms of birth and thus initiate a string of other medical interventions. Drugs used during labor depress the baby's life functions. Institutionalized birth separates husbands from wives, and babies from mothers.

The bedroom, by contrast, enables the spiritual dimensions of natural birth to flower. Support from father and friends can transform pain into exhilarating hard work. Only five percent of women with adequate prenatal care require hospital delivery. Statistics indicate that home birth reduces the need for surgery and drugs, decreases maternal complications, reduces infant mortality, and improves the health of the newborn.

The first-hand home-birth account here is excerpted from *Spiritual Midwifery* (The Book Publishing Company), written by midwives who have attended over 1,000 births on The Farm, a collective community in Tennessee. Midwives on The Farm encourage links between birth and other forms of bedroom spirituality, like sex. "Over and over again," states one, "I've seen that the best way to get a baby out is by getting it on with your old man. That loving, sexy vibe is what puts the baby in there, and it's what gets it out too."

A Bedroom Birth

Roberta: *I woke up around two o'clock Friday morning with light rushes. I felt like I was going to have my baby. I called Mary Louise and she came over to check me out. Joel and I decided to hang out together. We had a good time; it felt like we were preparing for our new baby. . . .*

I decided I wanted to get up and do something; I felt like working would bring on the rushes. I think what did it was mopping the floors. . . . Around ten o'clock . . . the rushes were heavy and very regular. It seemed to be taking a long time to open up. I thought it would take me forever to get to ten centimeters. . . .

Cara: *I got a call that Roberta was having heavy rushes. . . . When I got there, she was writhing with each rush and shaking. . . . Joel was sitting beside her looking worried. The whole scene was a bit grim for baby having. I got them kissing, hugging and had Roberta really grab on to Joel and squeeze him. . . .*

Roberta: *As the rushes got more intense, I felt more panic. At first I thought I couldn't go on, maybe even stop. But I knew that was ridiculous. What kept me together was having my family around me. . . . As morning came on, the rushes got more intense. I decided to get to work. By then I had learned how to do it and I felt more on top of the rushes. . . . Within an hour my cervix opened up the whole way and the baby was ready to come out. . . . It felt like everyone in the room and in our house was pushing with me.*

. . . On the next push the head popped out. . . . The next pushes brought the rest of the body out. . . .

Mary: *The baby came out and felt very floppy. . . . I knew he was in there—he even opened his eyes and looked at us, but his lungs were really full of junk and he wasn't breathing or crying at all. . . .*

Cara: *It was beginning to feel heavy. I took him because I had seen some really hard starters and it felt like this one was going to take all we had.*

Marilyn: *Mary and Cara said, "We're going to have to help him out." It was amazing tantric touch—as they were giving him mouth-to-mouth and oxygen, and slapping him. . . . Their arms and mouths were so intertwined and moving so fast they were giving their combined all to the baby, you couldn't tell whose was whose.*

Cara: *As I squeezed his heart, there was a time when he was grunting very shallow and I saw this pink aura of light come out of his heart and fill his upper body with energy. At the same time it filled up my heart and all these rushes of ecstasy were going from my heart to my head. Then he cried. . . . I looked at Joel and he looked . . . very calm, but there were tears in his eyes and I knew how heavy it had been for him. I felt the same way.*

Marilyn: *I could feel . . . one God-mind reaching out to this baby—breathing for him, then, finally breathing with him as he started. We were all crying and laughing, so fulfilled in our hearts that he was doing it, so grateful for this new child.*

Spiritual Midwifery (Revised Edition, Ina May Gaskin, copyright 1978, The Book Publishing Company, Summertown Tenn.)

Sex

For many people, sex is the most familiar aspect of bedroom spirituality. The bedroom is ideally suited for love's rituals. It is private. When the bedroom door is shut, people will not enter. Windows are generally curtained to provide seclusion from the outside. Bedcovers provide a final privacy for those who can't trust security until they feel it. The bed is as versatile a field of love as the house provides. It is soft, clean, and familiar with our bodies. The bed's simple form accentuates the inventiveness of love's positions.

Other bedroom activities nurture our sexy selves more indirectly, subtly transforming interest into desire. Here we store the clothes, scents, and amulets to make us more desirable. Here, just as regularly, we discard those devices for soft bedclothes, or nothing at all. And here, finally, we fall into those innocent embraces of sleep which hover suggestively between oblivion and arousal.

The bedroom as a place speaks to us of love. On another level, however, it is the deeper connection between inner and outer awareness suggested by bedroom activities which consecrates this place to sensual pleasure. It is not privacy which arouses us, after all, but the subconscious needs and impulses which are liberated when we are sure no one is looking. The forms of consciousness implied by beds are what seduce us. Beds suggest positions of vulnerability and trust which open us to love and connect us with the spontaneous sexual fantasizing which flowers during sleep.

Sleep and Dreams

In sleeping and dreaming we encounter the most pervasive domain of bedroom spirituality. Recent years have seen a virtual explosion of research on sleep dynamics. In laboratories all over the country, sleepers are being wired, monitored, and interrogated to discover the inner nature of sleep and its effect on our bodies. The picture of sleep that is emerging is an interesting one (for a good introduction, see *The Sleep Book,* S. Linde and L. Savary, Harper and Row Publishers).

The descent to sleep begins with a period of relaxation and serenity devoid of specific thought. Breathing slows and becomes regular, pulse drops, body temperature declines, and the brain emits characteristic bursts of electrical energy called alpha waves. The alpha pattern disappears within minutes, and we lose our sense of time. If awakened at this time, sleepers are unable to estimate how long they have been asleep. During this period of repose—the STAGE 0 phase of sleep—daytime concerns are still present in the mind, but associative forms of thinking take over to deal with these concerns in highly creative ways. The result is a form of light fantasy called hypnagogic dreaming, a mixture of brief conversations, body sensations, and hallucinations. If you want to get in touch with your hypnagogic dreams, you must awaken before you enter the next sleep phase. This can be accomplished by lying in bed with your forearm and hand balanced in a vertical position. As you drift off to sleep, you will be awakened when the muscle tone in your arm relaxes enough to cause it to fall over. As you regain consciousness, concentrate on the thoughts in your mind. These thoughts are hypnagogic imagery. One man, aroused through this technique, felt certain he had invented the perfect title for his book on chemistry. In the morning, he read what he had jotted down the previous night: *Twelve Bedsteads in Search of an Answer.*

Movement into the first stage of actual sleep—STAGE I—is marked by further relaxation and functional blindness. Even if your eyes were taped open during this stage, no images would register. For 10 or 15 minutes, sleepers in STAGE I sleep can be easily awakened, and upon arousal will customarily assert that they have not been asleep at all.

Sleepers next fall quickly into STAGE II sleep, a level in which brain waves grow larger and display rapid crescendoes and decrescendoes much like a musical performance. In STAGE III, which typically follows after another ten minutes, muscles are relaxed and both breathing and heart rate slow down.

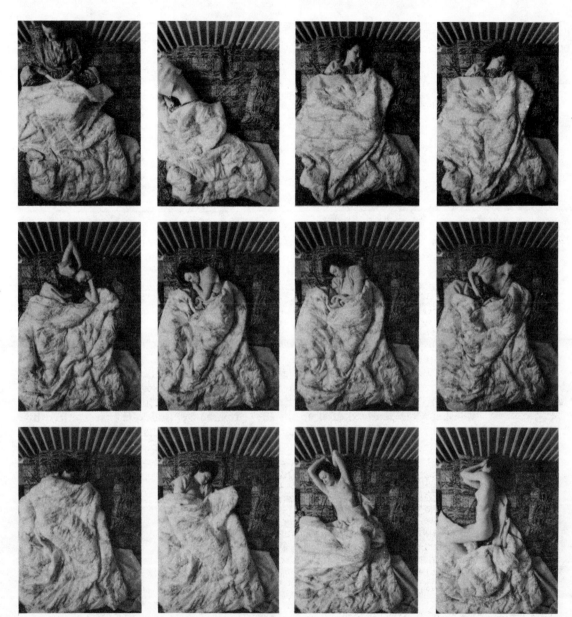

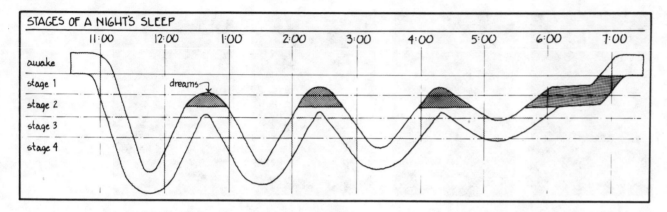

STAGES OF A NIGHT'S SLEEP

From here sleepers pass into STAGE IV sleep, an astounding form of human consciousness which forms the groundplane of bedroom spirituality. In this state, heart rate and temperature decline to their lowest level of the day. The brain is flooded with a new delta wave pattern, marking complete oblivion, which beats at pulses not so different from those of the heart. This stage of sleep is a requisite to both mental and physical well-being. If deprived of sleep for any period of time, the body will make up for Stage IV loss first, by including disproportionate amounts of delta sleep in subsequent nights. We are conscious of external stimuli during Stage IV sleep, but can recall nothing if awakened. Unremembered actions like sleepwalking, bedwetting, and mumbled sleep conversations usually take place during this stage.

Stage IV is home to one of the darkest forms of human experience—night terror—experienced by about 5% of children and somewhat fewer adults. Normal dreams, including nightmares, happen during lighter phases of sleep. Night terror occurs in the deepest stage of sleep, beginning with a jolt which accelerates bodily processes at an enormous rate. While nightmares represent a kind of focused anxiety, night terror, likened by psychologists to acute schizophrenic episodes, is characterized by uncontrolled, instantaneous panic. The deeper the sleep, the more severe the terror. Often the victim is propelled from bed and sent racing through the house in fright.

As our chart indicates, the first experience of Stage IV sleep lasts 60 to 90 minutes, after which the sleeper moves back through lighter stages of sleep to a period of dreaming. Every culture has understood that dreaming provides a special window on the mysteries of our inner life. Modern dream research, far from dispelling these mysteries, has drawn an increasingly detailed picture of a unique plane of spiritual and physical existence. Dreaming has many characteristics of an alertness even greater than that of waking life. Brain waves during dreaming are accompanied by fluctuations of pulse and blood pressure like those caused by intense bodily exertion or emotional agitation. Breathing is irregular, pupils dilate and contract erratically, and eyes race dramatically from side to side. Sexual hormones are produced during dream periods and powerful adrenal secretions become plentiful in the blood.

Through dreams we are linked to other realms of experience. Dreaming, for example, opens us to our most direct experience of intra-uterine life. As adults we dream typically 1 1/2 to 2 hours a night. Younger persons sleep more than adults, however, and spend more of the sleep time dreaming. Babies, research indicates, spend up to 60% of their entire day dreaming. It is thus possible that an entire life within the womb is spent dreaming, and that later dreaming is a lifelong reinterpretation of this reality.

Dreams link us with our sexual desires as well. Who can deny that sexual dreams describe an inner sexual identity as real as any we imagine for ourselves during the day? Religious interpreters have tried to pin responsibility for such matters on the devil.

"Satan transforms himself into various forms," wrote Malleus Maleficarium, "and by seducing the mind in dreams, holds it captive and leads it."

Freud set against this outer Satan a more troublesome inner one. Dreams, he held, were evidence of unconscious wishes, most of them sexual, which were unable to pass daytime censorship by the ego. Freudian dream analysis thus required an immense encyclopedia of analogies between dream objects and sexual experience. Under "architecture," for example, we read, "Rooms in dreams are usually women; if the various ways in and out of them are represented, this interpretation is scarcely open to doubt. . . . A dream of going through a suite of rooms is a brothel or Harem dream. . . . Steps, ladders or staircases, or, as the case may be, walking up or down them, are representations of the sexual act. Smooth walls over which the dreamer climbs, the facades of houses, correspond to erect human bodies."

Both religious and Freudian interpretations of dream sexuality are now being superseded by a simpler theory that recognizes dream sex as simply another aspect of our sexual selves.

Dreams have a creative dimension as well. Elias Howe, inventor of the sewing machine, worked for years on his discovery, but couldn't figure out how to arrange threading the needle. One night he dreamed that a tribe of savages was demanding that he finish his work or be put to death. As they shook their spears at him, he noticed that the tips had eye-shaped holes, the perfect solution to his needle problem. He woke up and drew the first design of the modern sewing machine needle.

In one study 98% of men and 40% of women said they had experienced orgasm in dreams. In two days of conversations with friends on this topic I uncovered: one ecstatic sexual reunion with a grade-school girlfriend dream, one homosexual encounter with a best friend dream, one two-week affair with Mick Jagger dream, one sexy touching dream, and one sexual resolution of a three-way affair dream. As if to parody this sexual dimension of dreaming, men have erections to accompany *all* their 1 1/2 to 2 hours of dreaming each night, whether erotic or not.

Religious thinkers have long understood the affinity between dreams and other spiritual realms. Jacob, we are told in the Bible, "dreamed that there was a ladder set up on the earth, and the top of it reached to heaven;.... and the Lord stood above it and said, . . . 'Behold I am with you wherever you go, and will bring you back to this land. . . .' " Jacob awoke from his sleep and said, "Surely the Lord is in this place and I did not know it."

Jung is the most powerful modern commentator on the spiritual dimension of dreaming. Having listened to some 80,000 dreams as a psychiatrist, Jung grew to believe that dreams alerted people to otherwise hidden dimensions of their experience. According to Jung, many dreams contain archetypes—symbolic representations of humankind's collective unconscious. Most people dream, more or less frequently, of disembodied voices which speak authoritatively to them in their dreams. If you wish to understand some of the religious significance of your dreams, presume, as have many before you, that this is the voice of God.

My Bed Is a Boat

My bed is like a little boat;
 Nurse helps me in when I embark;
She girds me in my sailor's coat
 And starts me in the dark.

At night, I go on board and say
 Good night to all my friends on shore;
I shut my eyes and sail away
 And see and hear no more.

And sometimes things to bed I take,
 As prudent sailors have to do:
Perhaps a slice of wedding cake,
 Perhaps a toy or two.

All night across the dark we steer;
 But when the day returns at last,
Safe in my room, beside the pier,
 I find my vessel fast.

Robert Louis Stevenson
A Child's Garden of Verses
(Charles Scribner's Sons)

Dreams provide us with a special perspective on our day-by-day existence. Some traditional cultures have a highly refined understanding of this relationship. The Senoi, a tribal people living in the central mountain range of the Malay Peninsula, conduct what amounts to a dream clinic every morning at breakfast. Sexual dreams, according to the Senoi, should always be carried through to orgasm. One's lover should then be asked for a poem, song, or dance which will express the beauty of this love to the group. A child who dreams of being attacked by a friend is told to inform the friend of the dream. The suggestion is offered that a malignant character has perhaps used the friend's image as a disguise, and that a recurrence might be prevented if the friend gave a present to the dreamer and was especially friendly.

Fritz Perls has popularized a form of dream interpretation based on the connectedness of dreams and daily experience. In his approach, everything in a dream sequence, including objects and places, is a part of the self. Everything is fashioned out of the life of the individual and reflects that life. Dreams, according to Perls, give the submerged portion of the personality, "underdog," a chance to speak out against the dominant portion, "topdog." Increasing awareness of dreams allows one to recover lost or distanced parts of one's self and thus achieve wholeness. Dream therapy based on these insights consists of role playing in which the dreamer acts out and extends the dream as seen from the perspective of people or objects it contains.

Death

Modern life has removed death from the bedroom. In the past it was natural for persons in extended families to stay in the home until death; in modern-day nuclear families this happens less. With the average American marriage lasting only seven years, and with half the population moving every five years, older persons frequently have no family homes to turn to. New developments in medicine have extended life expectancies, but at the expense of dignity in death. In order to receive the benefits of high technology in life preservation, people must enter the forbidding world of intensive-care hospitals or nursing home units.

Throughout human history, the death of a loved one has been experienced as a time of heightened spirituality. After witnessing another's death, the cycle of life—creation, growth, and degeneration—is illuminated in the most personal ways. It is a time that prompts the appreciation of friendships past and present, and a reevaluation of one's own life and pursuits. It is a time of mutual support for those most affected by the loss. For most, it is a time for religious renewal.

The bedroom is death's natural sanctuary. Here can be found the privacy, sense of belonging, and emotional support that form the best backdrop for this dimension of our experience.

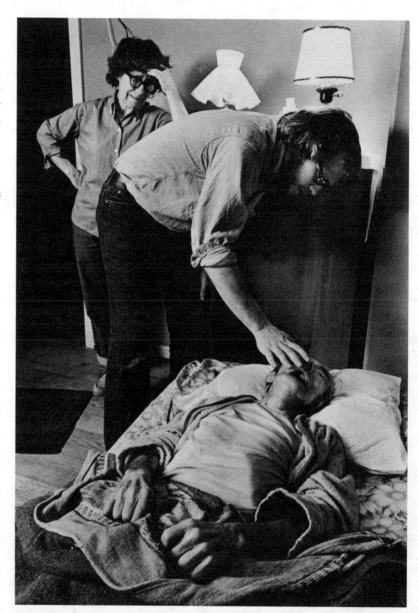

An encounter with death

I had a heart attack, and I found myself in a black void, and I knew I had left my physical body behind. I knew I was dying. . . . Immediately, I was moved out of that blackness, through a pale gray, and I just went on, gliding and moving swiftly, and in front of me, in the distance, I could see a gray mist, and I was rushing towards it. It seemed that I just couldn't get there fast enough to satisfy me, and as I got closer to it I could see through it. Beyond the mist, I could see people, and their forms were just like they are on earth. . . . The whole thing was permeated with the most gorgeous light—a living, golden yellow glow, a pale color. . . . As I approached more closely I felt certain that I was going through that mist. It was such a wonderful, joyous feeling; there are just no words in the human language to describe it. Yet it wasn't my time to go through the mist, because instantly, from the other side, appeared my Uncle Carl, who had died many years earlier. He blocked my path, saying, "Go back . . . go back now." I didn't want to go back, but I had no choice, and immediately I was back in my body. I felt that horrible pain in my chest, and I heard a little boy crying, "God, bring my mommy back to me."
quoted in *Life After Life,* Raymond Moody (Bantam, Mockingbird, New York)

The many manifestations of bedroom spirituality are deeply threatened by modern life. Hospitals insist that they are better caretakers of birth and death than the bedroom. Bedroom prayer is sanctioned by the church, but never accepted as a substitute for regular attendance at scheduled services. As we have tried to suggest, however, there is a profound appropriateness to home-centered spirituality. The rest of this chapter will indicate that as we broaden our familiarity with this realm, it can begin to show in the way we design and use our bedrooms.

Bedroom Fantasies

Here are several exercises to open you to some new dimensions of bedroom spirituality. Changing what you do in your bedroom will lead naturally to new ideas for fixing up the space. When you have completed one of these fantasy exercises, consider how it might affect your ideas about your bedroom.

Dream Exploration

You can learn a great deal about yourself, your life situation, and your personal spirituality by examining your dreams. But to examine a dream you have to remember it, and to remember it, unfortunately, you have to wake up within 20 minutes after it ends.

Try the following method for getting some dreams on paper.

1. Put a night-light by your bed. Aim it toward a writing surface and keep it dim enough to leave on all night.

2. Place a pencil and paper, or a tape recorder, by your bedside.

3. Before you fall asleep remind yourself several times that you want to remember a dream.

4. If you can't seem to wake up in time to catch your dreams, set a quiet alarm clock to go off two hours after you go to bed or about one hour before you normally wake up.

5. When you wake up, whether in the middle of the night or in the morning, think about the dream you just had. Do not wake up too quickly or you will lose the dream memory.

6. Write down the dream in as much detail as you can. Key aspects are usually enough to allow addition of detail the next day. Add as many associations as you can: experiences the dream recalls, who other people seem to represent, etc.

Placing a number of dream recollections side by side will give you a glimpse of your dream world. When you have collected a few, read them and make a list of the places mentioned —your "dream city"—and the people who appear in your dreams—your "dream community."

If you are interested in pursuing self-understanding through dream analysis, see Ann Faraday's excellent work, *Dream Power* (Perennial Library).

Nighttime Spirituality

Human beings are not the only creatures who sleep and dream. Each species has its own ritual balancing of activity in the outer world and retreat to an inner one. Horses lie down and sleep for up to seven hours a night. Cows sleep with their eyes open and continue chewing their cud. Dolphins seem to sleep for a couple of hours with one eye, then the other, closed. Cats have nighttime brain wave activity similar to that of humans. Although they cycle through a full "night and day" every 30 minutes, their rhythmic postural adjustments and dream activity during sleep are quite similar to ours. Throughout all species, rapid-eye-movement or dream sleep occupies from 15 to 25% of total sleep time. The following exercise will open you to the spiritual community of all sleeping beings. Do it some night as you are preparing to fall asleep.

Lie in bed, on your back. Relax all parts of your body completely for two or three minutes.

Let your mind roam like a spaceship over the earth. See yourself approaching first a continent, then a region of that continent, and finally a neighborhood, whether man-made or natural, within that region. Focus slowly on a single creature within that neighborhood—a human being, an animal,

perhaps even a plant. Watch as it goes through its own ritual of ending a day and preparing for rest. Observe quietly as it lies down and falls asleep. Understand that you in your sleep and this being are on the same plane of existence. Imagine in detail a dream which unites both you and the other dreamer on a plane of universal dream spirituality.

Bedroom/Clothes Survey

Since most people keep their clothes in the bedroom, this is a good place to compare how you dress with how your house or apartment dresses.

First, make a display of your own clothes. Clear your bed down to a neutral sheet or blanket. Take a varied assortment of your clothes from the closet—not just the latest or favorite ones—and lay them on the bed. Overlap each piece with the next so that a six-inch strip of each is showing. If you have very different clothes for summer and winter, or for formal and informal wear, you might want to represent these aspects of your wardrobe. Perhaps you have a set of clothes relating to military service, athletics, or yard work.

Now get some of your room's clothes as close together as possible. A good place to start is on the floor near a curtain. The array will be smaller than the one of your clothes, but there are many things you might include: sheets, pillowcases, bedspreads, rugs, curtains, and wallpaper.

Once you have constructed the two displays, play the stranger who has never met you or your room before. How would you describe the two sets of clothes? What addition would improve each display? What would your room look like decorated in your clothes? How would you look wearing the decorations of your room?

Bedroom Efficiency Survey

We have not emphasized efficiency in our discussion of bedroom spirituality. You might find it interesting, however, to see how your bedroom rates along these lines. Read the following questions and mark the "yes" or "no" boxes as appropriate. If a question doesn't apply, leave both boxes blank.

High Marks	Low Marks	
YES ☐	NO ☐	Do you have one bed reading light per person, aimed so that the bulb is not visible by the person who has gone to sleep? Give yourself two high marks if the light is on a rheostat.
YES ☐	NO ☐	Do you have a full-length mirror located so that you do not see any bright window light when you look at your image?
YES ☐	NO ☐	Is your bedroom located on the quiet side of your house or apartment?
YES ☐	NO ☐	Do you have at least 15 inches of standing space for making your bed along both sides?
YES ☐	NO ☐	Do you have a night light in your bedroom? (Seven thousand people die every year from bedroom falls.) Score two points if you can control your overhead light from the bed.
YES ☐	NO ☐	(A toughie) Are the light switches in your home located so that you can take your end-of-day lock-up tour without ever crossing a dark room?
YES ☐	NO ☐	Do your bureau drawers operate smoothly, without getting stuck or falling in your lap?
YES ☐	NO ☐	Is your bed located so you don't have to look at bright sky or sun when you wake up?
YES ☐	NO ☐	If your bed frame does not extend all the way to the floor, are there at least 8 1/2 inches of clear space underneath (hotel standards for easy underbed cleaning)?
YES ☐	NO ☐	Is your bed located away from winter window drafts?
YES ☐	NO ☐	Are your closets for hanging clothes at least 2 feet deep?

YES	NO
TOTAL	TOTAL

Goals/Solutions

The following pages contain ideas for fixing up your bedroom. To find the right solutions, however, you have to decide which goals are appropriate for you. Three possible goals—making a bedroom better for sleeping, using clothing inspiration for room design, and improving use of bedroom space—are examined.

If your goal is

To make your bedroom better for sleeping

 ## Quiet

First decide what sounds you want to block out. If the noise comes from outdoors, install storm windows. Deaden sound coming from the next room by installing heavy cloth, acoustic panels, or a wall of furniture or shelving between your bed and the source of the noise. A rug in your own room will absorb noise there as well.

Try a "white noise machine" (Sears) or a record of humming (Hammacher-Schlemmer).

 ## Support

Americans spend $1 billion per year on mattresses, so you might as well help spend it right. People with lower-back pain tend to sleep better on firmer mattresses. One style now available can be made softer on one half than the other, and firmest of all when a panel is slipped into a special slot in the center. You can make your own mattress firmer by slipping a 3/4-inch plywood board, one inch smaller than your bed, between box spring and mattress. Mattresses with individually pocketed springs (the Simmons Beautyrest line) do a better job of giving each part of your body the support it needs and keeping neighboring sleepers from being affected by each other's sleeping positions.

 ## Softness

Get a large fluffy pillow, to encourage oblivion, and a small fluffy pillow to accommodate those small-but-critical adjustments which keep your neck from getting stiff overnight.

 ## Climate

Locate your bed away from chilly window drafts. The ideal temperature for sleeping is 60 to 65 degrees Fahrenheit, not the 70 to 75 degrees most Americans sweat out each night.

 ## Stumble planning

Beforehand preparation for nighttime stumble-journeys to the bathroom, kitchen, or nursery can greatly improve anyone's sleep. Free these routes of all obstructions before you go to sleep, and put night lights along the way.

 ## Sleep potions

Try a glass of warm milk before bedtime. If its aura of restful nourishment doesn't put you to sleep, the amino acids it contains will. They break down to make serotonin, one of the body's sleep-inducing chemicals.

To use clothing as an inspiration for room design

 ## Shopping spree

Go on a shopping trip to a favorite fabric store with the goal of making something for your room (a cloth lamp shade, curtains, a bedspread, pillows, a plant-holder) and something for yourself (a winter scarf, a shirt) out of the same material.

 ## Queen for a day

For most people, clothes are a primary means of self-expression, representing hours of attention to color, style, etc. Yet most of this expression is hidden behind closet doors. The only clothes visible in most people's bedrooms are dirty ones. Make a "spotlight" place in your bedroom for a "garment of the week." Find a neutral background, such as a white door or piece of black velvet, and arrange a light so it will shine on the area. Put in a single clothes hook from which you can hang and admire a latest purchase or gift, an old standby, or a recent handmade effort.

 ## Earrings

New England farmers used to decorate their farmhouses with jewelry-like decorations—reflective glass balls—on lightning rods. In a similar spirit, you can make earrings for your bedroom (they should be about 10 times the size of the ones you wear). Imitate one of your favorite sets of earrings or construct something special out of Christmas decorations, pieces of chandelier crystal, drapery pulls, flashlight innards, salt and pepper shakers, etc. Use room earrings to embellish light or window-shade pulls, a full-length mirror, doorknobs, etc.

 ## Curtain wear

You can make spectacular clothes from cloth designed for houses. Use your own castoffs or find some at second-hand or antique stores. Make a uniquely elegant bathrobe from a chenille bedspread or brocade draperies (sewn together at shoulders and sides, with an opening at the front); use a drapery sash for a belt. A table cloth (old linen or flower-print extravaganza) makes a beautiful shirt and old lace, a wonderful camisole. Striking room fashions can be made, too, by recycling old fabrics: a bedspread from old lace doilies, curtains from damask tablecloths, lampshades from hand-embroidered handkerchiefs.

 ## Neutrality

Decorating your home in "neutral" colors will highlight any objects with brighter tones in a space. Buy yourself some similarly neutral clothes, which will focus attention on nearby highlights—namely yourself.

 ## Winter wardrobe

People dress quite differently in the winter than in the summer. Aside from another blanket on the bed, most bedrooms change very little with the seasons. Design a special winter identity for your bedroom: thick rugs, a snowdrift bedspread, a neck scarf for the bedside philodendron, a fur pillow, heavy curtains which can be pulled back during the day and closed at night to eliminate drafts.

 ## Body language

People hang literal images (paintings, photographs, samplers) on their walls, but are relatively timid when it comes to their clothes. Enliven your personal wardrobe with more such images: message t-shirts, earrings of miniature tools, picture lockets, photo-print shirts, sweaters knitted in natural scenes.

To make better use of the space in your bedroom

Bedrooms are frequently the most under-used rooms in the house. Although we have emphasized the spirituality of the bedroom in this chapter, a wide variety of "secular" activities are appropriate in this room as well.

 ## Less bed room

Smaller bedrooms can be quite filled with nothing in them but a bed. To get some space, try pushing your bed into a corner and replacing bed linen with a single, feather-filled comforter which serves as a sheet, blanket and bedspread and requires no side access for bed making.

Bunk beds are a natural in children's rooms, and are easily made up if you use sleeping bags with fitted sheet inserts. Place the upper bunk as high in the room as practicable so the space underneath can be turned into a desk area or walk-in closet when no longer needed as a bed. Beds which rise via counterweight systems into the ceiling, or Murphy beds which fold into the wall, are useful inventions for one-room apartments or guest rooms.

 ## Storage

Drawers on rollaway casters can be fitted underneath higher beds. Several smaller drawers are easier to move than a few enormous ones. Throw out your bedroom storage furniture (vanity, chest, bureau, armoire, night table) and get twice the storage space in half the room with a wall of modular storage.

 ## Sewing

Bedrooms make terrific sewing areas. You can use the bed for fabric layout, the bedroom mirror for fitting, and the closet or underbed drawers for fabric storage. Set the machine permanently in an area with adequate storage and lighting. Curtain it off by draping your latest cloth purchase over a fixed pole to hide the clutter.

 ## Bed-bath

The bedroom is a natural place to locate overflow bathroom activities. A bedroom sink can ease congestion at morning wash-up. A shower or tub creates a luxurious bedroom atmosphere of dream bathing and requires very little floor space.

 ## Room to breathe

Keeping one wall of your bedroom free of furniture will give even a cramped room a feeling of spaciousness. A similar principle applies to floors. A built-in storage wall containing desk and dressing-counter will free up continuous floor space and make the room feel larger.

Homework

Bedrooms are ideal places for desk and reading areas—quiet, out-of-the-way, private. Don't try to disguise such functions. Use appropriate task lighting, colors, plants, and visible storage so the reading area will provide an alternative focal point within the room. Try to locate a desk to the right of a window if you are right-handed, so as not to cast shadows on your work surface.

Bed Inspirations

1

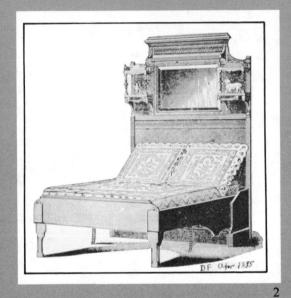

2

Spirited beds to prompt
your imagination: **1.** A
sumptuous bed/boudoir
from the reign of Louis
XVI. **2.** The Andrew's Improved Folding Parlour
Bed, 1885. **3.** A vaulted
sleeping arbor of pom-
pons. **4.** A funereal
matrimonial bed in the
Gothic style.

3

4

1

1. An art deco bed
sculpture. 2. A bed com-
mon in traditional domestic
French architecture which
doubles as a closet and sitting bench. 3. A German
bed filled to overflowing
with feather comforters.
4. A traditional Japanese
pillow, reported to keep
the head cool by allowing
air to circulate underneath.

2

3

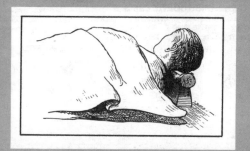

4

47

A Social Bed

Here is a bed for people who find that the comfortable, low-key quality of their bedrooms makes it one of the friendliest places in the house. Unfortunately, most beds are not set up for socializing. Most particularly, they provide very little support for normal sitting. It is usually possible to sit at the head of a bed, although even this is difficult in beds which slide away from the wall or have delicate headboards. Almost never, however, can a friend sit comfortably facing you at the *foot* of a bed. The "social" bed illustrated here solves this problem by creating two solid corners where large pillows can be placed to create a perfect environment for informal conversation. The shelf unit at the head of the bed has plenty of room for drinks, reading material, even a stereo tuner or tape deck. The shelf at the foot of the bed is sized to accommodate a TV. The "landscape headboard" is designed so you can cover the last three "hills" with fabric of your own choosing. The mood of the bed is established by your choice of fabric and can be changed from time to time. Thin stripes, calicos, and other small prints in seasonal colors will enhance the landscape theme. Big patterns, bright colors or solids will create a bold effect. A single light bulb behind the headboard casts a slanting light over the cloth-covered panels, accentuating their texture and providing a gentle indirect light for the room. The plans presented here fit a double bed precisely, but will serve equally well for a queen-size bed.

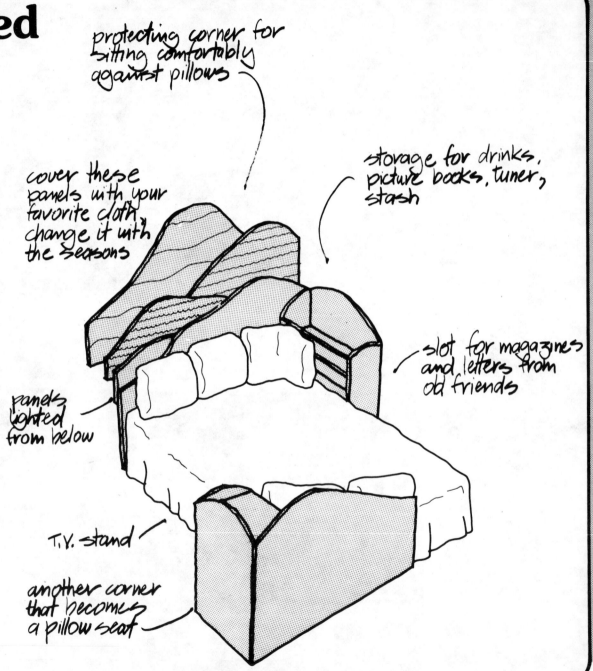

protecting corner for sitting comfortably against pillows

cover these panels with your favorite cloth change it with the seasons

storage for drinks, picture books, tuner, stash

slot for magazines and letters from old friends

panels lighted from below

T.V. stand

another corner that becomes a pillow seat

STEP 1. Obtain materials

- 2 sheets 3/4-inch plywood, each 4 by 8 feet, good one side.
- 1 sheet 1/2-inch plywood, 4 by 8 feet, good one side.
- 8 linear feet of 1 x 5-inch pine shelving.
- 11 linear feet of 1 x 8-inch pine shelving.
- 6 linear feet of 1 x 10-inch pine shelving.
- 24 linear feet of 1 1/4-inch square baluster stock.
- 6 number 8 flathead screws, 1 inch long.
- 36 number 8 flathead screws, 2 inches long.
- 11 stove bolts, 3/16-inch diameter, 5 inches long, with nuts and washers.
- 4 stove bolts, 3/16-inch diameter, 2 inches long, with nuts and washers.
- a handful of 2 1/2-inch finishing nails.
- fittings for one surface-mounted light-bulb socket.

STEP 2. Build headboard

Consult the diagram showing the headboard viewed from behind. Note that the panels closest to the bed (H and I) are constructed from 3/4-inch plywood and bolted to both the shelf unit and the box spring. This will provide the stability a backrest requires. The three panels behind (J, K, and L) are constructed of 1/2-inch plywood. Lay all the pieces out on the plywood, good side up, as indicated in the diagrams. Cut out the pieces with a saber saw.

Next construct the framework to support the three floating panels—J, K, and L. This framework fits against the wall and floor to provide extra stability. Floating panels attach to uprights with spacers, providing room for the cloth to be wrapped around the edges and pinned behind.

Panel I should be screwed directly to main panel H with 1-inch screws. Use 2-inch screws to construct the framework and secure it to H. Locate the center upright in the middle of H, and the two other uprights 9 inches in from each end. Attach floating panels to the framework with 2-inch screws from the *front* of the panels. All these panels have their bottom edges 30 inches above the floor. As seen from the back, panels L and J align with the right edge of panel H, and panel K lines up to the left edge. Wire the light bulb socket to main panel H as indicated.

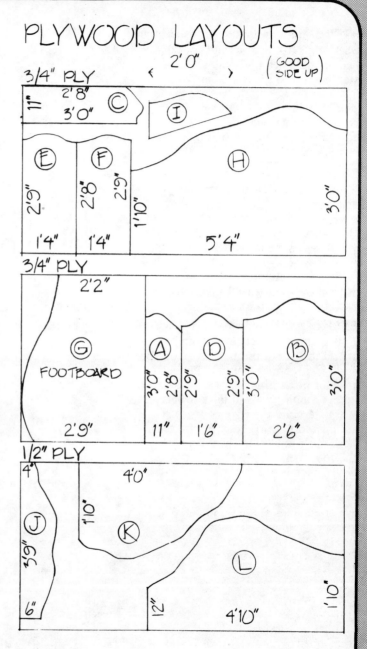

STEP 3. Build head and foot shelf units

Shelf units at the head and foot of the bed are designed and built as free-standing units. Sides are cut from 3/4-inch plywood. Shelves are made of pine shelving. Use finishing nails to construct units. Slats on the bottom of each shelf unit are for bolting to the box spring.

STEP 4. Finish surfaces

Sand edges and surfaces to remove splinters. To enhance the landscape quality use a forest green paint; make the panels appear to recede by mixing green and white to lighten the color of each panel moving away from the bed.

To cover the three floating panels with cloth, simply fold fabric around each one and pin it behind.

STEP 5. Assemble bed

Bolt shelf units, headboard, and footboard to the bottom board of your box spring with 5-inch bolts. If the bottom of your box spring is not big enough to accept a bolt, you will have to screw 2 x 3's around the edge of the box-spring and bolt to these. Secure the head shelf unit to the headboard and the foot shelf unit to the footboard with 2-inch bolts.

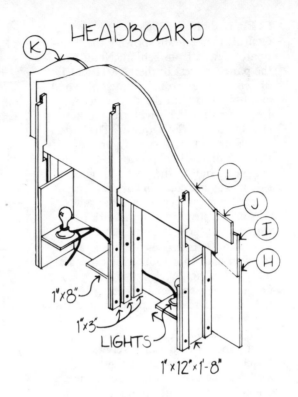

HEADBOARD

1"x8"

1"x3"

LIGHTS

1"x12"x1-8"

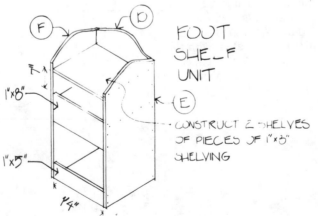

FOOT SHELF UNIT

E

CONSTRUCT 2 SHELVES OF PIECES OF 1"x8" SHELVING

1"x8"

1"x5"

4"

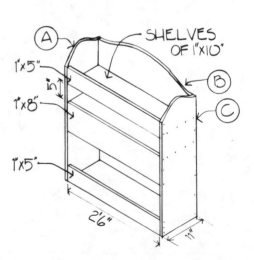

HEAD SHELF UNIT

SHELVES OF 1"x10"

1"x5"

5"

1"x8"

1"x5"

2'6"

1"

Fantasy Bed

This bed will transform your sleeping space for $40 and a weekend of simple carpentry. The design of the bed hints at dream castles with parapets and spires. Its most direct inspiration was the ornate facades of certain Italian cathedrals whose colorful twisting columns are set off by gold-leaf tracery. If oiled or stained, the bed has a unified natural look. It is easy to personalize and enliven the bed with colorful additions of your own. To decorate it for Christmas, try hanging strings of tinsel or Italian lights between the vertical columns. The slots directly beneath the two reading lights would make a natural spot for hanging necklaces or strings of beads. Although the completed bed has an air of intricacy, its construction is straightforward, consisting primarily of nailing uprights to a plywood back. The design presented here will work for a double or queen-size bed.

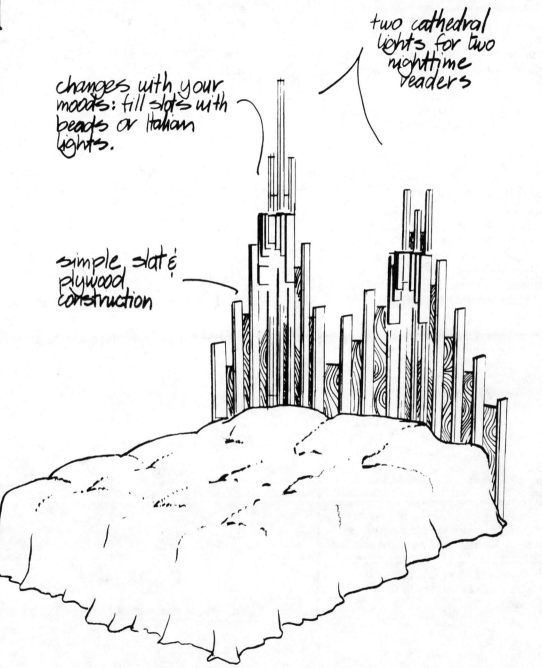

two cathedral lights for two nighttime readers

changes with your moods: fill slots with beads or Italian lights.

simple, slat & plywood construction

STEP 1. Obtain materials

- 1 sheet 1/2-inch plywood, 4 by 8 feet, good one side.
- 10 pieces, 4 feet long, 1 x 3-inch pine shelving, common grade.
- 7 pieces, 4 feet long, 1 x 2-inch pine shelving, common grade. (To save money, use a power saw to rip down the 1 x 2- and 1 x 3-inch pieces from a 1 x 5.)
- 10 pieces, 4 feet long, 1 x 1 baluster stock.
- 1 piece, 4 feet long, 1 x 6 inch pine shelving, common grade.
- small box of 2-inch finishing nails.
- 2 pull-chain sockets with 1-inch-long threaded nipples, a line dimmer, and 20 feet of electric cord.
- bolts necessary to attach to your bed (check to see what hardware is appropriate).

STEP 2. Construct headboard

Lay out the pieces to be cut from the 1/2-inch plywood as indicated in the diagram. Cut out and sand these pieces. Saw uprights to length indicated in diagram, sand, and attach to plywood with finishing nails. You will find it easier to attach all the 1 x 1's first, then the 1 x 2's, and finally the 1 x 3's. Run two boards end to end if necessary to obtain the needed length.

STEP 3. Construct lights

Cut pieces for lamps and nail together as indicated. Lamps should fit with their outer boards snugly against the uprights. Adjust the vertical location of the lamps to allow one person to read without light shining in the eyes of a bedmate.

STEP 4. Install headboard

The finished headboard will be quite heavy, but can be moved by two people. Simply placing the headboard behind your bed and tying it back to the wall will keep it secure. It is also possible to bolt it to a box spring or metal bed frame.

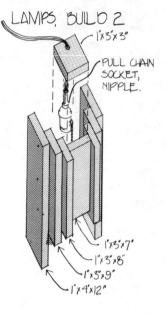

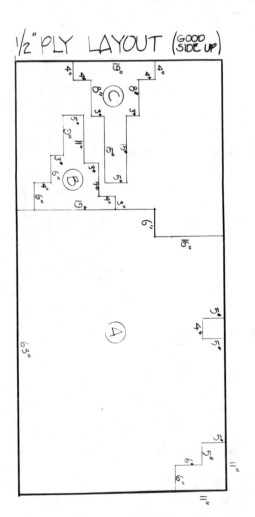

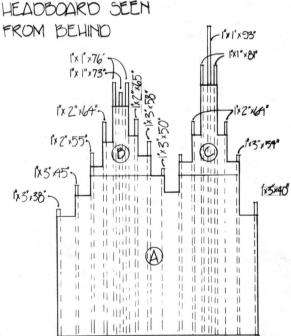

Bedroom Storage Wall

Bedrooms have a tendency to be too empty or too full. Here is a storage system for one which has grown cluttered with too many functions in too little space. Each bay in the system serves a different purpose. The one most forward in the drawing contains a workspace with a desk, tackboard, three shelves, and a light. Beside it is a

"dressing bay" with three drawers, a dressing counter, mirror, jewelry rack, and high shelf. A closet comes next, containing two rods for hanging clothes and a shoe rack. The closet and dressing areas are covered with a curtain hung on outsized rings from a pole above. An altar bay is next, with a spotlighted shelf for display of cherished objects. At the far end is a "greenhouse" with three shelves for

plants in pots, two rods for hanging plants, and several plant lights. A stack of simple, unfinished bureau units would make an elegant bay as well. The system is unified by boards running across the bays at top and bottom. The top board is used to hang lights with aluminum shades.

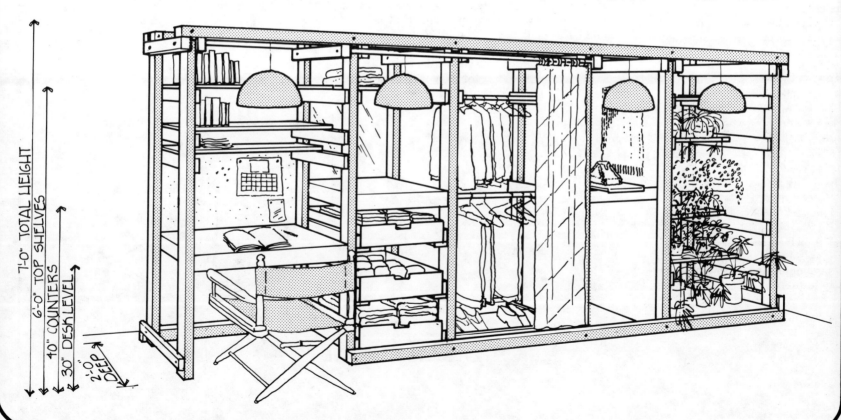

WORKSPACE   WARDROBE   CLOSET   ALTAR   GREENHOUSE

7'-0" TOTAL HEIGHT

6'-0" TOP SHELVES

40" COUNTERS

30" DESK LEVEL

2'-0" DEEP

STEP 1. Set dimensions

Measure the wall of your bedroom where you plan to place the storage system. If there are windows in the wall, locate them behind either a greenhouse or desk bay. Seven feet is a good height for the unit in most bedrooms. All bays are two feet deep. The altar and dressing bays are two feet wide, the rest, three feet. See the drawings for key dimensions within the bays.

STEP 2. Obtain materials

Because you will want to adjust the length and contents of the system to your own needs, the following instructions give only types, not quantities, of materials.

- Uprights and all crosspieces are 2 x 3-inch pine stock. This lumber should be straight but not necessarily free of knots.
- Braces under shelves are 1 x 3-inch common pine.
- Desk, countertops, and tray bottoms are 3/4-inch plywood, good one side.
- Shelves are 1 x 10-inch common pine shelving.
- Hanging rods are 1 1/4-inch wood closet pole.
- Homasote tackboard.
- 2 x 3's are bolted to each other with 1/4-inch roundhead stove bolts.
- Lights are hanging sockets with aluminum shades (sold as clamp-on reflectors).

STEP 3. Construct framework

Cut pieces to size and sand smooth. Build the ladder-shaped bay dividers first. Bolt the double braces at the top of each ladder to the uprights. If you are including a curtain, two of these braces should extend an extra 4 inches to hold the rod. Next, nail the 1 x 3 "rungs" of each ladder at appropriate heights to support the shelves and counters being placed within the bay. Nail these braces with two nails at either end to give the ladders strength. Construct desktops, drawers, and other units to be inserted between the ladders (see diagram for details).

STEP 4. Assemble bays

Bolt ladders in place to 2 x 3's running across the bays, top and bottom, front and back. Nail shelves and other units in place within the bays. If your unit sways from side to side, bolt it to the wall at several places along the top, or nail four 10-inch-wide plywood plates to the back of the narrower bays.

STEP 5. Finish surfaces

A light coat of linseed oil will give a good natural finish to most surfaces. You might want to give the desktop a coat of polyurethane or cover it with Formica plastic laminate.

STEP 6. Install lighting

Lights are hung through holes drilled in the top crosspiece. Aluminum shades that screw onto hanging sockets are available at most hardware stores. To make your storage system lighting your general room lighting, wire the lights to a ceiling or wall outlet governed by the room's wall switch. Another approach is to run all lights through a single pull switch whose cord hangs in front of one of the uprights.

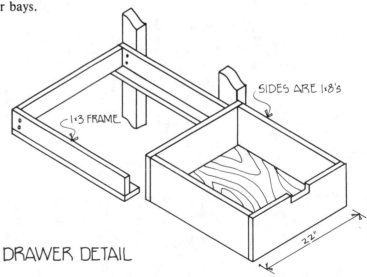

1x3 FRAME

SIDES ARE 1x8's

22"

DRAWER DETAIL

DESK & COUNTER DETAIL

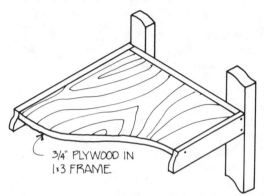

3/4" PLYWOOD IN
1×3 FRAME

SHELF DETAIL

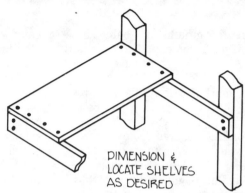

DIMENSION &
LOCATE SHELVES
AS DESIRED

HANGING ROD DETAIL

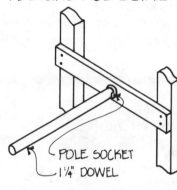

POLE SOCKET
1¼" DOWEL

SHOE RACK DETAIL

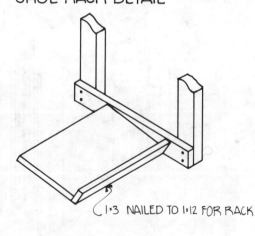

1×3 NAILED TO 1×12 FOR RACK

ALTAR DETAIL

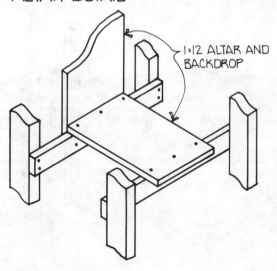

1×12 ALTAR AND
BACKDROP

55

Castle Cradle

The first few months of a baby's life are a magical time for all concerned. If you are lucky enough to have such a time in your life, you will probably want to mark it with special gestures within your living space. Many parents want their baby nearby for the first few months. The cradle shown here-brings your newborn to your bedside. The design has a little of the castle about it. You might find that it thus captures the fantastical quality of this period of your life better than a simple crib.

The cradle is designed to evolve with the family's needs. Its first use, as a cradle for a newborn, lasts until the baby weighs about 15 pounds. Special mounting allows it to rock or be pegged in a stable position. Hand-holds in the side of the cradle box allow it to be removed and used as a portable crib. When baby outgrows the cradle, the box can be secured in a sideways position, and the entire unit becomes a bedside stand with a deep shelf. A little later it can be returned to the child as a toy box.

STEP 1. Obtain materials
- one 4 by 6-foot sheet of 1/2-inch plywood, good one side.
- 1 piece of 1 x 5-inch pine shelving, 6 feet long.
- 2 pieces 1 x 4-inch pine shelving, 6 feet long.
- 2 pieces 1 x 3-inch pine shelving, 8 feet long.
- 2 pieces of 1 1/4-inch square baluster stock, 8 feet long.
- 1 piece of 1 x 12-inch pine shelving, 8 feet long.
- 1 piece of foam for mattress, 3 x 16 x 25 inches.
- 3 carriage bolts, 1/4-inch diameter, 3 inches long; 4 nuts and 4 washers.
- 2 eyebolts, 1-inch diameter.
- small box of 2-inch-long finishing nails.
- 8 number 8 flathead screws, 2 inches long.

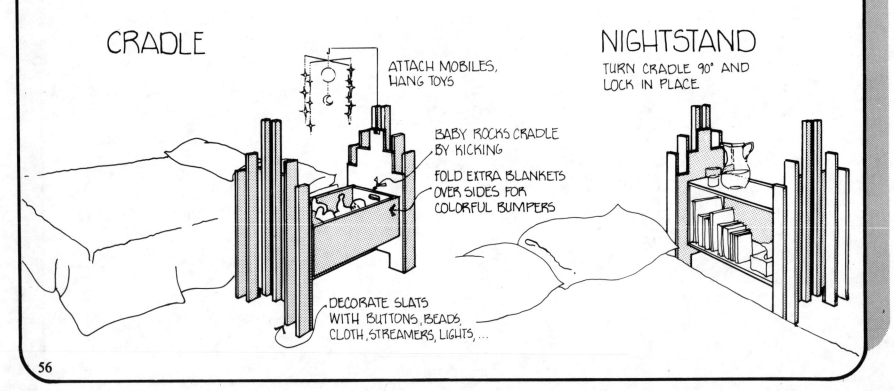

CRADLE

ATTACH MOBILES, HANG TOYS

BABY ROCKS CRADLE BY KICKING

FOLD EXTRA BLANKETS OVER SIDES FOR COLORFUL BUMPERS

DECORATE SLATS WITH BUTTONS, BEADS, CLOTH, STREAMERS, LIGHTS, ...

NIGHTSTAND

TURN CRADLE 90° AND LOCK IN PLACE

STEP 2.

Cut all wood to size and sand.

STEP 3.

Locate vertical slats and nail them in place.

Start with the 2 x 2 pieces and work outward. Construct cradle box according to the diagram. Locate the T-shaped brace between the end supports and secure it with screws.

STEP 4.

To hang cradle box from frame, drill holes 26 inches up from the floor in each end of cradle frame. Secure the carriage bolts in these holes with a nut and washer on either side so the rounded end of the bolt projects over the edge of the cradle box. Screw the two eyebolts into the top edges of the ends of the cradle box and slip them over the projecting carriage bolts to provide a swinging hinge. A third bolt locks the box in a non-swinging position when it is placed through a hole which has been drilled through one of the end supports and the lower part of the cradle box.

STEP 5.

Cover the foam mattress with a plastic bag to keep out moisture. Fasten the plastic securely and keep it covered with a fitted sheet to prevent accidental covering of the infant's face.

STEP 6.

Finish the wood. Linseed oil enhances the natural quality of wood, but the unit can also be finished with wood stain or lead-free paint.

½" PLYWOOD LAYOUT

4¼" 7" 4¼" 7"
5" 3" 3" 5" 3" 3"
4½" 4½" 4½" 4½"
19¼" 19¼" 42"

HEADBOARD FOOTBOARD

8¾" 8¾"
5¼" 4½ 5¼ 5¼ 4½ 5¼"
27"
8" CRADLE FLOOR

ENDBOARDS
(CONSTRUCT 2)

¼"x1¼"x44 ¼"x1¼"x44
1x4x33 1x3x39 1x3x39 1x4x33

- SAND ALL WOOD SMOOTH

- ATTACH SLATS TO FINISH SIDE OF PLYWOOD USING 4d FINISH NAILS

CROSSBRACING
(BOTH ENDS SIMILAR)

CENTER

DRILL 5⁄16" HOLE FOR ¼" DIAM. 3" CARRIAGE BOLT, NUT & WASHER EA. SIDE OF PLYWOOD

26"
4"

5⁄16" HOLE FOR BOLT-LOCK, FOOTBOARD & CRADLE

SCREW 2 PIECES OF 1"x 5"x 28" IN PLACE FOR "T"-SHAPED BRACE

CRADLE

3" FOAM MAT

25"
16"

1x12 PINE SIDES
½" PLYWOOD BASE

1" EYE BOLTS CENTER EA. SIDE

27"

4" HANDLES CUT IN CENTER

18"

Bedroom Inspirations

1

1. An English bedchamber from Knowle, Kent, containing a heavily draped bed structure to keep out castle drafts. 2. A spartan medieval bedroom depicted in a 15th century woodcut. 3. A Victorian bed nestled in a forest of pillows, lace tablecloths, wicker furniture, and art arrangements.

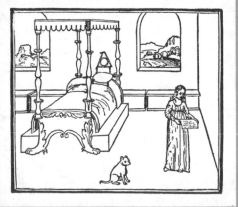

2

3

1. A bed that retires
discreetly within the wall
when its occupant gets
up. 2. The basement
bedroom quarters (two to
a bed) of the live-in maids
of England's Mamhead
House. 3. An evocative
pile of bedroom pillows in
a glade-like setting by
Atelier Martine.

1

3

2

A Sleeper's Bedroom

Here is a bedroom that draws inspiration from Robert Louis Stevenson's ode to sleep,
"My Bed Is a Boat" (see page 36). A sleeping craft, moored in the middle of a boat-shaped room,
bobs gently on a sea of pillows and billowing carpet.

The Room

The room here is unusually long and narrow, with a generous bay at the front, a configuration frequently found in older city brownstones. Placement of the bed and other furniture accentuates the directional quality of the room and launches your attention, like that of the sleeper, to what lies ahead and beyond.

Room orientation is an important aspect of design for sleeping. A northeast exposure is generally preferred because it permits morning sun to brighten up the space either directly from the east or indirectly from the north. (Getting morning sun into the bathroom can be equally important in brightening up the start of a day.) Rooms in this corner of the house are naturally cooler as well, a good quality for sleeping. Other living spaces, warmed by the afternoon sun, are thus saved for day and evening activities. Small-paned, double-hung windows like these have one disadvantage for the professional sleeper. On chilly nights they are likely to be drafty. Double-paned insulating glass, in larger sections, is generally the sleeper's favorite. Such windows also reduce sound transmission from outside—an important consideration in noisy city areas.

The Design

Zoning

The room is divided into two parts. The larger part, toward the window, is dominated by the bed and devoted exclusively to sleeping. The "forward" orientation of the bed places its back to persons entering the room. This unusual position focuses more attention on the sleeper's realm, while the incorporation of a back rest in the headboard keeps this position from compromising bedtime reading.

The second zone of the bedroom, in the foreground of the picture, contains two small areas on either side of the doorway—a dressing area with closet and bureau to the left and a desk area to the right.

Bedboat

The bed is built in boat form around a twin-size water bed. The head- and footboards are built up of 1 x 2- and 1 x 3-inch slats nailed onto 4-inch-wide horizontal ribs. Designed into the headboard is a smaller shelf for books and an alarm clock. Located aft right and left, and on the prow, are three chrome boat lights connected to a single switch and dimmer. If building such a bed is beyond your reach, scout local boatyards for a no-longer-seaworthy rowboat to use as a base.

Floors

Within the bed zone, the floor is covered with blue shag carpet in a shiny fiber. The rug is carried up in "waves" over the baseboard, where it is tacked and covered with a piece of quarter-round molding.

Colors

The ceiling has been painted a midnight purple-blue, with stars of key constellations in the positions they occupied at the moment of the sleeper's astrological birth. Stars can be painted in reflective yellow or purchased as a package of stick-ons that glow in the dark from Childcraft. Walls are painted sunset mauve, slightly pinker on the west wall than the east. Windows and other woodwork are left natural and the bedboat stained to match. A photo-mural of the sea ($80-$100 in wallpaper stores) covers one wall.

Lighting

A large Japanese paper-globe light hangs like a moon near the bed for general room lighting. There are boat lights on the headboard for bedtime reading. Two soft spotlights accentuating the desktop and a picture on the wall of the dressing area give these places a separate personality. A clamp-on over the desk allows flexible lighting for close work.

Personalizations

- Bed blankets are replaced by a cloudlike comforter in sea colors.

- A night light illuminates a moody Dulac painting from *Dulac,* David Larkin ed., Bantam Books.

- On the shelf at the head of the bed is a dream-capture clipboard with an attached night light and felt-tip pen on a string (see p. 39).

- The aquarium above the bureau provides real sea creatures for the room, an underwater glow from the aquarium light at night, and a quiet gurgling noise from the water filter.

- A half-dozen outsized cushion-pillows lie in the bedboat part of the room. Covered in a blue/white velveteen, they provide crests to the floor waves and make a seating alcove in the bay window.

A Sensual Bedroom

Here is a bedroom that takes its inspiration from the sensuous side of bedroom spirituality. Every surface is given a texture pleasing to the eye and touch. An outsized bed sets design motifs for the entire room.

The Room

The room here is typical of most master bedrooms. A sliding glass door is set in one wall, but the cavelike feeling of the place could easily be created in a room with tiny windows and poor views. The walk-in closet at the back of the room, while not a typical amenity, adds to the sensuous appreciation of dressing and undressing in the bedroom.

The Design

The bed

The room is dominated by a large bed sitting in one corner like an outsized, overstuffed chair. Large cushions, like those found in contemporary modular seating, are against the wall side of the bed (forming the "back" of the chair), and along its foot (forming the "side"). Three loose cushions of the same material spill over into a second relaxation area at the floor level. The mirror on the far wall extends the bed in another direction and provides a full-length mirror between the bed and the closet.

Curtains

The room is full of curtains, each providing a special effect. The bed, for example, can be turned into an enclosed chamber by pulling the curtain hanging at the foot around the two open sides. The curtain in front of the window, suffused by sunlight during the day or backlit at night, adds depth to a square room. The walk-in closet against the back wall is covered by another curtain which can be completely opened to display the textures of the owner's wardrobe. A final curtain is hung on the small dressing screen opposite the bed.

Textures

Each surface of the room is covered with a pleasing texture. Curtains hanging against the wall are nubby, open-weave cotton. Bed cushions are upholstered in slippery nylon. A long-pile rug covers the floor and is carried up onto the low platform on which the bed is located. The wall is covered with a wool wallcloth, the two shelf units with reflective Formica laminate. The Victorian chaise longue is tufted leather; the bedspread fur. While the textures of this room are strong, its colors are muted, coming from a family of whites, creams, and beiges, with a brown accent in the bed upholstery.

Lighting

Lighting is particularly important in a room which de-emphasizes light from the outside. Three types of artificial lighting are used here. The first accentuates the varied textures of the room. The long-pile rug, for example, is illuminated by two sources that shine on it from floor level and cast strong-textured shadows across its surface.

One of these is located under the coffee table. Its light is reflected across the rug's surface by the parabolic curve of the table's "foot." The second is a cove light located under the overhang of the bed. Recessed downlights around the edge of the room accentuate the texture of the wallcloth. A second form of lighting (another set of recessed downlights) places "spotlights" on the places where people are concerned about seeing themselves and being seen—the dressing-mirror area, and the bed. Finally, several special-purpose lights provide illumination in the relaxation area beyond the bed and in the walk-in closet.

Sex

It's only fitting that a sensual bedroom provide an especially comfortable setting for sex. The bed is set high off the floor to create an altarlike effect, but surrounded by soft cushions to provide a sense of protection and security. Bed and cushion heights are calculated to support a variety of postures. The full-length mirror speaks for itself. The sumptuous textures of the room create a cavelike quality that reinforces the privacy necessary for spontaneous play. The room's many curtains create a hide-and-seek atmosphere, especially appropriate in the dressing area where see-through Victorian lace beckons to new fantasies about even the most familiar bodies.

Bathrooms and Bodies

Bathrooms are confusing—the smallest but the busiest room in the house; a most private place, yet one where guests can lock themselves in and look around; a room dedicated to our bodies, but too cramped for the most rudimentary exercise; scene of the elegant bath and the workaday dump.

What drew such a crazy assemblage of activities—washing, elimination, shaving, medication, contraception, reading, masturbation, grooming, suicide—into one place? It wasn't always so. Medieval ladies bathed outdoors when they could; the Romans, in vast civic buildings. Not so very long ago, most Americans bathed in the kitchen, washed in their bedrooms, and had a completely separate "out" house for elimination. Europeans still have separate rooms for bathing and elimination.

In America all the activities that remotely involve water (except cooking) get crammed into one room because it takes less plumbing pipe to build houses this way. The logic extends to the vertical dimension as well. If you live in a high-rise, rest assured that precisely above your toilet is another one, and above that, another. Although it was an architect who located all of these activities in one place, it was a larger collusion that made the place itself small and mean.

Our house plans imply that body functions should be kept out of sight and out of mind. Within the bathroom, machinery dominates. Between sink, tub, toilet and shower, most bathrooms are quite crowded before the first person arrives. When we enter, the result is aggravation and chaos. Doors bump against knees, bottles break in the sink, drains clog, someone falls in the tub. Despite ourselves we succumb to the logic that body functions are unpleasant necessities to be tolerated and dismissed.

For all its confusion, the bathroom is an important room to set aright. Ours is an age of new body awareness, and here is the one room in the house that is *about* bodies. If there is pleasure in our bodies, then the bathroom is our pleasure dome. If there is body learning to be done, the bathroom is our school. There's not much space in there, but we can always find room for a luxuriant bath, a proud look at sparkling clean teeth, an invigorating shower, a lufa massage, or some steamy sex.

In a time when body-consciousness is evolving so rapidly, understanding how you relate to bathroom activities will guide you in reconstructing your bathroom. To prompt this understanding we will describe some "secret bathroom selves" and present several fantasy exercises on body themes. Descriptions of bathroom activities in other cultures will give you a fresh perspective on your own values. A few ideas for improving on machinery in the bathroom have been included, as well as a Bathroom Efficiency Inspection. Several pages are devoted to matching goals for your bathroom with practical suggestions for change. The chapter concludes with several how-to projects and sketches of three bathrooms that show how several ideas can be coordinated into an overall personality for the place.

Rejuvenations

1

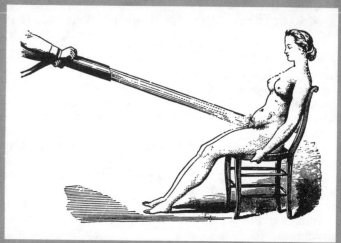

2

3

Three strategies for rejuvenation from earlier times:
1. A mechanical heat closet. **2.** A hydropathic treatment developed by 19th century French doctors for the treatment of abdominal maladies. **3.** Outdoor bathing, medieval style.

Secret Bathroom Selves

The Human Animal

Bathrooms can provide a special kind of rejuvenation to those open to the animal side of their nature. Rejuvenation by warmth is one part of it.

Throughout history rooms of the house (and their occupants) have huddled toward sources of heat. Colonial houses were often built around a large central chimney which serviced fireplaces in each room. During the coldest months, activities centered on the kitchen, a room where there was always an excuse to have a warm fire. Who would have suspected that the bathroom would become the place within the modern house for indulging in our creature need for heat? Between sunlamps, hot tubs, steamy showers, and the tropical room atmosphere that these generate, the bathroom provides our only year-round seduction to the pleasures of body warmth.

In many places the pursuit of warmth has produced a subculture all its own. The Finnish sauna tradition has sparked a new interest in sweat-bathing in this country. But perhaps the American Indian experience speaks most directly to those of us still trying to cope with the North American climate. Sweat lodges were used by Eskimos and Aleuts to the north, Yuroks and Okanagans to the west, and Chippewas and Omahas of the Great Plains. Most

frequently sweat-baths were relaxing interludes in an arduous day, but they often served medical and religious functions as well. In some tribes such baths provided ritual purification after a death in the village and initiation ceremonies for the young. Construction and use of the sweat house involved rituals recognizing the four elements: earth for the floor and heated rocks, water for steam, fire for heating the lodge, and air heated during the ceremony itself.

Heat generated for sweat-baths is fortifying to the body. Though the temperature within a sauna rises to between 160 and 200 degrees, homeostatic mechanisms within the body restrict body temperature gain to 1 or 2 degrees. Pulse typically increases during a sweat-bath from 70 to 125 beats per minute, with an accompanying increase in blood pressure and distribution of blood to the skin. Many claim that the sauna alleviates rheumatism and arthritis, that it clears nasal passages, activates sex hormones and cleanses the skin through sweating. Although research and experience generally support the beneficial effects of sauna, children, the elderly, pregnant women, and those with special health conditions (especially heart disease) should consult a doctor prior to taking sauna baths.

Other forms of animal rejuvenation take place in the bathroom—a splash of cold water in the morning, the tingle of a close shave, a shampoo. Showers have their own spartan appeal.

For 85% of American families the bathroom is the site of home first aid. It is here that we keep the salves, splints, and pills which soothe our aches and get us through the night.

Adams and Eves

Next to the human animal that we see in our mirror stand other selves, more aware of the social and sexual dimensions of the bathroom. These Adams and Eves understand the subtler messages conveyed by transparent shower curtains and towels draped over clean torsos.

After a stay at Baden-Baden, one of the many European resorts dedicated to the pleasures of bathing, the Florentine humanist Bracciolini wrote, "I think this must be the place where the first man was created, which the Hebrews call the garden of pleasure." The place, he reported, "resounds with song and music, and offers banquets on floating tables to the bathers. Garlands and crowns of flowers are thrown down (from the gallery) with which the ladies ornament their heads while they remain in the water. In the shallow part of the water they play upon the harp."

Our own bathtubs, though less resplendent, are no less primal. Here we can lie down and bob gently in a warm medium, recapturing the peace of inner body floating that was our life before birth. Oils, scents, clouds of warm bubbles are all at home here. Hail the one place in the house where, report the tireless sex surveyors, female masturbation exceeds that by men.

The Friendly Nudist

Bathrooms bring out the friendly nudist in people, especially children. Thirty percent of kids aged 2–10 walk nude to the shower (less than half as many adults do). Eighty percent of kids aged 4–5 share baths. The presence of very young children tends to promote nudism among parents, but when kids get a little older, a reverse effect sets in. Only one quarter of American parents object to being seen nude by children under 2, but half object to being seen nude by older children. Boys frighten adults more than girls; parental nudism starts to decrease when sons hit 6, but the presence of daughters doesn't change things until they reach 12.

Friendly nudism is the exception, not the rule, in American bathrooms. Three quarters of American families share the bathroom during teeth brushing, but only half during bathing, one in three for urination, and one in four for defecation.

Public bathing was quite common in the West until Elizabethan times. Among the most magnificent of Roman buildings were the thermae, or public baths. Here, as Gibbon notes, "the meanest Roman could purchase, with a small copper coin, the daily enjoyment of a scene of pomp and luxury which might excite the envy of the kings of Asia." Roman baths were used not only for cleaning, but as a place to meet and talk, exercise, gamble, and even read. Three activities were involved: a hot bath in a steamy chamber, a relaxing soak in warm water, and finally a dive into a cold water pool. During the Middle Ages, morning trumpets would announce the opening of the neighborhood steam bath. Most people undressed at home and walked to the bath naked, except for a valuable necklace or sword.

The Person of Refinement

For some people the bathroom functions primarily as a "backstage" for their performance in the world. Such bathrooms often take on qualities of the world outside: a rug, decorator cabinetry, period furniture. Bodily functions are hidden away. Stores specializing in bathroom furniture sell a variety of *chaises percées,* caned chairs which fit over the toilet to disguise its function. Queen Victoria's bathtub was located behind cabinet doors, leaving only looped chintz curtains, a fireplace, and a collection of paintings in evidence between baths. Such arrangements provide a special status revenge when the occasional guest wanders in. "And what did *you* come to do?" the room seems to ask.

Knowing your bathroom personality is important in designing a bathroom that will make you feel comfortable. Some people play the superstar in their bathroom, others the recluse. Yves St. Laurent has a design studio in his. Liberator bombers, returning from World War II, turned their tail turrets into bathrooms. Knowing who you want to be in the bathroom will give you direction on many issues: whether plants are appropriate, how to use mirrors, whether the place should be bright or dark, what kind of floor to install, whether to hang landscapes or nudes on the wall, etc.

The American Way

I will take occasion . . . to mention a practice to which I have accustomed myself. You know the cold bath has long been in vogue here as a tonic; but the shock of the cold water has always appeared to me, generally speaking, as too violent, and I have found it much more agreeable to my constitution to bathe in another element, I mean cold air. With this view, I rise almost every morning, and sit in my chamber without any clothes whatever, half an hour or an hour, according to the season, either reading or writing. The practice is not in the least painful, but on the contrary agreeable. . . . I find no ill consequences whatever resulting from it, and that, at least, it does not injure my health; if it does not in fact contribute much to its preservation. I shall therefore call it for the future a bracing *or* tonic *bath.*

Ben Franklin

Bathroom Fantasies

The bathroom is a natural location for flights of imagination. Martin Luther, we are told, did his deepest philosophizing there. Rodin named his tribute to the time-honored position "The Thinker."

To complete the bathroom fantasies that follow, read the directions, shut your eyes, relax and take as much time as you need to conclude the story through your own fantasizing. Exchange descriptions afterward if you are with a friend.

The Royal Bath

You are on a trip to Asia Minor. After several hard days' traveling you arrive in Istanbul. Friends have described an establishment where you can experience a miraculous bathing ritual. Be prepared, they say, to spend the afternoon. You search out the place in a dense neighborhood near the Golden Horn. The building looks like a cross between a mosque and an opium den. Imagine the sequence of baths, massages, and relaxations that come your way within. Include hot things and cold, active periods and quiet, small trays of appropriate food and drink, and the rooms or chambers that provide settings for each event.

A Great Dump

You are on a wilderness trek to your favorite natural area. A week has passed since you headed into unfamiliar territory. With each step the landscape grows more exciting. Today, if your calculations are correct, you will arrive at the most beautiful spot of all. During the morning's hike, nature calls but you decide to wait so you can relieve yourself in the most beautiful spot in the world. Imagine the last few miles of your trek, the bursting scenery, and the event you have anticipated so patiently.

Nudism Survey

Some bathrooms promote nudism while others restrict it. Here is a survey which will help stir your thoughts about nudism and thus help you decide whether you want more or less of it in your bathroom.

To fill out the survey, take the name of one person at a time from the list on the left. For each name, try to remember how old you were when you first saw that person nude. Mark an "X" on the line opposite that person's name at the appropriate age. If you never saw that person nude, put an "X" to the far right of the line. If a certain category does not apply, leave it blank.

When you have finished filling in the chart, connect all the X's with a line, starting at the top and moving to the bottom of the chart. The area to the left of the line is your "Zone of Innocence"; to the right is your "Zone of Experience."

Try having a friend or spouse fill in the chart and compare readings. If you can talk with your parents about such things, try having them fill out a chart. Were many of your nude encounters bathroom-related? Do you want your bathroom to be more or less supportive of nudism than the ones you grew up with?

AGE:	0	10 yrs	20 yrs	30 yrs	Never

Mark an "X" at the age you were when you first saw the following persons nude. For example, if you were 10 when you first saw a brother or sister nude, mark an "X" on the first line below age 10.

Brother or Sister _____

Father _____

Mother _____

A Friend (not a lover) of the Same Sex _____

A Friend (not a lover) of the Opposite Sex _____

A Lover _____

A Stripper _____

Bright Life Survey

Fantasy is a powerful tool for promoting body awareness and health. This exercise is designed to give you new perspective on your body's urge to health. By filling out the charts here you can create an image of your body as vibrant, healthful, and energetic.

Get a set of colored pencils or crayons. First look at the colors you have. Which color best expresses the way you feel about the healthiest part of your body? Starting with that color, and using any others you wish, fill in each part of the body outline in the Bright Life Chart in the brightest and most beautiful way you can imagine. Proceed one part at a time. Look at the chart; imagine where each part is located on your own body; and decorate freely.

We have included names for the major parts of the body represented on the chart around the outside. The thin line drawn just around the body represents the nervous sytem. The dotted line beyond that represents your "aura." Think of the aura as a magnetic field radiating from the body, expressive of the condition of all the subsystems.

When you have completed the chart, hold it in bright light. As you look at it, take a deep breath and imagine that you are blowing fire and light into the image. Enjoy your body image as a bright new planet in the universe.

The Bright Life idea comes from a beautiful book which emphasizes the role of good thinking in health, *The Well Body Book,* (Random House/Bookworks), by Mike Samuels and Hal Bennett.

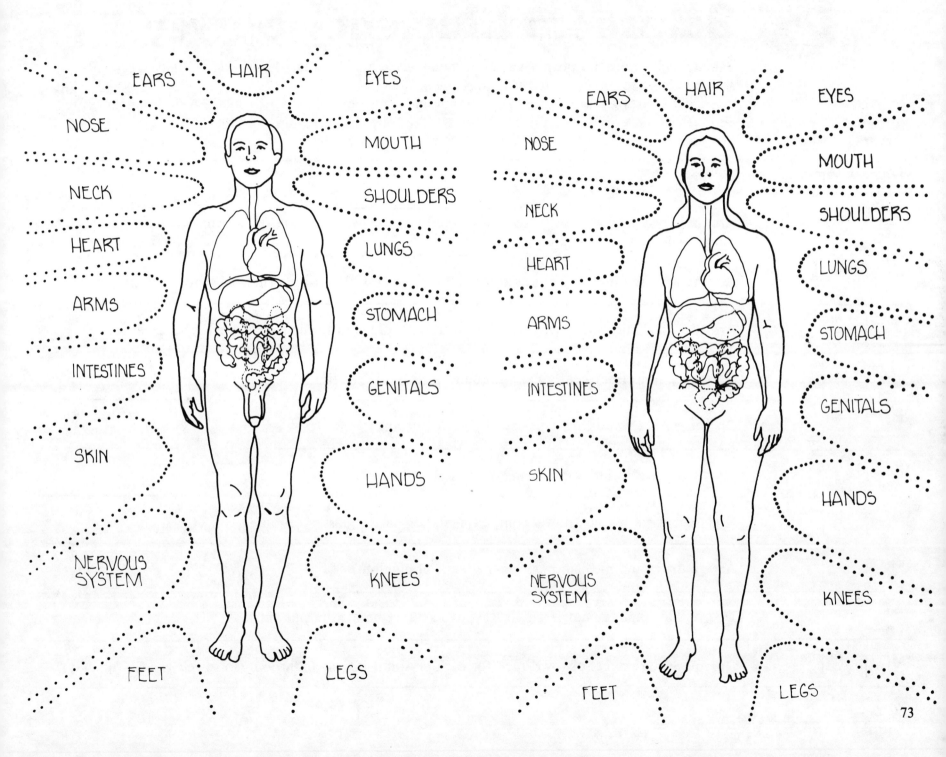

EARS HAIR EYES
NOSE MOUTH
NECK SHOULDERS
HEART LUNGS
ARMS STOMACH
INTESTINES GENITALS
SKIN HANDS
NERVOUS SYSTEM KNEES
FEET LEGS

EARS HAIR EYES
NOSE MOUTH
NECK SHOULDERS
HEART LUNGS
ARMS STOMACH
INTESTINES GENITALS
SKIN HANDS
NERVOUS SYSTEM KNEES
FEET LEGS

73

Bathroom Efficiency Survey

Twenty-eight thousand people will die in home accidents this year; 12 million will have accidents severe enough to restrict work or require medical attention.

Accident rates go up 20 times for children under one and for older people. To find out how safe and efficient your bathroom is, read through the following questions and mark the "yes" or "no" box as appropriate. If a question doesn't apply, leave it blank.

High Marks	Low Marks	
YES ☐	NO ☐	Do you have a place to hang a towel and bathrobe located not more than six inches from the shower?
YES ☐	NO ☐	Are there two grab-bars (with no sharp edges) next to your bathtub, one about two feet high, and the other about four feet high?
YES ☐	NO ☐	Are the windows in your bathroom located in an accessible position (not behind the bathtub)?
YES ☐	NO ☐	Are all water faucets arranged with hot to the left and cold to the right? Are they marked?
YES ☐	NO ☐	Is your bathtub floor nearly flat with built-in slip resistant finish?
YES ☐	NO ☐	Do you have a water-saving device in your toilet tank?
YES ☐	NO ☐	Do you have aerating water-saving nozzles on your faucets?
YES ☐	NO ☐	If glass is used in your shower compartment, is it safety glass?
YES ☐	NO ☐	Are all drugs and medicines out of the reach of children?
YES ☐	NO ☐	Do you have light coming from at least two sources beside the sink mirror?
YES ☐	NO ☐	Do you have two feet of towel rack for each person using the bathroom (so towels can dry quickly)?

YES   **NO**

TOTAL   TOTAL

Goals/Solutions

The next few pages present some specific ideas for making your bathroom more health-related, more sensual, bigger and brighter, and better for kids. If any of these goals suits you, read through the solutions suggested and set to work on one or two.

If your goal is

To make a bathroom better for kids

Given half a chance, kids will take to bathrooms like they do to summer vacation. Where else in the house can you lock the door, play with water, and be nude? In order to set up a good bathroom for kids, make it easy to clean, child-sized, safe, and fun.

 Child-size

Install a six-inch molding board around your bathroom, about two feet from the floor. On it put the kids' towel racks, toothbrush holders, clothes hooks, mirrors, and bins for shampoo, bandages, and tub toys. For access to adult-size sinks and apparatus, build a stand-on cube, one foot on each side, that will slide under the sink when not in use.

 Kid-proofing

Consider washbasins with anti-splash rims; door locks you can open from outside; child-proof locks on medicine cabinets; thermostatically controlled showers to prevent scalding; and non-slip rugs and toilet seat covers.

 Bubble splash

No-splash nozzles on sink and shower faucets (the kind that fill the water with little air bubbles) will reduce the mess created by water play.

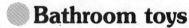 **Bathroom toys**

Some good bathtub toys include pump-and-splash dolls, rubber-band paddle-wheelers, submarines that rise and sink, floating ducks, swim goggles, and water pistols.

 Double bath

Install a large-size bathtub, with the controls to the side. Now you can hop in with the kids, or they can have a friend join them on a hot afternoon.

 Mud-bath

Construct a "mudroom" near an outside door of your home. Include a shower, sink, toilet, and lots of storage space. Tile the whole room so you can hose it down when it gets dirty. Use it for showers when you are especially dirty, for messy projects like finger painting, for shaking off when it's rainy, for dog washing or plant misting, and for storing winter boots and coats.

 Child-designed

Go to a store with a wide selection of shower curtains and towels for children and adults. Let everyone choose a towel. Lay them all out on the counter to see how they look together, and select a shower curtain that unites them all. Find a clear plastic shower curtain and let the kids decorate it using permanent magic markers.

To make a bathroom more health-related

Bright life

Mount your Bright Life Chart (see p. 72) in the bathroom where you can look at it each morning. Paint your bathroom in the colors you used for the chart so that even after you take it down, the whole room will reflect the good energy you feel in your body.

Hot towels

Heating your bath towels helps them dry faster (fewer germs), keeps you from chills (fewer sneezes), and feels great. Chromed pipes plumbed through the hot water feed will accomplish this pretty well. Baths and showers generally use enough hot water to warm things up. Electrically heated towel racks are also available. These can provide a little extra room heat in winter.

Examination

The bathroom is the best place to have a close look at your body. (*The Well Body Book* contains a good exercise for getting acquainted with your body through a mirror.) Install two floor-length mirrors opposite each other so you can get both a front and back view at the same time. Install an illuminated close-up mirror for micro-examinations.

Health chart

Mark off a piece of chart paper in days along the bottom and put it up in your bathroom. Becoming aware of your own health rhythms is the first step in preventive health care. Mark your weight and any health symptoms you want to track: indigestion, headaches, sleep, sinus congestion, allergy attacks, etc. You can chart more than one variable on a single graph by establishing different vertical scales. If there are kids around, chart heights, weights, colds, etc. Very young children won't be able to mark things on the chart, but they will learn a lot from watching their health lines go up and down.

M.D.

Find room for a "medical poster of the month" in your bathroom. Some of these are quite beautiful, and all are informative. Best bets: the cut-away pregnant lady, heart system, eyes, and of course, the time-honored cross-sections of male and female reproductive systems. (Obstetrically related posters can be obtained through the Maternity Center Association in New York.)

First aid

Set up a first aid corner in your bathroom. Hang a well-supplied first aid kit on the wall. Post instructions for emergency heart resuscitation, choking, and treatment for shock. Paint the wall in a supergraphic of the colors and pattern of the first aid kit.

Steam treatment

A water-tight shower or bathtub stall can be turned into a steam room by installing a small steam generator and vapor-proof doors.

If your goal is

To make your bathroom more sensual

● See-through

Buy a transparent shower curtain or one with Baroque nudes in outline.

● Lovelight

The glaringest bathroom light turns to candle glow with the simple addition of a rheostat. As you turn the power down, the light moves toward a flesh color tantalizingly flattering to skin tones. Add a couple of strategic mirrors and put the *Joy of Sex* on the bathroom reading shelf.

● Group heat

Install a sauna near your bathroom for good sensations, good health, and good times. A ready-made model from Baths International sells for $545 and holds one person. Build a sauna for three yourself for $1,000. Converting an abandoned hot water heater into a sauna rock heater will save you lots of money on equipment (see *The Sauna Book,* Harper and Row, for details).

● Body color

Get a set of color-matching cards from an art supply store. Find the color closest to your own lips and skin, before and after a tan. Use these shades to set the color scheme for your bathroom. If anyone peers in, you can camouflage yourself by standing against the wall.

● Hot time

Warm your bathtub by raising it on one-inch blocks and using the space underneath as the hot-air duct for the bathroom heating system. Buy a hot-lather machine to heat your favorite shaving foam. Install slab heating in the floor of your bathroom so that your feet are the first things to get warmed in nippy weather.

● Water massage

Install a whirlpool machine in your tub, a massage head in your shower, or, if you're still sore, a padded toilet seat.

● Showerful

A shower stall 40 inches by 40 inches will provide enough room for two to shower at the same time. Tile it with your favorite colors, add a soft light, tune the shower to a tropical mist, and soap up.

● Polish

Reflective surfaces will make your bathroom seem bigger. Silvered glass mirrors are best where you need an accurate image, but acrylic mirror can be cut to fit odd spaces with wood-working tools. One-inch-square mirror tiles create a mystifying effect on counter or wall surfaces. All of this sparkle is complemented by glossy paints, chrome fittings, and sparkle light fixtures.

● Bathroom fantasy

Fantasy worlds take up very little space in a bathroom. Frame a roadmap of your favorite part of the country and mount it next to the toilet.

If your goal is

To make your bathroom seem bigger and brighter

Those who build houses are usually too embarrassed about bathrooms to have real heart-to-hearts with their clients over the topic, so bathrooms usually wind up small and dingy. With a little ingenuity, however, even the smallest bathrooms can be made to feel bigger and brighter.

 ## Places

Giving parts of your bathroom their own personality will make the room seem larger. Such places needn't take up much room—a plant corner, a set of shelves for books and display, a gallery wall, visible storage of colorful linen, a Hollywood vanity mirror. Give each place special lighting which goes on when the bathroom light is turned on.

 ## Bath room

A bathtub or shower can occupy as much as one-third of the space within a bathroom. If you can open up the tub and shower areas, so they feel like alcoves off your bathroom instead of separate places, the room will feel larger. This can be accomplished by hanging plants and a grow-light inside the bathing area, using transparent shower curtains or door, and continuing the color scheme of the bathroom into the area. If there is a window on the other side of your tub, show it off with home-stained glass.

 ## Rearrange

Consider putting your new shower in the bedroom or under the stairs instead of in the bathroom. Use the liberated space in your bathroom for a sunlamp, greenhouse, or mirror area. Replace old sinks or toilets with triangular fixtures designed to be tucked tidily into corners of the room.

Color

With all its towels, facecloths, shower curtains, bathmats, linen storage, curtains, and rugs, most of your bathroom is made of cloth. Getting lively sympathetic colors for these textiles can brighten your bathroom. Find bath linens in the brightest colors you can imagine; then buy enough matching cloth at a fabric store for a six-foot-square drape in front of your regular shower curtain.

Bathroom Inspirations

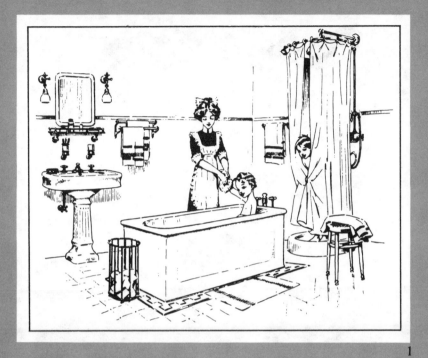

1. A turn of the century bathroom from a Kohler Company catalogue. 2. A medical rain bath controlled by the doctor from his observation platform, France, 1860. 3. A portable prairie outhouse. 4. Several traditional Japanese towel racks.

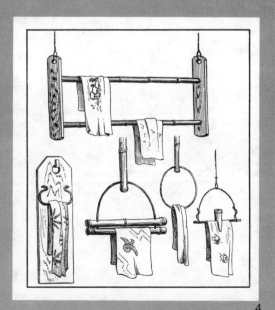

1

2

3

4

1

2

Aura Mirror

Included in the Bright Life Chart earlier in the chapter (p. 72) was a place to color in your "aura"—that psychic emanation that mystics see hovering around each person's body. Presented here is an aura mirror which surrounds a clear mirror image of yourself with fractions and multiplications of that image. Whether these will reveal your aura depends on your own psychic energy (and perhaps whether or not you have had your morning coffee). In any case, it will frame your present mirror with shimmering reflections of the lights and colors in your bathroom. It can easily be made in a few hours, for less than $10.

STEP 1. Obtain materials

- a mirror. A larger mirror will give you more room around the edge to work with. If your present mirror is too narrow, buy a larger one, or extend it by gluing strips of chipboard around the sides on the back of the mirror.
- aluminized reflective Mylar sheet vinyl, .003-mil thick, with adhesive backing. A two-foot length, 52 inches wide, is just enough to surround a 20 x 60-inch mirror. Local art or architect supply houses will have this material, or you can order it from Charrette Inc., Woburn, Mass.
- some cardboard.
- white glue.

STEP 2.

Measure and cut the Mylar vinyl strips you need to surround your mirror. Try to make a band 6 inches wide around the mirror.

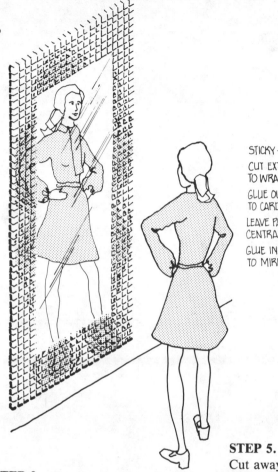

CORNER DETAIL

USE **WIDE** MIRROR (FULL OR HALF SIZE) OTHERWISE BUILD OUT FROM EDGES WITH CARDBOARD

1' WIDE CARDBOARD STRIPS GLUED TO MIRROR EDGES

STICKY-BACK ALUMINIZED MYLAR:

CUT EXTRA ROW OF SQUARES TO WRAP AROUND SIDES

GLUE OUTER SQUARES TO CARDBOARD

LEAVE PAPER BACK ON CENTRAL SQUARES

GLUE INSIDE SQUARES TO MIRROR

STEP 3.

Score the Mylar vinyl into one-inch squares using the dull edge of a butter knife and a ruler. Lay the material on a pile of newspapers and press hard when you score it, so each square will form a little convex mirror.

STEP 4.

Cut your cardboard into 1-inch strips and glue these around the edge of your mirror, on the front, as indicated in the diagram. These strips raise the outer edge of the squares a little so they will reflect more of your image.

STEP 5.

Cut away the paper backing from the inner row and the outer two rows of squares, as indicated in the diagram. Position the strips of squares around the mirror. First press the inner row of squares to the mirror. Then stretch the material tight and press the outer row to the cardboard strip, wrapping the outermost row around the edge of the mirror so it can be glued to the back. The middle rows of squares are left with their paper backing on because they form smoother mirrors that way.

STEP 6.

Attach mirror to wall.

Body Furniture

Here are two simple projects that can put a little body in your bathroom. Most bathrooms are under-equipped with storage and mirrors. If you have a three-foot section of free wall in your bathroom, try constructing one of these units framed by twisting body shapes. With their human curves, they alleviate the boxy feeling of most small bathrooms.

All you need is one sheet of 3/4-inch particle board—a material slightly more dense than plywood and a little harder to cut, but one which gives sharp splinter-free edges and smooth surfaces for painting. The Korpine and Novaply brands of particle board are stronger than the more common "underlayment board." Lay the pieces out on the board using the 6-inch grid indicated on the diagram. If your ceiling is lower than eight feet, you will want to adjust the height of the upright body shapes to fit snugly between floor and ceiling. Cut out the pieces with a saber saw and sand the edges slightly to avoid chipping. To install either unit in a house with a wooden floor and ceiling, screw the bottom piece to the floor and two furring strips to the ceiling as indicated in the drawing. The upright body shapes may then be screwed and glued securely to these. If you are unable to attach supports to your floor and ceiling, you must make the unit independently stable by screwing two braces of 12-inch pine shelving between the upright body pieces against the back wall of the unit. The stabilized unit can

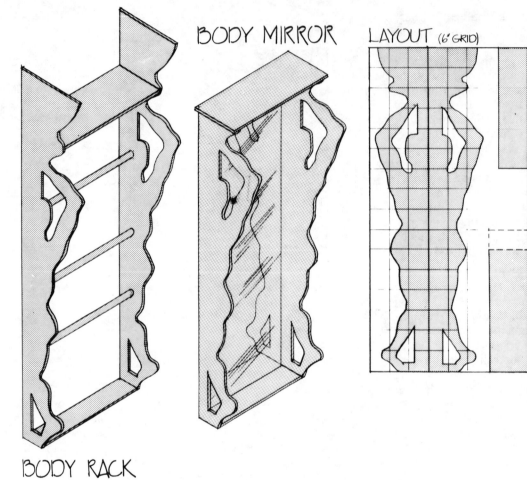

BODY MIRROR

LAYOUT (6" GRID)

36" BOTTOM PIECE

36" SHELF, TOWEL RACK

42" TOP ON MIRROR UNIT

BODY RACK

then be held back against the wall with wire securing the top of the unit to the ceiling molding at two points.

If you are building the mirror unit, you will need a 3- by 7-foot mirror. If you cannot find one this large, adjust the width of the unit accordingly (mirrors less than 30 inches wide will be overwhelmed by this frame). The mirror should be hung directly on the wall, not attached to the frame.

Shower Planter

There is a natural affinity between plants and showers. The warmth and moisture of the bathroom make it more like a greenhouse than any other place in the house. All those plants you never get around to misting automatically get a dose every time someone takes a bath or shower. The combination works from the human point of view, as well. Here is the one place in the house where we want to feel at home with nothing on. The harsh lighting and cold floors of most bathrooms, however, provide an inhospitable environment for such exposure. A few plants in there with us can make the place feel more like a garden and less like a plumbing machine. Here, then, is a simple device that will allow you to share your bathtub or shower with some friendly plants. The idea comes from Ethan Anthony, a student of mine with a lot of experience in fixing up people's homes.

A clear plastic tube, filled with water, is suspended from the ceiling near the bathtub. Plants grow hydroponically (in the water) and cascade over the edges to create an organic shower curtain. A fish tank water filter, fitted into one of the holes in the tube keeps the water clean and creates a pleasant bubbling sound overhead.

You must select plants suited for the light and moisture conditions of your bathroom. Placement and pruning of plants is important as well. Although many species will thrive on moisture and heat, almost all will be scalded if touched directly by hot water from the shower. The location for the shower

planter shown in the drawing—just outside the shower curtain—is thus especially appropriate. At the foot of the shower, toward the ceiling, is another natural place to hang two or three shorter tubes. An "L"-shaped tube could hold plants in both of these positions and be served by a single bubbler.

STEP 1. Obtain materials

- clear acrylic tube, 1/4- or 3/16-inch thick, 4 inches in diameter.
- a one-foot-square piece of 1/4- or 3/16-inch thick clear acrylic.
- a small bottle of acrylic cement (a clear, thin fluid which dissolves the plastic and reconstitutes it in a bond as strong as the plastic itself).
- a one-inch diameter rubber stopper from a scientific supply house.
- one 3-inch-long, 3/16-inch-diameter threaded hook or eyebolt, with two washers and nuts, for each two feet of tube.
- hydroponic plant holders to secure plants in holes along the top of the tube.
- a small, continuous-action water filter.

STEP 2. Build plant tubes

Cut squares from the sheet acrylic to fit over the ends of the tube and glue in place (see diagram). Drill a one-inch-diameter hole in the lower side of one end plate for draining the tube when necessary. Plug the hole with the rubber stopper. Cut holes along the top of the tube for inserting plants. The size and shape of these holes is determined by the hydroponic plant holders you have purchased. The

plants should sit just above the water line when the tube is 2/3 filled with water. Attach eyebolts or hooks about every two feet along the top of the tube with nuts and washers inside the tube and outside. Locate the hooks close enough to the plant holes so you can reach inside to hold the inside nut with your fingers.

STEP 3. Install

Hang the tube from the ceiling with screw hooks, expansion bolts, or toggle bolts as required. Fill tube about 2/3 full of water and insert plants. Place water filter inside tube and plug in.

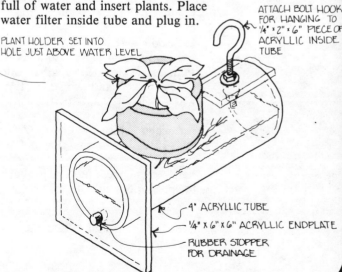

PLANT HOLDER SET INTO HOLE JUST ABOVE WATER LEVEL

ATTACH BOLT HOOK FOR HANGING TO 1/4" X 2" X 6" PIECE OF ACRYLLIC INSIDE TUBE

4" ACRYLLIC TUBE

1/4" X 6" X 6" ACRYLLIC ENDPLATE

RUBBER STOPPER FOR DRAINAGE

A Social Bathroom

No more squeeze-by, one-at-a-time, and wait-till-I'm-finished. Here's a bathroom that provides a great environment for lots of people to be in at the same time. Big, comfortable, with a natural feel, this room encourages so many pleasurable activities it could replace the kitchen as the central room of a liberated household.

The Room

At 150 square feet, the space in which this bathroom has been constructed is about three times the size of most bathrooms. It could be created, however, by a renovation that adds the space of a large closet, part of a hall, or half a typical bedroom into an existing bath. Minimization of replumbing, do-it-yourself carpentry, use of roughcut lumber, and avoidance of costly cabinetry can keep renovation costs down.

The Design

At the far end of the room is the most popular toilet in the house. It is located out of the mainstream of bathroom activities to provide just the right amount of privacy and access. Plants growing in the counter- and doortop-level windowboxes in this area will be perceived as a barrier by those concerned with privacy and a permeable screen by others. With an expansive view on one side and an intimate bonsai world on the other, it is hard to imagine a more engaging place to spend a few minutes of every day.

Sauna
The enclosed corner behind the bathtub contains a sauna. For serious students of the sweat-bath, the bathtub can be filled with icy water.

Relaxation Area
Toward the front of the bathroom is a generous space for just hanging out. A low seat on one side, next to the tub, makes a good place for adults to sit while bathing children. Two seats opposite flank a massage table which folds into the wall like a Murphy bed. When lowered, the table provides a padded counter-level surface with room to stand on either side. It can be used for massage, relaxation exercises, children's climbing games, or backgammon. Nearby is ample space for hanging towels and clothes. A wall-size mirror in condensation-free acrylic encourages the natural curiosity of the nude and doubles the perceived number of guests at bathroom functions. A sunlamp is installed in the ceiling. Although there never seems to be enough space for it, calisthenics and other active forms of exercise are natural bathroom activities. Working up a good sweat has long been recognized as a special form of deep cleansing. Above the relaxation area is a horizontal ladder, one of the most useful indoor exercise devices. When the massage table is folded into the wall, there is enough room for vigorous exercises like jumping rope or for quieter disciplines like yoga.

Tub
In the center of the bathroom is a large combination shower-tub. Its 40-by-40-inch size allows simultaneous bathing and showering by more than one person. A shower curtain is used instead of sliding glass doors because it allows more kinds of privacy. An opaque shower curtain turns the shower into a room-within-a-room, defined at ceiling level by the "window-box" beam. Installation of a more transparent curtain creates a playful, hide-and-seek privacy. Pulling curtains back allows the option of opening the tub to the larger relaxation area nearby.

Sink Area

Double sinks encourage multiple morning use of the bathroom. A large vanity-area allows household activities like shampoos, baby changing, and messy children's play to take place in the bathroom. Above the sinks are two medicine cabinets, a radio, open shelf storage for linen, stereo speakers, a small refrigerator, and a hot and cold water dispenser for bathroom cocktails.

Climate

If people are to spend lots of time in the bathroom, its climate must be carefully tailored to the needs of exposed bodies. The floor of this room, for example, is of rubber-surfaced natural cork, a nonskid material (especially important for older people and children) that is warm to bare feet. The sauna, which provides its own microclimate, helps keep the rest of the bathroom warm when in use. A few splashes of water on the sauna rocks as people leave will fill the whole bathroom with steam and make the plants ecstatic. The tub area, closed in at the top by the box beam, is another microenvironment which can be brought to a much higher temperature than the whole room.

A Bathroom for Bodies

Here is a bathroom that takes the "bathrooms and bodies" theme of this chapter seriously. It is difficult to stay clothed in this room where the storage closet, towel rack, and even a full-length mirror have already undressed. The space here is not large, but each part of it has been tailored to the needs of a different bodily function served by the bathroom.

The Design

Bathing Area

Bathrooms in most homes are disastrously small places. The cramped quarters and overlapping of uncongenial activities which result make feeling at home there difficult. Care has been taken in this design to provide a measure of privacy for the various bathroom functions. The bathing area, for example, has been enclosed by a wall with two arches, one containing linen storage, the other a curtained entrance. This simple expedient, combined with appropriate lighting within the tub area, turns the shower into a true bathroom whose climate and exposure to the rest of the house can be adjusted by successive occupants.

Toilet Area

The toilet is set into a small niche which emphasizes its quality as porcelain sculpture (its organic form is a not-inappropriate presence in this room). Psychological separation from other bathroom activities is obtained by the low wall between toilet and sink containing shelves for reading material and a two-handed toilet paper caddy.

Sink Area

The sink is framed by an arched opening with a fitted mirror. In the topmost part of the opening is strong incandescent lighting for close-up tasks like shaving. Down one side are open shelves forming a medicine cabinet whose contents are accessible but hidden from general view.

Storage Wall

Opposite the toilet is a wall serving a variety of bathroom functions. Each of its bays is framed by dividers cut in shapes suggested by the human body. The first bay is a full-length mirror which frames the body of the observer with body images to either side. The second is a combination storage shelf and towel rack. On the back wall is a set of open shelves for linen storage.

Color

For the walls, a flesh tone light enough to make the bodies of the room's inhabitants seem especially colorful; for the floor tiles, dark ocher; for "orifices" of the room (the slots between double arches over the sink, toilet, and shower entry), deep red made even deeper by recessed lighting in these areas.

BY JEROME SIMON

87

A Refined Bathroom

A most refined setting for those inclined, by nature or upbringing, to the discreet interpretation of bathroom functions. The genteel presence of antique furnishings and classical architectural references create a cultivated but luxurious atmosphere.

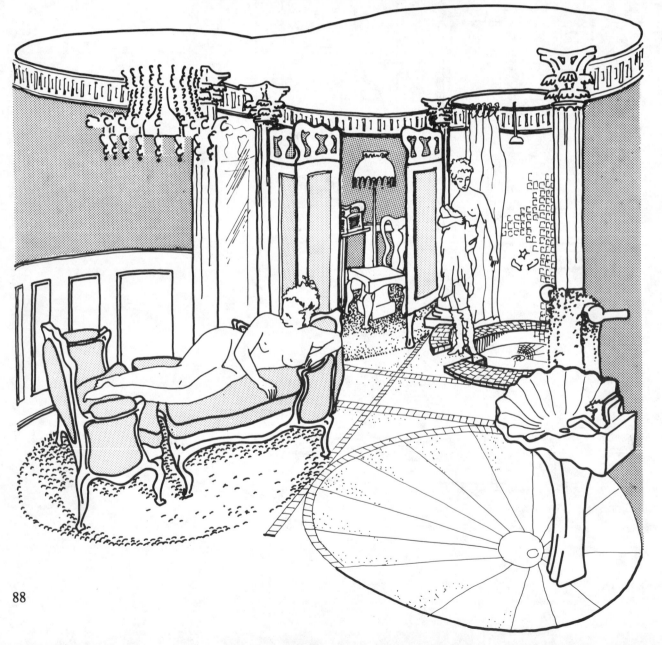

The Room

Getting nontraditional functions into the bathroom helps give it an air of refinement. Here we have added some "drawing room" and a touch of "natatorium." Such additions demand more space. The plan here requires a room 12 by 16 feet, a size that could be attained in most houses by adding half of a nearby room to the bathroom (the other half would naturally become a dressing area). Not an inexpensive bathroom, renovations, fittings, and furniture described here could easily cost $20,000 to create. In the spirit of our other room designs, however, we present it for its connotative qualities and describe achievable as well as extravagant features of its design.

The room is entered from between the paired columns to the right. Windows have been covered in adding the circular subareas at each corner of the space. Although it is generally preferable to have a bathroom open to the outdoors for ventilation and natural light, this room's complete isolation from external influences adds drama to the world it creates within. If you have windows in your bathroom, addition of sumptuous curtains can make the place feel more refined.

The Design

Bathing Circle

Each of the four circular areas contains a major bathroom function. To the immediate right of the entrance is the bathing area, a sunken tiled pool whose lowest level can serve as an out-sized tub. The step around this area provides a sitting bench when the curtain is drawn and the area becomes a large shower. The tub and walls are tiled in an electric blue.

Toilet Compartment

The next zone is a most genteel toilet compartment. In it is a Queen Anne *chaise percée*. We felt it appropriate to complement this piece with matching Queen Anne floor lamp and adjustable book holder.

Lounge

Included in the third zone of our refined bathroom is one of the most sensuous pieces of furniture ever conceived, a carved walnut *duchesse brisée,* consisting of a *bergèe en gondole* and an extended lounge rest. It dates from about 1759, a dynamic period in the history of furniture when designers were doing for the wooden supports of their pieces what architects had done for stone in the Gothic cathedrals. The result was an organic art form dedicated to the most discriminating forms of relaxation. Even unoccupied, this double piece speaks of sybaritic postures and mysterious couplings. It is hard to imagine inhabiting either portion of it in innocence. In this room it serves as arbiter of taste, host to the bathroom lounge, and couch for sunlamp treatments from the fixture hidden in the chandelier overhead.

Sink Area

The fourth zone of the room is a washing area, containing sink, towels, and storage for toilet articles. The sink is a conch-shaped fixture in onyx. The floor is tile again, in quieter colors from the same blue family as the shower, laid in a pattern that radiates from the foot of the basin.

Entry

The back of the door and the wall directly across from it are covered in mirror. The view upon entering is thus yourself, in an infinitely regressing colonnade.

Living Room Friendships

4

Living rooms shelter the friendships that sustain our lives. The best living rooms are memory books of quiet conversations with old friends, boisterous parties, and heartfelt reconciliations with loved ones.

A kind of craziness sets in, however, when we think about decorating the place. Because it is also our home's face to the world, fixing up the living room occasions more soul-searching and disagreement than any other task of home design.

The approach taken throughout this book—basing physical design on the emotional dynamics of a room—leads us to begin here with a general discussion of friendships and the nature of places that nurture friendliness. A "friendship survey" will help you appreciate the nature of your present friendships, and two exercises will reveal how these relationships are accommodated in your present environment. Several living rooms and how-to projects are then followed by illustrations of living rooms designed for entertaining, family use, and making maximum use of small spaces.

Intimate Friends, Colleagues and Acquaintances

Friendships differ widely in the needs they serve and the understandings they represent. We all have three kinds of friends: colleagues, intimate friends, and casual acquaintances. Of the three, intimate friends are perhaps the most essential. Only with our closest friends can we be known as we really are. Intimate friends play an important role in affirming our identity over time. In periods of crisis, our close friends remind us that we have the resources to survive. Wise friends know they can never solve our problems for us, but how soothing is the attention of one who cares. Often, just voicing the problem that weighs us down suggests its own resolution.

Intimate friendship is important to physical as well as emotional well-being. In a survey of 300 New York women, those who had no friends they could describe as "confidantes" reported more negative moods (tiredness, irritation), more depression and more physical distress (headaches, palpitations, dizziness, and breathlessness).

Families are an important source of intimate friendships. A study of women's friendship patterns in a Mid-western city of 50,000 indicated frequent interaction between family members. One in five visited a relative outside the nuclear household every day; nine out of 10 visited relatives at least twice a month. When asked who they "felt closest to," both middle- and working-class women listed a sibling first, a "girlfriend" second, and parents third.

Colleagues in work are a second important type of friendship. American culture has a deep ambivalence about friendship in the work setting. The person who can do without colleagues has always been a favorite of American folklore—like the solitary cowboy who rides out of nowhere to settle range wars and unsettle women's hearts. Equally compelling, however, is the image of barnraising, that wonderful communal activity in which neighbors come from miles around to help a farmer with a task he is incapable of handling alone.

There are many practical advantages to carrying out a job with the help of colleagues. The most valued executives are those who can facilitate collective action. Almost any contemporary business or service now involves coordinated action by a variety of people with differing loyalties, interests, and outlooks. In such situations, colleagues play an indispensable role in challenging assumptions and promoting empathy with the many points of view involved.

Casual acquaintances offer a third kind of friendship. Through them we keep in touch with the wider dimensions of human experience. Sports are one source of acquaintances. Through sports friendships, we can act out bodily the dramas of competition and vanquishment that stand frustratingly veiled in everyday experience. A hundred organizations in every neighborhood attest to the pleasures of casual companionship—veterans groups, fraternal organizations, consciousness-raising groups, and kaffee klatsches for the adults; scouts, corner hangouts, field hockey, and majorettes for the youngsters. Many religious and political organizations, though nominally dedicated to higher purposes, are best understood as another expression of the need for companionship.

Each person's need for these three kinds of friendships differs. Some people are better at one kind than another. Some activities, like traveling together, foster intimate friendships; others, like spectator sports, promote more casual relationships. Similarly, some environments facilitate one kind of friendship more than another. The goals/solutions section of this chapter focuses on suggestions for changing your space to promote each of these three kinds of friendship.

Your Seven Friends

Tucked away in sociological journals are some compelling facts about friendships. If you are like the average American, the studies indicate, you will have seven close friends. Of these, three will be related to you by blood or marriage and two will live within two blocks of your home. Of the four who are not relatives, three will be of the same sex as you and similar in age and education. Someone will move in or out of this circle of close friends only once every four years. Of these seven, say the sociologists, only two will be intimate friends as we have been using that word. (The typical American, for example, has only one or two relationships in which lending or borrowing more than a cup of sugar plays a part).

So the sociologists confirm what our hearts already know—how precious are those few people we call friends, how close, indeed, we are to having none at all. For every one of us with more than two intimate friends, there is another person with one or none.

Living Room Inspirations

1

Two evocative living rooms from the past: **1.** A large chamber in Speke Hall, Lancashire, England, with a fireplace which has become a small room and a table constructed like a stage. **2.** A hall vaulted with bamboo trusses in which a 19th century Chinese merchant is receiving friends on a platform covered with thick mats.

2

2

3

Three visions of what living rooms can be and do: **1.** A soft Victorian parlour, filled to overflowing with evidence of its inhabitants. **2.** A stainless steel and glass confection, perhaps the most famous living room of the 20th century, by Mies van der Rohe. **3.** An ominous turn-of-the-century reception room in which the chairs haughtily turn their backs on each other.

1

The Half-Hearted Friends of Friendship

Marriage

Getting married is our most direct way of seeking intimate friendship. Knowing how rare such friendships are suggests new respect for an institution that aims to last "till death do us part." Marriage promises an increase in casual acquaintances as well, through association with the friends and relatives of one's partner. Statistics, however, point to a more disappointing reality. The average American marriage now lasts but seven years. Unfortunately, divorce is as good at crippling intimate friendships as marriage is at creating them. Folklore wisely alerts us to the difficulties of establishing in-law relationships with a spouse's relatives.

Figures concerning the fate of more casual friendships in marriage are sobering as well. For most people, marriage means a slackening of attention to other friendships. In one-third of marriages, for example, none of the husband's close friends before marriage becomes a friend of the couple.

In one *Psychology Today* survey, single people named "friends and social life" as the most important factor in their general happiness. For married people, however, this factor fell to sixth place, behind their partner's happiness, success at work, sex life, and personal growth. Studies indicate that women's close friendships reduce in number from seven to five after marriage. For the typical woman, then, getting married means losing three good friends and gaining one.

Work

Work-related friendships are the exception rather than the rule in American society. Two-thirds of those interviewed in one study reported "hardly any" or "no" friends from work associations. Friendships with a boss are usually awkward—it is difficult to form an authentic relationship with someone who holds the key to your income and career. People in like positions, on the other hand, tend to be wary of each other's bids for recognition and advancement. Promotions often affect friendships adversely, as many a line worker who advanced to the position of shop foreman has discovered.

Neighbors

People who live nearby are a surprisingly important source of close friendships. We have already mentioned that two of our seven close friends are likely to live within two blocks. Studies indicate that people who live in low-rise multi-family housing count as good friends half the people who live next door, one quarter of those who live two doors away, and one-tenth of those who live three or four doors away.

In small towns, where the circle of potential friends is restricted and living patterns are stable, neighborliness can become a way of life. In one study of a Midwestern town, people said they counted half of all their neighbors as good friends.

Not everyone finds neighborliness so rewarding, however. It is much rarer for friendships to be formed around apartment corridors than neighborhood streets, for example. Upper-class people generally form fewer of their friendships along neighborhood lines. In some studies, half of middle-class people reported having *no* close friends from the immediate neighborhood. Most neighborhoods are unable to provide the elderly with adequate friendships. Older persons who have moved into housing for the elderly report half the loneliness of those who stay in their old neighborhoods.

Implications for the Design of Social Space

Our Friends Have Been Here Before
Our most important friendships are few and stable. It is hard to imagine "impressing" our closest friends with our living rooms. They are in and out of our house all the time. These people like us *because* of the crazy way we fix up our space. It is interesting to think of all the living rooms of these close friends as an extended common space where everybody hangs out. We feel more like hosts than guests when a party is thrown in any of these living rooms. The trick, then, is involving closest friends in decisions about the design of your living room. We have included a number of suggestions for accomplishing this on p. 104.

The Art of Visiting
Most of the enjoyable time you spend with friends will be in other people's environments. In one study, people reported spending about three evenings a month out with friends. If you are one of the many people who find visiting harder than hosting, try cultivating the art of enjoying other people's space. Get involved in the everyday aspects of your friends' lives—those random concerns from car repair to keeping warm in winter that fill our homes with meaning. Find activities that involve rooms other than their living rooms—joint cooking or gardening, for example.

The Unimportance of Living Rooms
Many households would be happier if an awkward living room were converted into a centrally located children's room or project area. For many people such spaces promote more social interaction than a place for formal entertaining.

Shared Design of Shared Space
People can never seem to agree on living room design. Design of common space was the precipitating issue in the departure of one of my roommates several years ago. My wife-to-be, Deborah, had just moved into our apartment, and we wanted to mark the happy shift in our lives with some much-needed renovation of our space. When we approached our third roommate, he said he was very interested in the improvements but couldn't turn to them for six weeks. Our hearts sank. We had no idea if we would have the time or interest for such an effort in another week, much less six. We went ahead with the changes, trying to involve him as much as possible, but our relationship never recovered. He moved out not long after.

Designing a living room unfailingly holds us to account for our social pretensions. Even worse, the dialogue always gravitates toward issues of taste and style. Almost everyone feels insecure on such ground. Reducing design issues to questions of "taste" changes the atmosphere. If the main issue is one person's taste versus another's, the winner's status is vindicated, the loser's debased.

But there are ways out of these dilemmas. Try approaching living room design piecemeal. Hang a picture or move furniture around with the understanding that it will be switched back in a month. You will be much less anxious about making changes if you have a chance to see how they feel.

Plan for activities first and style second. Almost every living room can benefit from better planning for casual reading or TV viewing, for example. Children's play happens naturally in the living room; plan a play and toy storage area that does not compromise adult enjoyment of the room. If there is more than one person in your household, recognize that everyone has a stake in the living room. Find out what everyone likes and dislikes about the room as it now stands. Have each person describe the ideal living room. Discuss what activities should and shouldn't go on there. Commit yourself to expressing something of each person's identity in the common space. Let each person select an object for display on the mantelpiece or create a rotating exhibit with a "display schedule" posted nearby.

Living Room Fantasies

Here are two fantasies to help you understand your feelings about friendship. The first one prompts you to imagine the kind of party your parents might throw; the second leads you on an imaginary adventure with some do-or-die colleagues.

Your Parents' Party

Imagine how your parents might throw a party. If you are already familiar with their present style of entertaining, try thinking back to what they might have done when they were your present age. What kind of an occasion is being celebrated? Are preparations precise or haphazard? Who is invited? Close your eyes, relax, and imagine coming to the door as one of the guests. Is the evening quiet or noisy? What do you talk about with the other guests? How long does the party last and how does it end? Who cleans up?

Stranded in the Jungle

Here is a fantasy about feelings of solidarity and colleagueship. Before reading further, think of four people who are friends or colleagues. Imagine that you have convinced these people to take a vacation together in Brazil. An excursion there takes you by small plane over the heart of the Amazon jungle. Suddenly the plane's engine sputters, and the pilot announces you are going down. He manages to glide to within a mile or so of the Amazon before crashing, but your flightpath has taken you 1,000 miles from the nearest civilization. As you recover from the shock of impact, you hear the first friend whose name came to mind crying out with a broken leg.

Close your eyes and relax into a fantasy of the events which befall you in your efforts to return to safety.

Where Is Your Living Room?

In order to make your home a comfortable place for friends you must first find out where visiting actually takes place. To do this, you will need a house plan (see p. 22) and a short list of friends (see previous survey). Look over the lists of names and mark an "X" on the plan where any people who have visited you recently spent time within your house or apartment.

When you have completed the exercise, see where most of your X's fall. Any surprises? Does most of your entertaining take place in the living room or in some other part of the house? What does your survey suggest would happen if you turned your living room to another use altogether? What can you do to make the other parts of your house more sociable? Perhaps

just keeping them in a little better order would make you feel better about them. Bedrooms and kitchens (common "second living rooms") often lack comfortable seating. Perhaps you should be thinking about new chairs for these places rather than the living room.

Friendship Survey

Here is an exercise that will help you see your friendships in perspective. It asks you to list the people in your circle under three categories: intimate friends, colleagues, and acquaintances. Listing friends may seem a little callous at first, but much insight can be gained through the exercise.

Do not differentiate between "family" and "friends." If you have a small family, that is a fact of your life,

as is a family that falls more under the category of acquaintances than intimate friends. We have put "acquaintances" in the middle of the chart so you can put friends who are not quite intimate or true colleagues in an in-between position.

Once you have completed the list, look at it from a geographic perspective. Do you have a lot of long-distance relationships? Do two out of your seven

closest friends live within walking distance of your home as we suggested was typical for the average American? Mark the people on your list that you have known for two years or less. How many of your friends have you known since childhood?

Does the list feel long or short in any of the three categories?

Intimate Friends
People who know and like you as you really are, and with whom you share personal problems.

Acquaintances
People who know you by name and with whom you look forward to friendly conversation or joint activities.

Colleagues
People who work side-by-side with you and make your work day happier and more productive.

Names

Sitting Inspirations

1

2

Chairs imply characteristic ways of sitting and being together. Imagine the different ways people would greet each other in these chairs: **1.** A French *duchesse* from 1762. **2.** An American kangaroo sofa. **3.** A regal German chair. **4.** A circular upholstered bench from France.

4

3

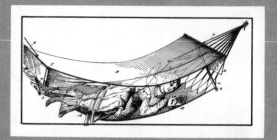

Chairs are a natural object of inventive attention. These examples should encourage your own flights of imagination: **1.** A health jolting chair. **2.** A wearable walking chair. **3.** A mechanized hammock. **4.** An early dentist's chair. **5.** An inflatable relaxer.

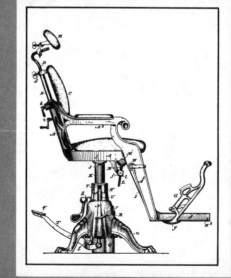

1

2

4

5

3

1

2

1. An elegant, high-backed chair you can build with number 2 pine. 2. A sofa designed with friendship in mind. 3. A traditional Japanese sitting arrangement in which a robe captures heat from a small brazier. 4. A tree stump rocking chair.

3

4

Style Survey

Style in furniture and interior decoration has often been driven by social aspiration. It is important to disengage the two. Each piece of furniture, wall pattern, and accessory in your home contains a whole world of meaning concerning our collective history. Each piece speaks subtly about ways of socializing, attitudes toward nature, concepts of bodily comfort, and the particular craft tradition that brought it to life.

To complete this survey of the styles that can be found within your home, make a brief list of three or four furnishings in several rooms of your house—tables, chairs, beds, etc. Include, if you like, artwork, curtains, and wallpaper. Do not be selective.

Just write down the four or five things that make any particular room in your home what it is. Then place every object in one of the style categories of the chart, from Greek to International. Find some category for every article. Treat each object like a riddle. Only one clue has been provided—a picture of one chair designed in each style. Many items will puzzle you because they seem to fall in no particular style, but look carefully for any connection to one of the styles listed. Often you will be forced to make a decision on the tiniest of details. Our categories are very general. If you are able to name a more precise style than the ones we have listed, go ahead. Once you have decided on a style for an object, mark

an "X" on the appropriate date for that style and at the location on the world map where that style originated.

When you have completed the survey, see how broadly your house represents the universe of furnishing style. (If you would like to learn more about a particular style or era, look for a book on it in your local library.) Often a small but heartfelt addition—an Indian bell or Victorian plant stand—can bring a whole new world of cultural reference into your home.

Domestic life has been a major theme of artists throughout the ages. You can pay homage to a favorite period by placing an evocative work of art depicting a home from that time on your wall.

Style Categories

Greek 300–500 B.C.	Oriental date varies	Medieval 500–1450	Spanish Renaissance 1500–1700	French Rococo 1700–1750

For each object you have listed, place an "X" by the date associated with its style.

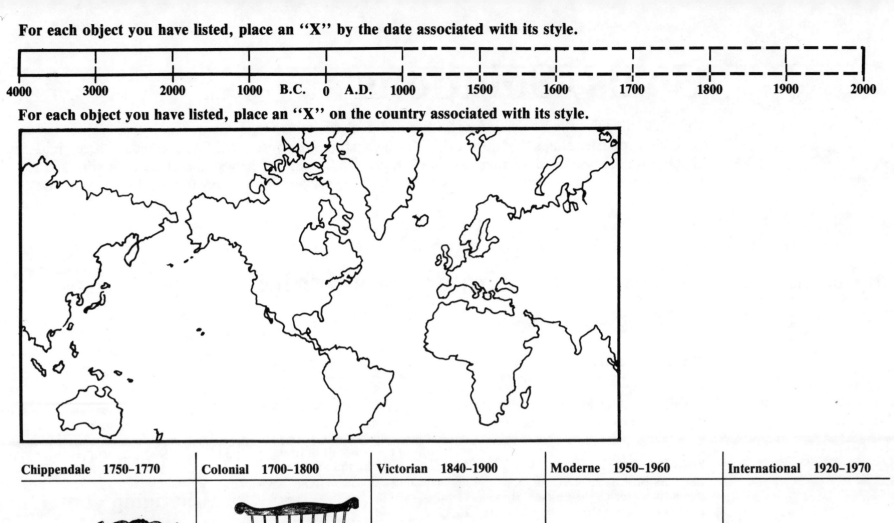

| 4000 | 3000 | 2000 | 1000 | B.C. | 0 | A.D. | 1000 | 1500 | 1600 | 1700 | 1800 | 1900 | 2000 |

For each object you have listed, place an "X" on the country associated with its style.

| Chippendale 1750–1770 | Colonial 1700–1800 | Victorian 1840–1900 | Moderne 1950–1960 | International 1920–1970 |

103

Goals/Solutions

This section begins the translation of wishes and analysis into change. Goals relating to each of the three kinds of friendships described earlier in the chapter are considered. For each goal, three kinds of solutions are proposed, changes in yourself, changes in your activities, and changes in your space. The final pages of the chapter enlarge on this last category with how-to projects and comprehensive designs for living rooms.

If your goal is

To improve intimate friendships

Changing yourself

Empathy

Pick up on your friends' real concerns. Imagine the answer to two questions for a close friend: "What is most bothering me this month?" and "What is making me particularly happy these days?"

Fewer Answers

Learn to listen. Don't feel you must find answers for all the personal concerns your friends share with you. Try just restating what a friend is saying to ease the expression of things that are difficult to talk about.

Nothing Special

Live the everyday with your intimate friends.

Your Own Best Friend

The better you feel about yourself, the more you'll be able to give your friends. Accept the next challenge in your own personal growth.

Co-counseling

Co-counseling is dedicated to the idea that we are each other's best life counselors. The program will get you together with another person you find sympathetic, give you brief but effective training in counseling each other, and set you free to meet once a week on whatever concerns you. Its success derives from the power of intimate friendship. Look up the co-counseling organization in your area in the phone book.

Changing your activities

Play

Get together with a close friend and plan an activity that appeals to your "natural child"—a campout, building a treehouse, ice skating. . . .

Date a Friend

Give a close friend some of the good energy you pour into dates. Wear something special, think of a good place to go, anticipate "discovering" that friend's life.

Birthdays

When are your closest friends' birthdays? Put them down on your calendar and throw the party this year.

Share

The most authentic way to gain intimate friends is to share more of your own joys and problems with others. With how many people do you talk over your finances or your love life?

Changing your space

Planning

Next time close friends come over, mention any plans you have considered for fixing up your space. You will find it hard to resist taking their opinions into consideration, and they will feel more a part of your life and home.

Shopping

Invite close friends to help you shop for household furnishings. They will get vicarious pleasure from all the money you are spending, and you will feel less exposed in what can be a pretty anxious activity.

Evidence

Get reminders of your closest friends into your space. If they spend time at a hobby or craft, ask them to create something for your living room. Make a photo-gallery in a hallway that they star in.

Openness

Be your vulnerable (as well as stylish) self in decorating. Try a crazy color or outrageous fabric in your living room. Guaranteed to endear you to your closest friends even if they can't stand it.

Cleanup

Involve close friends in everyday environmental maintenance. Spend a Saturday raking your yards or painting a porch floor.

If your goal is

To get better at making casual acquaintances

 ## Changing yourself

Pastimes

Talking about "nothing" is the ground plane of all friendship. Thomas Harris, in *I'm OK, You're OK* (Avon Books), mentions some common "pastime" topics—"Who Won?," "Grocery," "Ever Been?," "GM or Ford." Such conversations form the basis for selecting acquaintances from the many people we speak with each day, and reaffirm people's interest in each other's lives.

Contract

Agreements between casual friends (who calls whom, what to talk about, etc.) are usually tacit and thus often betrayed. Articulate some of these agreements to yourself and stick by them.

Changing your activities

Togetherness

Reach out to others who have fewer acquaintances than you. Visit a home for the elderly. Get involved in a Big Brother association.

Entertainment

Find some smaller-scale spectator events that interest you—jazz clubs, chess tournaments, drag racing.

Good Neighborliness

Start a regular neighborhood kaffee-klatsch.

Support

Take an initiative in your own growth that also puts you in touch with other people—est, a women's or men's support group, Parent Effectiveness Training.

Changing your space

Free Store

Look for opportunities to give home furnishings away to your friends—the double bed you are replacing with a queen-size; an outsized plant stand; bookshelves that no longer fit; a rug that has fallen into disfavor. Start a basement collection of odd pieces of furniture from flea markets and friends' houses, and keep your eyes peeled for friends in need.

Avocations

Create environments for avocations in your home—a darkroom, a potting shed, a woodshop—and entertain in these rather than your living room.

Entertaining

Take the steps necessary to make you feel comfortable with casual entertaining at home. (See p. 118 for some suggestions.)

Another Place

Get together with a few friends and rent a small vacation home in the country. It will enlarge your circle of acquaintances and give you a good environment for enjoying time with friends.

If your goal is

To improve colleague relationships

Changing yourself

Bad Thoughts

It's easy to become a negative person on the job. Work organizations always respond to danger signals and bad reports but seem quite able to do without positive feedback. Negative people have an easy time being listened to but a hard time finding true colleagues.

Work Friendships

Don't dole out your work friendships according to work status. Treat your workplace like a family reunion where everyone is kin.

Advice

Be open to "second opinions" about your work. This will improve your performance as well as facilitate colleague relationships.

Changing your activities

Cease-fire

The hardest people to communicate with in an organization are those at exactly the same level as yourself. The natural competition in this relationship always seems to drive out meaningful colleagueship. These are precisely the people you have most to share with, however. Try reaching out to find ways of cooperating that minimize the destructive effects of competition for both of you.

Food

Humanize an early-morning work session with pastries, a late afternoon one with a six-pack, and an all-nighter with pizza.

Aid

Volunteer to help co-workers with their tasks. Smaller gestures (taking over during a break, reviewing a report, helping out in a last-minute rush) are greatly appreciated and not usually seen as threatening by those responsible for assigning tasks.

Changing your space

Workplace

Humanize your work space by bringing in non-work features—a terrarium or picture calendar if you have to think small; a wall hanging or tack board if you have more latitude.

Status

Be unconcerned about the status associations of your work environment. Don't insist on the precise furniture and office location granted to people at your level. Be generous in moving your work station around to accommodate others. Cultivate a self-centering that does not rely on petty distinctions within the environment.

Evidence

Get some evidence of your co-workers' presence into your own work space. This can be results of projects they have completed (reports, drawings, etc.) or just some art that you know they will appreciate as much as you.

Visitors

Make your work space easy to visit throughout the work day. Give people who stop by place to sit or lean. Don't arrange things so people have to come completely into your space to say hello. If you have a desk, place one side toward the entry to your space to ease interaction with passersby.

Sofa/Bed/Table

Here is the ultimate in multipurpose furniture. As illustrated in the three drawings here, what starts out as a comfortable two-person sofa plus easy chair converts easily into an elegant dining table for four plus side table, and just as easily becomes a double bed for guests. The essence of the design is a U-shaped frame of natural wood. This frame creates the arms and back of the seating unit and the headrest for the bed. Two cushions placed directly on the floor create the seat of the sofa and chair. Another slightly tapered cushion becomes the back. When the seat cushions are assembled on the floor, they create a double bed which can be secured with a fitted sheet. When the frame is turned 90 degrees, the back of the sofa becomes a tabletop for eating or desk work.

SOFA & CHAIR

DINING TABLE

DOUBLE BED

107

STEP 1. Obtain materials.

- 3 sheets 4 by 8-feet, 1/2-inch, plywood, good one side. If you prefer the appearance of particle board or Texture III plywood (scored to look like boards), use these materials. If you do use particle board, insist on Korpine or Novaply brand, both stronger than the "underlayment board" carried by most lumberyards.
- 40 linear feet of 1 x 4-inch, Grade A
- pine shelving.
- 40 linear feet of 1 x 3-inch, Grade B pine shelving. This wood is to be used for the inside furring strips and need not be finish grade. It *is* important, however, that it be exactly one-inch narrower than the edging board.
- a box of 2-inch finishing nails.
- wood glue.
- seat cushions as indicated in the diagram. You may want to order these, precut and covered, from a foam cushion store. Cushions are sized to create a double bed when placed together on the floor, and a comfortable seat when stacked. It is important that the seat be 16 inches off the floor and not sink more than a couple of inches under a person's weight. If two pieces of dense 8-inch foam will not accomplish this for you, try three pieces of 6-inch foam instead.

HORIZ. SECTION

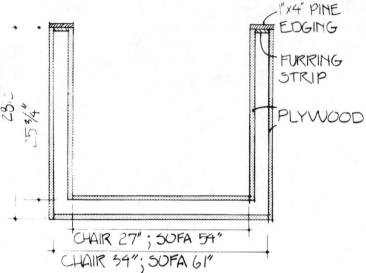

CHAIR 27"; SOFA 54"
CHAIR 34"; SOFA 61"

VERTICAL SECTION

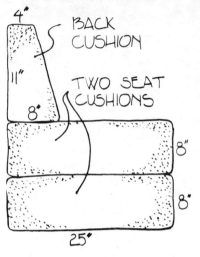

LAYOUT
ON 4'x8' SHEETS OF 1/2" PLYWOOD

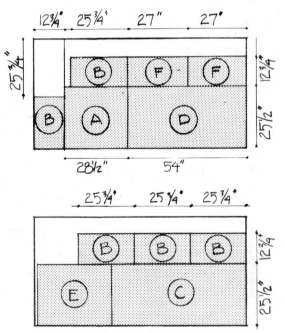

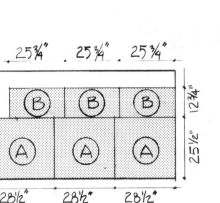

STEP 2. Build frame.

Lay out and label the pieces as indicated on the sheets of plywood. There are 6 types of panels, all 25-1/2 inches high (some inside panels must be cut in two pieces to fit economically on three sheets of plywood).

Type A: outer sides of both units, 28-1/2 inches wide

Type B: inner sides of both units, 25-3/4 inches wide

Type C: outer back of the sofa, 61 inches wide

Type D: inner back of the sofa, 54 inches wide

Type E: outer back of the chair, 34 inches wide

Type F: inner back of the chair, 27 inches wide

Consult the diagram to construct the frames.

STEP 3. Finish surfaces.

Sand all surfaces carefully. A coat of linseed or tung oil will give a simple natural finish. If you have used plywood and want to use a stain or varnish finish, first rub the frames down with a "prewash" of four parts denatured alcohol and one part shellac. This will keep the broad grain of the plywood from being even further accentuated by your final finish.

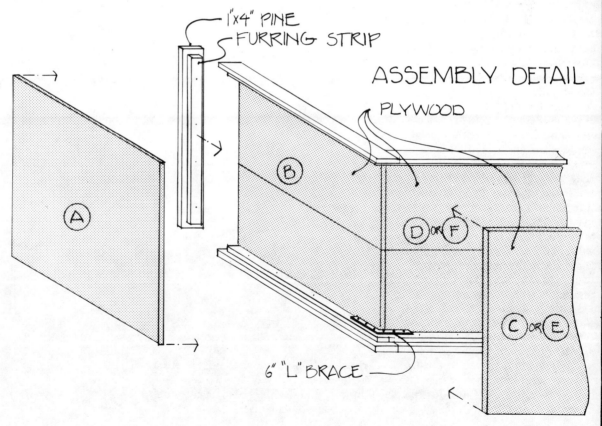

1"x4" PINE FURRING STRIP

ASSEMBLY DETAIL

PLYWOOD

6" "L" BRACE

Plant World

Bringing a lot of plants to your living room is one of the easiest ways to transform it. Their presence will enliven the place in a way that is difficult to achieve by any other means. Plants are constantly changing—thriving, failing, going dormant during one season, blossoming in another. You will find yourself experiencing your living room quite differently as soon as you start taking care of plants there. Where sunlight falls in the room suddenly becomes very important, as temperature differences within the room. You will find yourself visiting a room with plants more frequently, to care for them and catch up on the latest developments.

Getting a number of plants together can make them a strong presence in any room. The plant world described here does this in a way that is elegant enough for any living room.

The unit consists of plant boxes hung by ropes from a frame. Each box holds potted plants on its top surface and provides a place to mount plant lights underneath in a way that hides fixture and bulb from view. A great deal of flexibility is built into the system. There are many natural places to hang plants (the single holes in the top crosspieces). The boxes holding potted plants are easily moved up and down along the rope (no hardware or knots needed). Boxes can be moved from one "bay" of the unit to another just as easily. By leaving the center bay entirely empty, you can use the unit to frame a window or a doorway. On moving day,

you need only remove the boxes from their ropes, unscrew the two top braces, and use the boxes as carrying trays for your plants.

Boxes hold plants above & grow-lights below.

Boxes move up & down as plant family & light needs change.

Unbolt & untie to move around your apartment or across town

Arrange plants against wall or as room divider. Two units make a greenhouse.

STEP 1. Obtain materials.

- 7 pieces, 1 x 10-inch common pine shelving, 8 feet long.
- 2 pieces, 1 x 12-inch common pine shelving, 8 feet long.
- 4 pieces, 1 x 6-inch common pine shelving, 8 feet long.
- 4 pieces, 1 x 5-inch common pine shelving, 8 feet long.
- 2 pieces, 1 x 4-inch common pine shelving, 8 feet long.
- 1 box 2-inch finishing nails.
- 16 number 8, 3-inch flathead screws.
- 8 lag screws, 1/4-inch diameter, 2 inches long.
- 16 number-8, 2 1/2-inch, flathead screws.
- white glue.
- 100 feet of 1/2-inch, 3-ply sisal rope.
- light fixtures which take two 2-foot-long fluorescent bulbs (1 cool white, 1 warm white). Buy as many as you feel your plants will need.
- 2 stove bolts for each light fixture, 3/16-inch diameter, 2-inches long.

STEP 2. Build boxes.

The width of the boxes will be set by the width of the 1-inch by 12-inch pine shelving used as the box floor (see construction diagram). Use 1 by 10-inch pine for all box sides. Drill rope holes as indicated in "box side" diagram, and use the first side as a template for the rest. Wind rope in and out of holes as shown. Friction will hold the box in place. Use 2-inch finishing nails and white glue to hold boxes together. Check the overall length of the boxes to see that the light fixtures will fit snugly inside. Attach light fixtures with stove bolts screwed through the ends of the boxes into the press-out holes on the ends of each fixture.

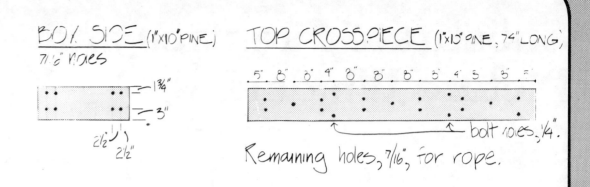

BOX SIDE (1"x10" PINE)
7/16" holes

1 3/4"
3"
2 1/2"
2 1/2"

TOP CROSS PIECE (1"x10" PINE, 74" LONG)

5" 8" 8" 4" 8" 8" 8" 8" 5" 4" 5" 5"

bolt holes, 1/4".

Remaining holes, 7/16", for rope.

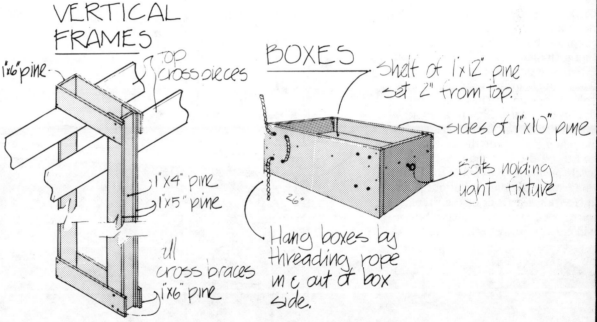

VERTICAL FRAMES

1"x6" pine
top crosspieces
1"x4" pine
1"x5" pine
all cross braces
1"x6" pine

BOXES

shelf of 1"x12" pine set 2" from top.
sides of 1"x10" pine
Bolts holding light fixture

26"

Hang boxes by threading rope in & out of box side.

STEP 3. Build frame.

According to diagram, secure pieces to each other with screws. Assemble unit by bolting top crosspieces to frame with lag screws. Install rope-hung boxes as shown.

Substitute Fireplace and Picture Window

Living rooms benefit from the focus and drama provided by a fireplace or picture window. But what do you do if your living room lacks these amenities? Here are a couple of suggestions for "substitutes" that are easily built and can be moved from place to place. The designs are a bit tongue-in-cheek, but the point is not to pretend you have a fireplace, but to play with the qualities that a fireplace can bring to a room. Either one or both of these projects will create a strong new presence in your living room. They were both designed by Jerry Simon, a friend who is part artist, part carpenter. The carpenter part made the designs easy to construct; the artist added several levels of meaning to make the "substitute" more than an imitation. A small coffee table in front of the fireplace mirror or hearth of linoleum bricks will enhance the effect.

Substitute Fireplace

STEP 1. Obtain materials.

- 1 piece of 1/2-inch plywood, 4 x 6 feet, good one side.
- mirror or reflective Mylar, 3 by 4 feet.
- mantelpiece of 2 x 8-inch pine, 6 feet long. If you want to go for broke, use a beautiful piece of oak or mahogany.
- light oak or walnut varnish.
- 2 feet of 1 x 8-inch pine shelving.
- six, 3-inch long, number 8 flathead wood screws.
- permanent black felt-tip pen.
- masking tape.

STEP 2. Construct fireplace.

Cut fireplace front and brackets according to diagram. Attach mantelpiece.

STEP 3. Finish fireplace.

Sand wood and give entire fireplace one coat of varnish. The grain of the plywood should now stand out strongly. Draw the black panel lines on the front of the fireplace with felt-tip pen. Let varnish dry thoroughly and outline panel "shadows" with masking tape. Give these shadows a second and third coat of varnish.

STEP 4. Mount.

Assemble and mount mirror and fireplace on wall with mirror clips, nails or bolts.

Picture Window

STEP 1. Obtain materials.

- 4 pieces, each 6 feet long, 1 x 4-inch common pine shelving.
- 1 piece, 3 feet long, 1 x 3-inch common pine shelving.
- 2 pieces, 5 feet long, 1 x 2-inch common pine shelving.
- 2 square feet of 1/4-inch-thick plywood for plates to hold frame together.
- color poster of clouds.
- small box of 7/8-inch wire nails.
- small can of sky-blue acrylic paint.
- 3 x 6-foot piece of mirror or reflective Mylar.
- spray adhesive.
- satin-finish polyurethane.

STEP 2. Construct frame.

Cut out and sand pieces for frame. Fasten them in place with small plates of plywood and wire nails. Use dimensions indicated for a 3 x 6-foot window. Adjust dimensions if your mirror is a different size. Fill seams with wood putty and sand smooth. Paint entire frame sky blue.

STEP 3. Add clouds.

Cut the cloud forms from your poster and glue them to your sky-blue frame with spray adhesive. Wrap the cloud forms around the sides of the frame when you come to an edge. Give the entire frame, including the clouds, a coat of polyurethane.

STEP 4. Mount.

Mount frame over mirror and hang both on the wall with mirror clips.

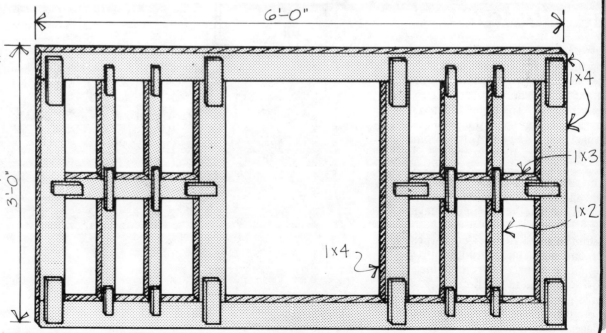

113

An Efficient Living Room

Efficiently designed and arranged furnishings allow this room to function not only as a relaxed living room, but as a study, a dining room (the sofa becomes a table seating four for dinner), and a guest room (sofa cushions plus chair cushions make a full-size bed).

The Room

This 11 by 13-foot room is about as small a space as you can convert into a workable living room. The problem does not lie in getting living room furniture into such a small space (it will fit one way or another), but in preserving a sense of grace and an uncrowded atmosphere. This room illustrates a number of design tactics which can help give multipurpose rooms a sense of openness and ease.

The Design

Diagonal Layout

Laying out major pieces of furniture on the diagonal helps give this room a depth and complexity that foursquare rooms often lack. The rug is the major diagonal organizer—next time you rearrange your living room, try turning the rug 45 degrees. Its lines are picked up by a diamond painted on the ceiling, the substitute fireplace in the corner, and the built-ins along one wall. This diagonal arrangement makes excellent use of corners, especially important in small rooms. One corner has become a desk area. Another creates an open space in front of the window (too often in small rooms, windows get blocked by furniture and thus lose their ability to add variety to the spaces within a room).

Focus

Living rooms always benefit from the presence of one or two focal points which orchestrate the overall effect of the space. In this room the substitute fireplace in the corner serves this function. It consists of a triangular box with a painted design of an arched fireplace opening on the front. The box is brick-red, the design dark brown. On top is a triangular mantelpiece of 4-inch-thick wood on which objects can be displayed.

Illusions of Spaciousness

Several devices in this room make it seem larger than it is. Rooms feel more spacious when they are designed with a *continuous flow of lines*. In this room a valance line flows around the room at the ceiling. This valance carries the color of the ceiling down onto the walls and coordinates the window shades, the built-in desk area, and the cove lighting over the display stand. *Simple window treatments* enlarge space. Here, an outsized reed blind has been placed within a large cove at ceiling level. When pulled down, the shade creates a floor-to-ceiling panel of texture that fits into the overall design. Leaving *one wall free* always makes a room seem larger. Avoid placing furniture along all walls of a room if you want to make it feel more open. *Horizontal* rather than *vertical design* opens up space. A banded wallpaper in subtle tones of yellow and brown has been chosen for the walls, creating more lines that flow around the room and make it seem larger.

The Convertible Sofa

The matching love seat and armchair are do-it-yourself furnishings with unusual versatility. Two eight-inch cushions of dense foam piled on the floor within each U-shaped wooden frame provide a comfortable sitting place; a sloping bolster of the same foam provides a back rest. Removing the cushions and tipping the wooden frames forward creates two elegant tables that seat four or six for dinner. Sofa and armchair cushions are sized so that laying them alongside each other on the floor creates a full-size bed which can be held in place with standard-size fitted sheets. The wooden structures can be built inexpensively out of 3/4-inch particle board edged with 1 x 3-inch pine (a light stain will bring out the elegance of this combination).

Work Area

In the corner of this room is a built-in work area with a secretary's chair. The desk, aiming directly into the corner, disappears when the triangular section that creates it is lifted out and placed in its alternate location against the wall. A slot shelf at desk height allows desktop paraphernalia to be hidden away neatly when the desk is not in use.

Efficient Lighting

Wall-mounted lamps are one of the most efficient means of lighting you can employ. The Luxo extension lamp along the back wall, for example, can provide a spotlight for the substitute fireplace, gently wash the ceiling with light, or be aimed downward for a reading light.

Personalizations

- At one corner of the rug is an antique "corner chair," designed on the diagonal just for the kinds of spaces this room creates.
- Homemade car-part sculptures: a mantel display of car bumpers; on the shelves, a hubcap and taillight display; under the cove lighting at the end of the shelf unit, a chromed crankshaft sculpture.

A Family Living Room

A house within a house, filled with places for family members of all ages to carry on their leisure activities without intruding on each other.

The Room

This room design, unlike most of the others we have included, would be difficult to duplicate without building a new house from the ground up. Still, it shows some of the ways that architectural design can help create homes from the heart and may prompt your thinking about new ways of subdividing the space you already have.

The idea is to provide semiprivate spaces for the many leisure activities appropriate to family life, from TV viewing and somersaults to quiet reading and snuggling. Such activities almost always benefit from mutual interaction. Kids love to play near their parents where they can get instant feedback and support. Most adults, as well, like to carry out projects like sewing, making presents, casual reading, and watching TV where others can see what is going on and get involved if they wish. To avoid conflicts, however, it is important that overlapping activities be explicitly planned for in advance.

The Design

To the right in the drawing is a sunken lounge area for storytelling, visiting with guests, and falling asleep in front of the fire. The built-in sofas around the edge surround a carpeted area some seven feet across, large enough for spreading out around a game of backgammon on the floor, but small enough to keep an intimate distance between persons seated around the periphery. The fireplace is designed, in homage to Frank Lloyd Wright, as a room unto itself. The broad hearth running along two sides of the room is completely open to one side. The corner thus created under the lower mantel is the coziest place in the house when a fire is going. The two compartments further along the hearth are for storage of kindling and firewood. One of the important principles in designing a true family room is to recognize the presence of all family members. The fireplace helps in this regard by providing two mantels, a low one where children can arrange displays (like a toy village), and an upper one where adults can safely place cherished objects (like an antique clock collection).

Behind the fireplace area and up two steps is a study with a bay window. Here adults can retire to read, sew, fix a bicycle, or balance the household checkbook without isolating themselves from the flow of family activities. Several old-fashioned windows have been recycled as a divider between the study and fireplace areas. The generous opening to the central hall is fitted with double French doors although

these can be removed to provide closer connection between the study and other living room areas.

Back and to the left is a children's play area, separated from the rest of the living room by a low divider of shelves for toys and games. At one end of this divider is a raised TV box, a simple device originally designed for institutional dayrooms where use of a TV tends to preempt all other forms of socializing. To make one for yourself, construct a box out of plywood large enough for your TV to slide in and out easily. Line the inside with carpet to absorb all the sound except that going directly toward the viewer. Face it away from other centers of activity so the picture won't be distracting, but be careful not to aim it at a window (reflections on the screen make daytime viewing difficult). Also included in the play area are built-in benches along the wall (to reduce clutter in a hard-to-organize area), a corner of carpeted steps for "peanut gallery" TV viewing, a child-size desk, and a wall-size zoo photomural (available from your local wallpaper store for about $90).

One of the most difficult problems in joint use of family space is accommodation of noisy and quiet activities at the same time. Carpeting helps reduce noise. Open-plan schools find that this alone brings sound levels for multipurpose space within an acceptable range. Lowered ceilings, and accoustic ceiling tile over especially noisy areas, help too.

A Living Room for Entertaining

Here's a room that feels like a party even when no people are in it. When visitors do arrive, they find themselves seduced by a host of environments—dance floor, bar, music arena, grand parlor, perching ground. . . .

The Room

This room takes as its starting point a plain, high-ceilinged room some 25 feet long, like many of the living rooms found in elegant-but-past-their-prime city apartments. The entry to the room can be seen near the center of the drawing; windows are in the wall opposite. The ceiling has been lowered over the central third of the room to help subdivide the space, allow special lighting effects, and help provide sound insulation between zones of the room.

The Design

Each portion of this room provides a different environment for guests to enjoy.

Club Lounge

The zone to the front contains period overstuffed chairs. People who relax here attain some of the status of the periods represented, through the enfolding ambience of these pieces. Not very many people can sit here, but those who do are to be envied. An arrangement like this needn't be expensive. We bought four soulful old chairs like these for $80 (they are terribly out of vogue). Kids love the rooms within rooms they create and bounce happily from arm to arm for hours.

Perching Ground

Just beyond these chairs, in the middle third of the room, is a sculptural arrangement of square pedestals. In everyday use, these pedestals create a display space for valued objects (each pedestal is matched by a corresponding spotlight box hung from the ceiling). When entertaining begins, most of the display objects are stored away, and the pedestals become stools of varying heights for guests to perch on. *Heights* of the pedestals are calculated to provoke intimations of domination and submission by placing people unexpectedly above or below their friends. Distances *between* stools are set according to principles of social distances given definitive articulation by Edward Hall, the guru of "social space" (1 1/2 to 2 1/2 to 4 feet for less intimate conversing). When these pedestals are occupied by people, the spotlights above turn the area into a display of your friends.

Music Arena

At the far end of the room is a music place. An electric keyboard beckons to those interested (a volume control allows people to project as much or little of their music as they wish). On the wall, displayed along a supergraphic musical score, are play-along instruments: tambourines, thumb-harp, tom-toms, and maracas. On the low table next to the keyboard, within easy reach of guests, is the stereo.

Bar

Next to the door is a bar constructed in the same vocabulary as the pedestals and lowered ceiling. Bars add a touch of nightclub to a room for entertaining and set up a primordial person-to-person relationship—close enough to touch but no presumption of friendship. Placing the bar at a right angle to the wall keeps one half of it from becoming "dead" and allows head-to-head heart-to-hearts.

Slide and Movie Screen

Painted in white on the wall is an area for projecting slides or movies. When not in use, it creates a wall-sized design which subtly evokes the home light shows that go on there.

Colors

The strong sculptural design of the bar, pedestal area, and ceiling is best complemented by quiet colors. Deep tan for the walls, moving to darker shades of chocolate on the ceiling, a beige rug, and glossy off-white for the pedestals.

Mirrors

Large mirrors over the bar and behind the pedestal area multiply these zones and the people in them to infinity.

Kitchen Pleasures

You can't always have the job, or the lover, or the house you want. Eating, however, is one desire everyone can indulge. Gratification is what kitchens are all about. Everyone has a favorite kitchen pleasure—the sense of well-being that comes from a full pantry, or the smell of an oven full of cookies, or the pride of a complex recipe carried out successfully. Because the kitchen is so full of pleasure, it becomes a natural site for all kinds of social activities, from children's games and family hanging out, to afternoon coffee and evening cocktails.

Getting the kitchen you want is not quite as easy as getting the food you want. Understanding what pleasures you want most from this room will make the job a lot easier, however. This chapter seeks to evoke some of these pleasures and suggests ways to translate them into physical design. Included are exercises to help you understand your attitudes toward eating and cooking, surveys that analyze the way your kitchen operates and suggestions for emphasizing the nurturing quality of a kitchen, improving its operation for children, and making peace with the workaday nature of many kitchen tasks. The chapter concludes with a number of how-to projects and room designs which show how you can begin the transformation of your own kitchen.

Psychological Pleasures

For most people, physical hunger, as signaled by the hunger pangs of an empty stomach, is a relatively uncommon reason for eating. When, for example, was the last time you started a meal because you were really hungry, not because it was mealtime. When was the last time you ended a meal because your hunger pangs had subsided, not because you'd cleared your plate, were stuffed, or had something else to do? When physical hunger does occur, it can almost always be satisfied by a surprisingly small amount of food. Almost all of our eating is motivated by psychological, not physical, hunger. Everyone has a special menu of personal needs that can be satisfied through food.

The best introduction to the psychology of hunger is Leonard Pearson's *The Psychological Eat Anything Diet* (Popular Library), a book that helps people lose weight by finding exactly what foods satisfy their emotional needs. The promise for those who tend to overindulge in food (or kitchen decorating) is this: If you eat the right foods, it won't take much to gratify your needs. If you don't, no amount will bring satisfaction.

Eating for Reward

One of the major reasons we eat is to reward ourselves. Most of us have been rewarded with food for as long as we can remember. As children, we were given ice cream on pleasure outings, cake on our birthdays, and dessert if we ate all the things we didn't like. The urge to reward oneself through eating is most typically satisfied with sweet foods—chocolate, ice cream, cakes, pies.

Psychologists have come up with an easy way to tell exactly which foods will satisfy your needs at any given time. Much of the time we eat food just because it is there. In addition, a lot of food attracts our attention by "beckoning." Food that you really

Security Foods

A second major reason that people eat is to feel cared for and secure. Feeding, after all, was the major way our parents showed love for us as infants. Breast feeding makes the link most directly—through body warmth, eye contact, and sustenance flowing from one body to another. But the association of food and security goes far beyond infancy. At what age, for example, did you begin cooking more meals for yourself than your mother cooked for you? In our culture several special foods are associated with security: breads (warm from the oven), turkey and roasts (Thanksgiving dinner), pies (grandmother's apple crumb). Similarly, some kitchens convey this feeling of security. Warm lighting, wood, cloth textures, and visible abundance of provisions hum security to many people.

Cultural/Ethnic Foods

A final psychological need that is fulfilled through eating is affirmation of cultural identity. The importance of this need is indicated by the number of public eating places which take national foods as their theme. Cultural solidarity creates a sense that others are trustworthy and concerned with our fate, that individual lives form a continuity with the past and have meaning for the future—in short, that we are not alone.

want, however, will "hum" to you. If you can think of a food without actually seeing it, and if you crave it, rather than just feel you would enjoy it, then it is "humming." A sure way to see if some food is humming is to ask yourself if you would feel *cheated* without it. Psychologists advise people who are overweight to eat *only* foods that hum to them but as many of these as they please. People who do this conscientiously find themselves eating more frequently, but often ignoring regular meals altogether.

Most cultures celebrate a variety of rituals around food. In cultures where food was scarce, the successful hunt was often marked by a ritual distribution of food, including symbolic consumption of choice elements. Some food rituals are spiritual: Passover, Communion, Ramadan. Others mark stages in the family cycle: weddings, family reunions, the arrival of adulthood.

It is only appropriate that kitchen design reflect these links between cultural identity and eating. A theme can be established through visible storage of the woks, pasta makers, soufflé dishes, and culture-specific foods helps as well. Much ethnic cooking has a distinctive aroma. Storage of some spices to promote room smells, rather than preserve freshness, would bring smiles of recognition from knowledgeable guests.

Color and pattern play a role as well. The sea-blue of popular Grecian art or the organic patterns of Islamic tile can inspire wall, floor, or table designs. The kitchen is an excellent place to use colorful folk art motifs that might be out of place in other rooms of the house. With a homemade stencil (cut out of a file folder and shellacked so it won't absorb paint), folkloric designs can be handpainted as borders around kitchen walls and cabinets.

Physical Pleasures

Among the physical sensations associated with eating, we have already mentioned hunger pangs, that gnawing sensation most often satisfied by warm, filling foods like bread or potatoes. Hunger can originate as an ache or hollow sense in the back of the throat.

Sweet, cold things generally work best to satisfy this physical sensation. Sometimes hunger comes as a sensation in the mouth—a feeling that you want to "sink your teeth into something." This feeling is most directly satisfied by crunchy food like pretzels or crackers. Hunger can originate in the tongue and lips as well. When you are in a lip-smacking mood it generally signals a desire for licking and sucking foods like ice cream, a tall drink, or candy.

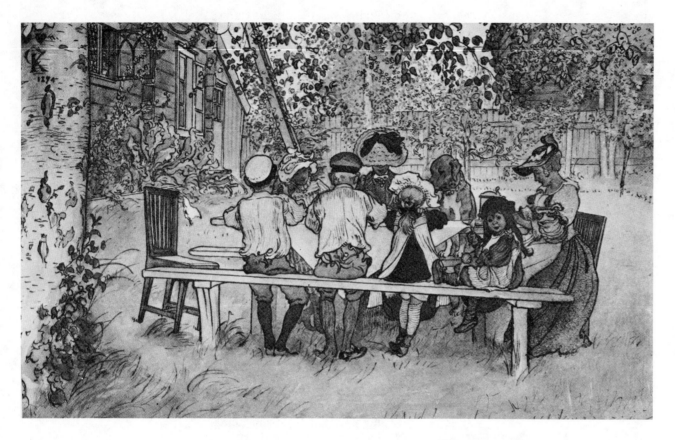

Social Pleasures

Eating is a time of being together. For most people, the family meal is the central activity shared with the people they love. Children recount days at school, adults their time at work. Special stories are saved up so the whole family can hear. Slights suffered during the day are aired and the soothing balm of group attention applied. Humor is encouraged. Events in the world outside are mediated through the concern of people who really care. Was a playground insult on or off the mark? Did a job interview go badly? Let's hear the whole story.

Mealtime gatherings can bring out the worst as well as the best in people. In families overattentive to appearances, mealtime becomes a theater of reprimand and denied expression. Elbows off, hands on, close your mouth, forks to the left, soup before salad.

The social dimension of eating affects nutrition. Several years ago, a team of New York City nutritionists examined the effect of diet on the physical well-being of low-income children. They asked families to list all the food they ate in a typical week, and as an afterthought, threw in a question about the atmosphere at the dinner table. To their amazement the social atmosphere of eating did more to explain health and physical growth than the amount or nutritional content of food eaten. Children who ate the most meager meals in a calm atmosphere did better than kids who had to cope with anger and hostility while eating, or those who just grabbed something from the refrigerator on the run.

The right physical environment will heighten the social pleasures of eating. Dining spaces are often more formal than warranted by their use. Repainting with a bright color can begin to change this. Let all the people who eat in a space participate in fixing it up. (If you are concerned about the taste of children, select two wall colors, two pieces of artwork, and two lamps, and let the children choose the one to be used.)

There is much to learn from the way good restaurants create positive spaces for eating. With so many people eating in a single room, restaurants have to make a special effort to give each table a sense of containment and sufficiency. Plants, low walls, and high bench backs all help define the space "belonging" to a table, as does the table's alignment with wall features. Something of this restaurant coziness can be added to a home dining room through controlled lighting. Lights can be turned down to a glowing yellow by using a dimmer. The effect immediately draws people into a circle of familiarity. On p. 137 are plans for a "fellowship light" with an embracing roof-like shape which throws strong light on the table and soft light on the diners' faces.

The Pleasures of Cooking

Imagine a job with the following characteristics: You can work one hour a day, or eight, depending on your mood. The tasks involved are easy to master. You are not expected to be an expert, but slight improvements in skill are lavishly rewarded. The raw materials involved are natural and bring

you in touch with the fundamental life processes of growth and regeneration. Recognition of your accomplishments comes fast and from the heart. Others anxiously await your production and come running as soon as you say it's ready. Pay is low, but there is no dress requirement and you work at home.

Such is cooking, the hardest work that goes on in the house, and potentially the most rewarding. Unfortunately, many families compromise the natural pleasures of cooking. The job is viewed as second class and given to one person, no time off, no assistance. False praise—"Isn't your mother's meat loaf delicious?"—replaces real appreciation for time generously given.

In our group household, we get together once a week and choose nights to cook. People who like to mount big productions can work up to them all week. No one feels pressured. Equity emerges naturally through regular conversation about who does what.

With so many cooking aids available today, it is easy to find an involvement

with cooking that feels right. Convenience foods and time-saving cooking devices can reduce meal preparation time to almost nothing for those disinclined to spend time in the kitchen. At the other extreme, gourmet shops, TV cooking shows, specialty magazines, and a never-ending supply of novel food preparation devices cater to those who consider their cooking a point of personal pride.

Cleanup as Gratification

Last in our list of kitchen pleasures is cleanup. Getting pleasure from kitchen cleanup is not as farfetched as it might seem. A good cleanup can be the most satisfying accomplishment of the day. The object is simple and clear. Every exertion brings visible progress. It doesn't take forever, and you know when you are done.

Part of the pleasure is clearing out the deadwood—ruthlessly doing away with things not pulling their weight. Some normally gentle people find satisfaction in the more violent forms of kitchen sanitizing—pot scouring, blasting sink traps, and search-and-destroy missions against insects. Similarly, food shopping needn't be drudgery. Trips to secure groceries are a vestigial link to our ancestors' dawn to dusk search for food. We, like they, can get pleasure from gathering in food, filling our storehouses, and celebrating the abundance of life. On p. 142 are plans for a pantry which attempts to express this sense of abundance.

Kitchen Fantasies

Here are several fantasies that explore feelings about food and eating.

One Conscious Meal

Because social interactions tend to dominate mealtime, most of us have lost touch with the messages our bodies send us about eating. Begin this exercise by finding a time when you can eat completely alone. Wait until you feel definite sensations of hunger, then carry out the following steps:

STEP 1. Understand your hunger. Decide where in your body hunger is originating—stomach? throat? mouth? all over?

STEP 2. Choose which food to eat. Before you go to the kitchen, decide what food would best satisfy your hunger. Choose only foods which "hum" to you, not ones that "beckon." Keep the number of different foods to a minimum. One food and one drink is plenty. Prepare the food for eating.

STEP 3. Eat the food you have chosen. Do not allow any other distractions during the meal. No magazines, TV, or company. Find the best environment within the house for conscious enjoyment of the meal you have chosen. Consider places other than the kitchen or dining room—a study, porch, living room, or outdoor spot. As you eat, physical responses will be taking place within your body involving glands, muscles, and organs. You won't be able to feel all of these, but with careful attention you will be able to track the following kinds of sensations for up to a half hour after eating: feelings of hot and cold, feelings of pressure and emptiness, feelings of movement, and sounds. Consider that these signs are messages which your body is sending you about your eating. Judge them by how they make you feel—satisfied, uncomfortable, contented, relaxed.

Family Dinner

For many people, childhood family experience was defined by what happened at the dinner table. Recreating such a meal from your childhood can reveal a great deal about yourself and the way you eat. Find a quiet spot, shut your eyes and imagine a family meal from your childhood. Where are you before dinner? How are you called to the table? Imagine your plate. What do you like most on it, what least? What is said at the table? Who does the dishes?

Ethnic Feast

Invent your own ethnic eating experience. Pick the foreign country whose cooking you most enjoy. Think of one or two good friends to have an imaginary meal with you there. Close your eyes and be transported to a beautiful region of that country, heading for a restaurant known for its food and atmosphere. Walk slowly up to the restaurant. When do you first notice a special smell? Who else is eating there? How is the table set and what are the waiters like? What courses do you select? How is the meal concluded?

Kitchen Inspirations

This early photograph of a high plains chuckwagon provides an evocative image of outdoor eating, American style.

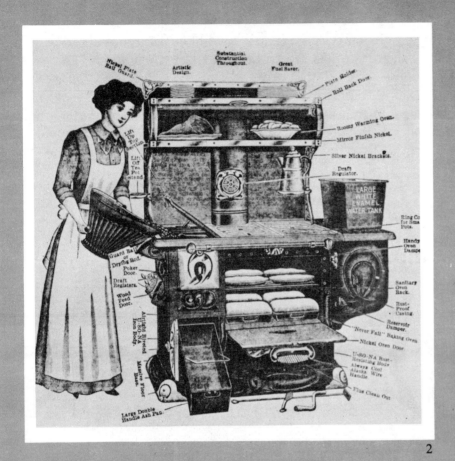

2

THE BIG HOOSIER

1

Two kitchen fixtures that become kitchens in themselves: **1.** Hoosier metal cabinet, purchased for over two million American households. **2.** A wood-burning stove from the 1911 Sears Roebuck catalogue.

Moods and Foods Survey

What we want to eat is often determined by our emotions. Take a pencil and fill out the following chart to see what foods are associated with your moods. Down the left is a list of moods. For each of these, fill in the first column of the chart with foods that you would find appropriate if you were in this mood. List several foods if more than one comes to mind. In the next column, list people that it would be appropriate to eat with if you were in that mood. Don't hesitate to repeat names or indicate that it would be most appropriate to eat alone. In the last column write the name of a place you might go out to eat if you were in that mood. If nothing comes to mind, just continue with the other questions.

When you have completed the exercise, ask yourself which moods your present kitchen tends to express, and which it would benefit from expressing more.

Moods	Foods What food would be appropriate to eat if you were in this mood?	Company With whom would it be appropriate to eat if you were in this mood?	Restaurants Where would it be appropriate to go out to eat if you were in this mood?
Self-indulgent, feeling like you deserve something special.			
Sociable, in a mood for getting together with friends.			
Nostalgic, filled with fond memories of your childhood.			
Harried, almost too busy to bother eating.			
Lonely, in need of care and consolation.			

Kitchen Efficiency Survey

Kitchens are the workroom of the house. When things go wrong there, your whole day can suffer. The following test will help you analyze the efficiency of your kitchen's layout and equipment. Read the questions through and mark the "yes" or "no" box as appropriate. If a question doesn't apply, leave both boxes blank. Total up the high and low marks to see how your kitchen rates in overall efficiency.

High Marks   **Low Marks**

YES ☐   NO ☐   Is the area above your stove free from storage?

YES ☐   NO ☐   Is your sink located efficiently *between* the refrigerator and the stove?

YES ☐   NO ☐   Do you have 2 feet of counter to either side of your sink, 2 feet to one side of the range, and 1 foot 3 inches next to the handle side of your refrigerator?

YES ☐   NO ☐   Is your pantry located so the sun never shines directly into it?

YES ☐   NO ☐   Is the total distance from sink to stove to refrigerator to sink—what kitchenologists call the "work triangle"—between 12 and 20 feet?

YES ☐   NO ☐   Is your kitchen arranged so that no circulation paths go through the "work triangle"?

YES ☐   NO ☐   Does your refrigerator door open properly from the left or right, as suits its location in the kitchen?

YES ☐   NO ☐   Do you have a "toe space" under all cabinets so you don't have to lean over so far, and to ease cleaning?

YES ☐   NO ☐   Do you have special lights for sink, range, and mixing areas so that you never work in your own shadow?

YES ☐   NO ☐   Do you recycle glass and tin cans and compost your organic garbage?

YES ☐ NO ☐   Do you have a stove vent?

YES ☐ NO ☐   Do you have a mixing counter three feet long?

YES ☐ NO ☐   Do you have 10 feet of cabinet frontage below counter height and 7 feet above?

YES ☐ NO ☐   Are all the places where you would walk or stand in the kitchen at least 4 feet wide?

YES ☐ NO ☐   Are your counters no more than 2 feet deep when there are cabinets above?

YES ☐ NO ☐   Is your garbage disposal switch located at least 6 feet from the unit?

YES ☐ NO ☐   Does your kitchen face north or northeast to avoid hot sun while you're cooking?

YES   **NO**

    TOTAL   **TOTAL**

132

Paper Cooking Survey

Careful location of utensils and food can greatly reduce the physical exertion required by cooking. The number of steps taken around the kitchen in cooking breakfast can be reduced from 500 to 200, say efficiency experts. Dinner exertion can be reduced by 500 steps, washing dishes by 550. Tracing some of your cooking habits on paper will give you a fresh look at them. You need a plan of your kitchen to begin (see p. 22 on drawing a plan of your house or apartment). For each of the following items, mark an "X" where the item is *stored,* an "X" where it is *first used*, and connect the two with a line.

Mix Area Items

- flour or baking mixes
- powdered sugar
- cooking oil

Sink Area Items

- onions
- potatoes
- cleaning liquids

Range Area Items

- hot cereal
- spices
- coffee
- spaghetti

Serving Area Items

- cookies
- silverware
- peanut butter
- cold cereal

Imagine what steps you could take to shorten the lines you have drawn on your kitchen plan. Where would items go if you put them at the closest possible point to where they were first used?

Kitchen experts say the four categories above mark the four major work areas of any kitchen. How would you rearrange your kitchen to make these work areas more efficient?

Goals/Solutions

To begin the translation of hopes and aspirations into concrete ideas for fixing up your kitchen, we include a variety of practical suggestions grouped under four goals: giving your kitchen a greater sense of security and nurturing; making it a more direct source of reward and pleasure; making children more at home; and easing the repetitive quality of kitchen work.

If your goal is

To get more feelings of security and nurturing from your kitchen

Tried and true

Get a copy of your mother's favorite cookbook (or your grandmother's recipe box) and cook up some childhood favorites from the original texts.

Security Foods

Indulge in your security foods more frequently. Highlight these foods in your kitchen by getting a new breadbox, potato bin, pie stand, or cookie jar as appropriate.

Protecting shapes

If you are undertaking a kitchen remodeling or addition, keep in mind that parts of a room which are protectively enclosed by a low ceiling or partial wall will feel especially sheltered.

Lighting

Many kitchens are illuminated more like factories than homes. If you want your kitchen to feel warm and cozy, use incandescent, not fluorescent, lighting, and arrange different lights to shine on each of your work and eating surfaces.

Good smells

To extend nurturing feelings all over the house, turn your oven vent off and cook things like Indian pudding, pork shoulder, bread, or baked beans that take all day to prepare and smell great.

Nostalgia

Things from the past give some people feelings of security and well-being. On a small scale, you might bake in old-fashioned tins, beat eggs with a turn-of-the-century egg beater, make kitchen lights out of kerosene lanterns, or display a set of Currier and Ives prints. On a larger scale, you might get an old-fashioned stove or "Hoosier beauty" metal cabinet system with built-in flour and sugar sifters and a wooden-match dispenser.

If your goal is

To get more feelings of reward and pleasure from your kitchen

Color

Could you find more pleasurable colors to paint your kitchen and the places you eat? How about spring green or waterfall blue? Introduce colorful patterns—whether Art Deco, Colonial, or primitive—through stencils, patterned curtains, or wallpaper.

Reward foods

Find out what foods "hum" to you when you feel a need to be appreciated. Invent ways to make these foods visibly present in your kitchen with a see-through cookie jar, stemmed cake plate, glass candy box, chocolate chip dispenser, and the like.

Big production

Celebrate the preparation of foods you enjoy. Get an ice cream maker, espresso machine, corn popper, expensive cake decorator, or donut machine.

Extras

Keep well-stocked with the little rewards that make everyday meals special: Indian lemon-pickle chutney, Dutch cocoa, fresh Roquefort dressing, ground nuts, Chinese five-spice, real maple syrup.

Projects

It is always rewarding to be surrounded by things you are proud to have made. If you do craftwork, photography, or carpentry, get some of it into the kitchen. If you want even more strokes, try sanding down the floor to natural wood or replacing one of your kitchen windows with a greenhouse bay.

If your goal is

To make a kitchen better for children

Counter

Construct a two-sided counter in your kitchen where kids and adults can easily cook together.

Kids' place

Make a sitting place in your kitchen where kids can do their projects, whether food-related or not, out of the way but still part of kitchen activities.

Shopping

Involve kids in shopping—checking to see what you need, deciding between brands, being responsible for picking up two or three items in the supermarket.

● Safety

The kitchen is the most dangerous room in the house for kids. Get a stove with controls on the upper surface and burners set back from the front edge. Turn handles of cooking pots toward the wall. Install childproof locks on cabinets for knives and household chemicals.

● Children's level

Store foods that kids can prepare on lower shelves where they can reach them. Make a special place for children's cookbooks. Get broad-based stools and boxes for kids to stand on when working at adult-height counters.

● Floor

Kids spend a lot of time on the kitchen floor. For their purposes, the best floor is warm and slip resistant. Cork tile would be excellent, with a throw rug in a children's corner where toys are kept.

If your goal is

To ease the boring, repetitive qualities of kitchen work

● Fresh perspective

If you find a task boring, stand outside your body and watch yourself doing the work. Be open to pleasurable dimensions of the task, no matter how small—the sound of water in the sink, a piece of sky out the window, the smell of a clean floor.

● Equipment

Get your tools working with, not against you. Indulge in a new vacuum cleaner or garbage disposal. Get an appropriately sized carrier tray for household cleaners.

● Ritual

Submit to the ritual of the task at hand. There is no kitchen task more "boring" than the central Zen attitude of "just sitting." Let the repetitive aspects of the task at hand become your mantra and emerge relaxed instead of anxious.

● Architecture

If you are building a new house or remodeling an old one, insist on effort-saving architectural features: kick space under all cabinets, splashbacks on counters, floor coverings that do not show dirt, a trash compactor, insulating glass, plenty of storage space for food and kitchen utensils, washable wall surfaces in key locations.

● Share

Share the arduous work. You can never enjoy a task you are doing *against* someone else. Talk house chores through with all household members and divide them up equitably.

Fellowship Light

Here is a dining table lamp which reinforces the sense of fellowship we look for from mealtime. Rather than drawing attention to itself, this lamp showcases the eaters below by sheltering them with a rooflike shape. Two bulbs light up the cloth "roof" of the lamp from within. This gentle, indirect illumination sets the faces of people sitting around the table softly glowing. Out of the slot in the lower side, however, comes direct, unshielded light for the table surface directly below. This has the effect of placing the meal in a kind of spotlight. Everybody (especially the cook) will appreciate the way this highlights the nurturing gesture of preparing a meal for friends. The lamp is designed so you can give it a special personality with the cloth you select for the roof. A favorite piece of material from grandmother's chest would create a Victorian effect. Fall colors would give the room a warm feeling. Striped cloth would create a carnival effect. Drape a number of materials over the finished light to see which one you prefer.

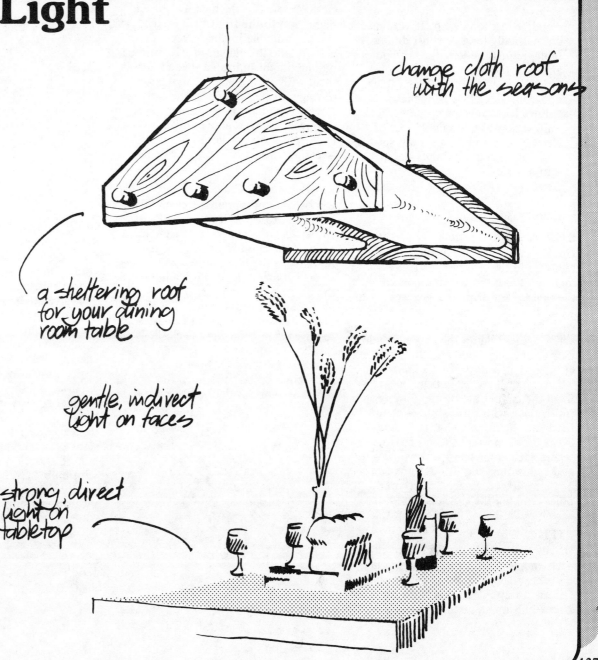

change cloth roof with the seasons

a sheltering roof for your dining room table

gentle, indirect light on faces

strong, direct light on tabletop

STEP 1. Obtain materials.

- 5 closet poles, 1 1/4-inch-diameter wood, 4 feet long each. If you have an unusually long or short dining table, adjust the length of the poles, and thus the lamp.
- 1 piece of plywood, 1/2-inch thick, good one side, 28 x 28 inches square.
- fittings for 2 surface-mounted light bulb sockets, including 25 feet of electric cord and 2 light bulb shields, 6 inches in diameter, that clamp onto the bulbs.
- 2 yards of cloth at least 42 inches wide.
- a dozen 3-inch finishing nails.

STEP 2. Build the wood framework.

Cut the end pieces according to the template in the diagram. Drill 1 1/4-inch holes as indicated to accommodate the poles. Test drill on a piece of scrap wood to make sure the hole provides a snug fit. When drilling holes in the actual pieces, clamp the two ends and a piece of scrap wood and drill them all at once. This will prevent splintering when the drill comes out the back. Sand the endpieces and the dowels and finish them with oil, paint, or stain. Insert all the dowels so they extend 2 1/2 inches beyond the endpieces and secure each connection with white glue and a finishing nail through the edge of the endpiece. Leave both center poles defining the slot unsecured, to ease installation of the cloth roof.

STEP 3. Wire lamps.

Install two light bulb sockets, one on each endpiece. Dimensions of the lamp have been carefully set to insure that light will fall out directly onto the table below but not shine in people's eyes.

Light is blocked to the sides by the cloth "roof," to the back by the end-piece, and to the front by a 6-inch shield (available in dime stores) that clamps onto the bulb itself. Use surface-mounted light bulb sockets and attach them with screws that will not show through on the outside of the endpiece. Locate each light in the center of its endpiece, 8 inches above the bottom edge. Wire the two lamps in parallel (see diagram) so only one cord emerges from the top.

STEP 4. Install Cloth.

Choose an appropriate piece of fabric and cut it to a width which will just fit between the endpieces. Staple one edge of the cloth to one of the center poles; turn the pole so the cloth wraps around it a couple of times and secure the pole to the end piece with a finishing nail (no glue this time). Let the nail extend a tiny bit so it will be easy to remove when changing the cloth. Wrap the cloth around the three fixed poles to create the "roof," then staple it to the second center pole; turn this pole until the fabric is tight and secure it with a nail.

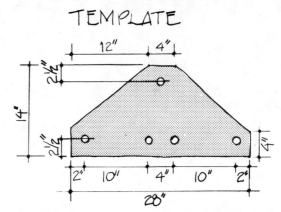

END PIECE TEMPLATE

STEP 5. Hang lamp.

Screw two eye hooks into the top of the end pieces. Secure two hooks in your ceiling with eye hooks, bolts, or expansion shields, as appropriate. If you have an existing ceiling lamp over your dining table, remove it and wire the fellowship lamp to the same outlet. If you don't, plug the lamp into an existing wall socket and install a line switch at a convenient height. Dining room lamps should always be on a dimmer so they can be turned to a level which illuminates the table but does not glare (see p. 194 for instructions on installing dimmers). Once the lamp has been installed, experiment with bulb size and adjustment of the small shield on each bulb for the most pleasant effect.

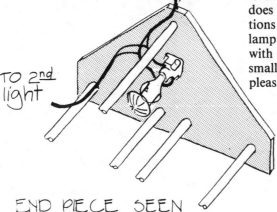

TO 2nd light

END PIECE SEEN FROM INSIDE.

High Chair

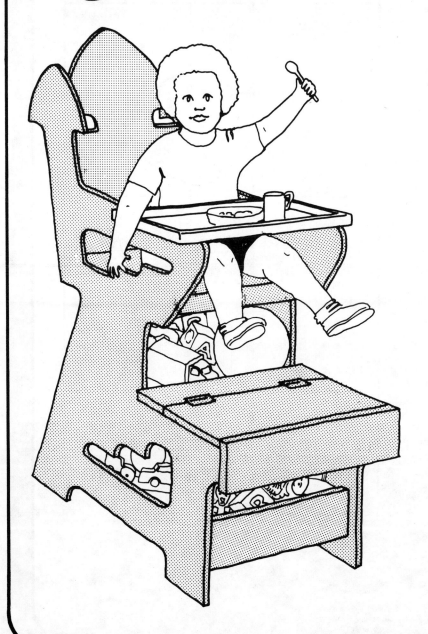

There is a long period in a family's life when children are old enough to be present at the table, but too small for conventional chairs. The high chairs you can buy these days are functional but ugly, and if you have to have one around, you will probably find it the most visible piece of furniture in the kitchen. Because kids tend to use the kitchen as a second playroom, this high chair contains a place for storing toys. The small step on the front lifts up to reveal a large toy bin. The step serves an additional function. When some kids hit the "I-can-do-it-myself"

WOODEN TRAY FROM BELOW

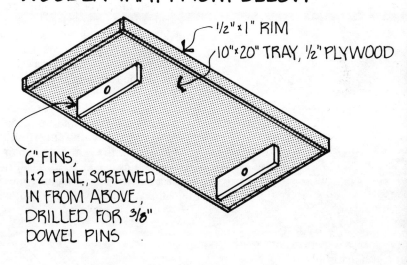

½" x 1" RIM

10" x 20" TRAY, ½" PLYWOOD

6" FINS, 1 x 2 PINE, SCREWED IN FROM ABOVE, DRILLED FOR ⅜" DOWEL PINS

phase, just putting them in a high chair can set off a tantrum. With the addition of this step, independent kids can climb peacefully into the chair themselves from about 18 months up. But the happiest quality of this chair is its thronelike shape. Most high chairs do little to welcome kids to the kitchen. Some antique versions have spirit, but they are expensive, and often unsafe. This sturdy high chair has a style all its own—a good place for someone to eat a year to two of meals, and a pleasant piece of furniture to have in your kitchen or dining room.

STEP 1. Obtain Materials.

- one 4 by 6-foot piece of 1/2-inch plywood, good one side.
- one 8-foot length of 1 x 10-inch select pine shelving.
- 40 2-inch-long, number 8 flathead wood screws.
- 2 hinges with 2 x 3/4-inch leaves.
- fine sandpaper and polyurethane finish.
- seat strap (purchase or make one from an old belt or luggage strap).

STEP 2. Purchase or construct tray

Check with your local children's furniture store to see if they will special-order a high chair tray for you. The molded plastic ones are strong and easy to wash. Find one that is attached by spring-loaded pins that pull outward to release the tray from the chair. Drilling several holes in the arms of the chair will allow this kind of tray to be used on a wooden chair you construct. If you purchase a tray, set the width of the chair to meet the width required by the tray. We have included plans for a wooden tray as well. It should be rectangular (17 by 10 inches) with a one-inch rim to catch spills. Give the tray three or four coats of polyurethane to stand up to repeated washings. Four fins underneath secure the tray to the arm of the chair when dowel pins are inserted. Drill the holes at a slight slant so jiggling the chair will not cause the pins to fall out.

LAYOUT
ON 1/2" PLYWOOD   (EACH SQUARE IS 6" x 6")

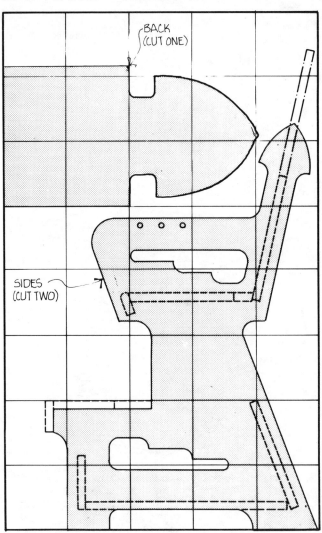

BACK
(CUT ONE)

SIDES
(CUT TWO)

CUTAWAY VIEW

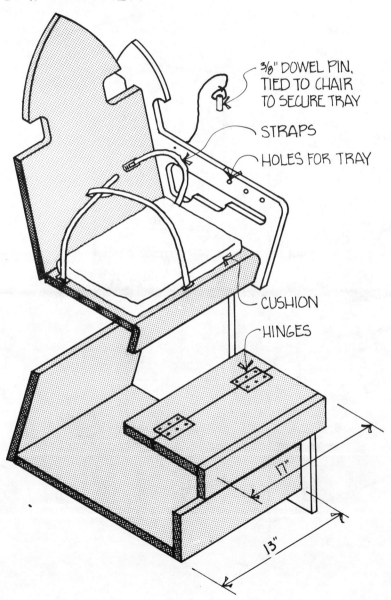

3/8" DOWEL PIN, TIED TO CHAIR TO SECURE TRAY

STRAPS

HOLES FOR TRAY

CUSHION

HINGES

17"

13"

STEP 3. Cut out pieces for chair.
Cut the two sides, the seat back, and the bottom of the toy bin out of the 1/2-inch plywood. Layout for the side pieces and seat back have been included on a 6-inch grid to help you draw these accurately. Cut all remaining crosspieces from the pine shelving. The distance between the two sides, and thus the length of all these pieces, is 15 inches (unless you have purchased a tray of different dimensions). Sand all pieces carefully. Round all edges of the high chair to avoid splinters and chipping of edges when the chair is moved around.

STEP 4. Assemble.
Screw crosspieces forming the seat, toy bin, and step together securely before screwing them in place between the side pieces. Attach a seat strap (young children need a section of strap that comes up between their legs).

STEP 5. Finish surfaces.
Fill all holes into which screws have been countersunk with wood putty; let dry and sand smooth. Two coats of polyurethane will give a strong, water-resistant finish to the chair. If you want to add decoration, be sure you use lead-free paint. A small seat cushion can be added.

Abundant Pantry

One of the keenest kitchen pleasures is the sense of well-being that comes from a full pantry. Here is an outsized piece of furniture which Deborah designed as a walk-in pantry turned inside-out. It was designed for our kitchen (the short end goes against the wall), so you will probably want to adjust the plans for your own needs. Ideas in the design can be used separately or clustered together in a unit like the one shown. At the bottom level is a roll-out bin for childrens' toys or potatoes and onions. At the same level are several vertical slots for cookie sheets, baking pans, large pot lids, oven racks, etc. Vertical storage of these items avoids the bone-chilling din that results when a pan is pulled from the bottom of a horizontal stack. One level up is a deep shelf, the only element which continues uninterrupted around all three sides of the unit. The dimensions of the shelf were set to accommodate gallon-sized jars for storing grain, flour, nuts, beans, and the like. At about table height is another large bin. In our household, this bin is used to hide the inevitable pile of bags, mittens, books, and tools that gathers each week. Removing either the shelves or hanging racks above this level permits conversion of this area into a kitchen work surface. At the end of the unit on this level are several slots where spatulas, cooking spoons, eggbeaters, etc., can be stored on end. Two poles for hanging cooking pots are bolted to one side of the unit.

On the opposite side are three shelves for visible storage of cans and packages. Between the two uprights on the end are narrow shelves for spices. The top two spice shelves are sized for quart- and pint-sized canning jars. A lamp hidden in the cantilevered "fascia" above spotlights these two shelves and the rows of spices. The instructions that follow contain only key information so you can plan and build a unit that meets your own particular needs.

STEP 1. Obtain materials.

- 4 x 4-inch stock for posts.
- 1/2-inch plywood for bottoms of storage units (use 3/4-inch plywood for working surfaces).
- 1/4-inch-diameter machine bolts for attaching crosspieces to posts.
- pine shelving for shelves, braces, fascia, and sides of storage units.
- 2 x 2-inch stock for pot hanging rods.
- one light socket.
- casters for rollaway bin.
- 2-inch finishing nails.

STEP 2. Build subparts.

Construct vertical storage unit, rollaway bin, utensil storage unit, and counter-level bin separately.

STEP 3. Assemble unit.

Bolt subparts and fascia to posts. Use two bolts per post wherever possible to provide resistance to cracking. Size, cut, and install shelves.

STEP 4. Finish wood.

Linseed oil is the easiest natural finish although light stain or varnish might be more appropriate for your kitchen.

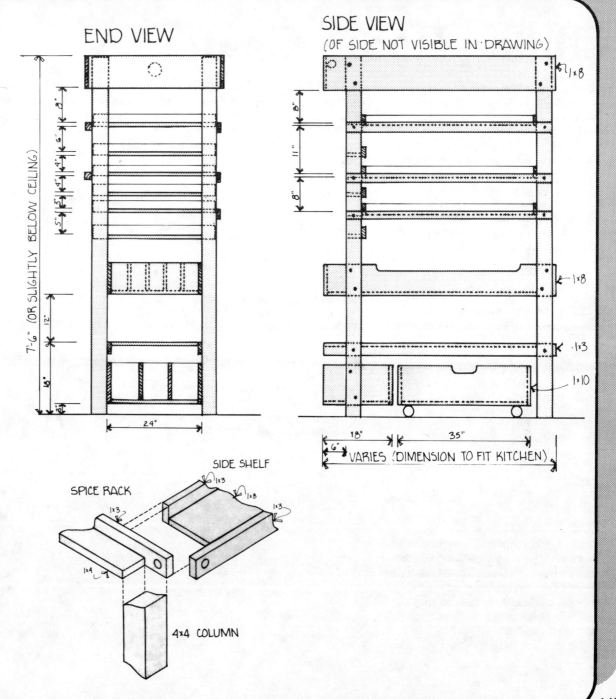

END VIEW

SIDE VIEW
(OF SIDE NOT VISIBLE IN DRAWING)

SPICE RACK

SIDE SHELF

4x4 COLUMN

Dining Room Chair

The relaxed atmosphere of after-dinner conversation is often cut short, not because there is somewhere better to go, but because we can't sit still on the hard chairs any longer. Here is a very inexpensive, do-it-yourself dining room chair with a curved back and seat that will encourage people to stay at the table for hours. It is designed by Chuck Plaisted, an architect friend who has built three generations of the chair, improving it a little bit each time. Yours will thus be one of the great-grandchildren of the original, still doing service at his dining room table.

STEP 1. Obtain materials.

- 2 feet of 5/16-inch hardwood dowel.
- small box of 2-inch finishing nails.
- wood glue.
- one bundle of 1 x 3-inch wood strapping (some of the cheapest wood you will find at the lumberyard).

STEP 2. Make legs.

Cut out the three pieces required to make each leg (see diagram for exact shapes). Clamp all four upright pieces together to cut the 3/4-inch slots in the top before assembling. Nail and glue legs together.

STEP 3. Make chair seat.

Cut side pieces for chair bottom with a saber saw (see side view diagram for shape of curve and notch that must be taken out of bottom corner). Nail and glue slats of chair bottom so that the seat will be 15 inches wide at the back and 19 at the front. Install the front and back slats first and then the center ones.

STEP 4. Cut pieces for backrest.

Cut the first curved backrest support, the one at the level of the arms of the chair. Cut the second curved backrest support which fits into the notches on the chair bottom. Cut the five slats that make up the back of the chair.

STEP 5. Assemble pieces.

Carefully set distance from chair bottom to floor as indicated on diagrams. Nail chair bottom to legs for temporary hold until dowels are inserted. Chair legs are attached to chair bottom with four dowels per side. Drill 5/16-inch holes for these dowels, insert glue, drive the dowels in place, and saw off the ends. Because the dowels should extend only about an inch and a half into the chair leg, they will not be visible from the side of the chair. Nail and glue backrest slats to the two backrest supports. Assemble "T"-shaped armrests, glue them in their slots, and attach backrest support at this level.

STEP 6. Apply finish.

Sand as necessary and apply a light coat of linseed or tung oil. Polyurethane will give a shiny, easy-clean finish if you prefer.

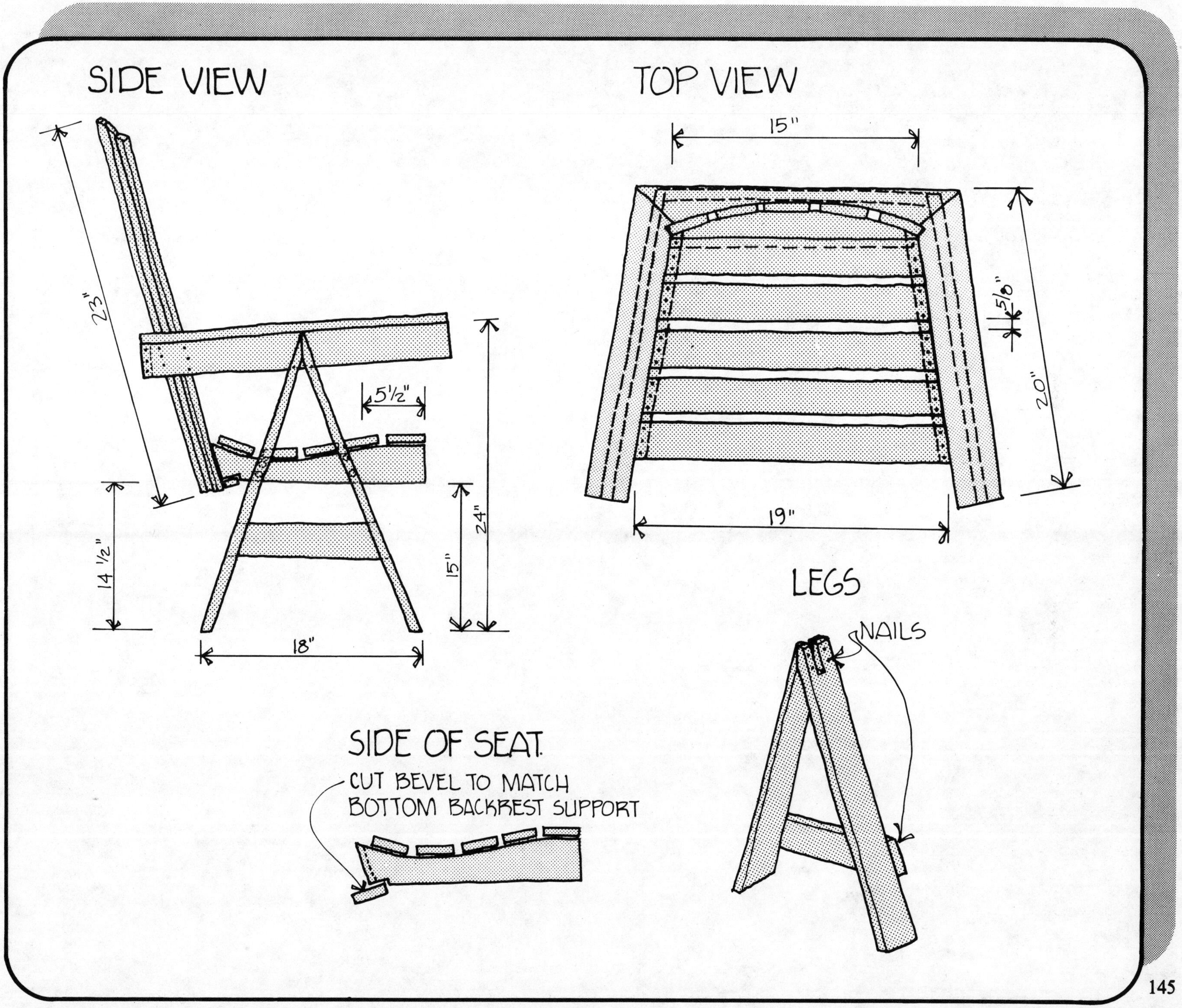

SIDE VIEW

23"

5½"

14½"

24"

15"

18"

TOP VIEW

15"

5/8"

2·0"

19"

LEGS

NAILS

SIDE OF SEAT.

CUT BEVEL TO MATCH
BOTTOM BACKREST SUPPORT

145

Kitchen Inspirations

An early American kitchen
scene.

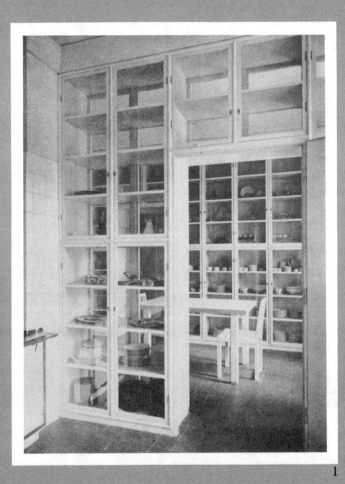

2

1

1. A kitchen pantry with the flavor of a scientific laboratory. 2. A basement kitchen equipped to provide food for a large household. 3. A farmhouse kitchen in the traditional Japanese style.

3

A Cook's Kitchen

Here is a kitchen for the person who takes cooking seriously. Each part celebrates a phase of cooking by giving it the space and organization it demands. The room design, including the drawing of it presented here, comes from Jerry Simon, an architect who is as good at building spaces like this as he is at designing them.

The Room

This cook's kitchen has been designed to fit in a room 16-feet square, larger than most kitchens, but not out of the question for people who could add the space of a pantry, hallway, or part of a dining room to enlarge a modest-size kitchen. The room opens to a dining room in the foreground of the drawing and has one window to the outside, over the sink.

The Design

Lazy Susans. Three corners of the kitchen are occupied by outsized cylindrical storage units that pivot around metal axles at their center. The units are large, 4 feet across, to allow storage of items like food boxes which would fit awkwardly on a circle of smaller diameter. Industrial-scale hardware is necessary for these units, especially the ball bearing plates that hold the trays in place around the central pipe, but any carpenter could design and install them. These room-size lazy Susans take the most neglected parts of any kitchen —the corners—and turn them into storage centers. The same gesture frees up the broad wall areas between corners for use as counter space.

The cylindrical unit in the foreground contains a section for plates, glasses, and other diningware. When this section of the unit is rotated toward the kitchen, it is easily loaded from the sink and dishwasher area nearby. When the table is being set, the same section is rotated to face the dining area across the broad counter.

The open unit in the back of the picture is a compact pantry. Each two shelves of this unit rotate independently so that an entire selection of grain jars or packaged foods can be viewed without having to rotate the full unit.

The third unit is shown with its sliding wood-slat doors closed. Its upper section is a temperature- and humidity-controlled storage closet for vegetables and fruits. Most of the rotating bins within contain wire bottoms for freer circulation of air. Below is a circular storage shelf for outsized pots and pressure cookers.

Central Island

In the middle of the kitchen is a workspace containing a sink with a garbage disposal. Its central location makes this an efficient place to carry out projects requiring proximity to stove, sink, refrigerator, or pantry. The heavy wood top of the island is mounted on a set of storage cabinets. On the ceiling above the counter is a circular hanging rack for cookware.

Lighting

The room is surrounded at ceiling level by a continuous soffit. Within the soffit are downspots which bathe the counters with light. The inner surface of the disk-shaped structure above the central island is a diffuser for lights hidden behind.

Vertical Storage

The vertical panels on either side of the cylindrical units hide storage slots for flat cooking utensils like cookie sheets, and vertical racks for smaller items like spices. Two of these are shown in the open position at the rear of the picture.

An Eater's Kitchen

At first glance, this kitchen for eaters, also designed by Jerry Simon, looks more like a restaurant than a home. But take away the starry-eyed couple, the distracted businessman, and the couple looking at the scenery out the window, and you have a modest-sized kitchen-dining room that emphasizes eating instead of cooking.

The Room

The space which this room occupies measures 17 by 12 feet. An efficiency kitchen is unceremoniously packed away in one corner while a variety of eating environments claim the majority of space. The average person coming home from a day's work stops in the kitchen to figure out what to cook for dinner. Should it be a major production like lasagne, or a minor one like a big salad? The question one asks when entering this world is not "What should I cook?" but "Where should I eat?" The location and pace of the meal is set first—eat-and-run burger stand, cozy breakfast nook, or formal restaurant. Only then does one go to the freezer and pop the appropriate dish in the microwave oven.

The Design

Stand-up Counter

A small counter with a stool is the fast-food department in this kitchen. A small section of mansard roof covers the area. Against the wall are a menu, hamburger condiments, and a napkin holder. Here is where you wash down that leftover piece of pizza with a soft drink.

The Breakfast Nook

In the center of the back wall is a booth with rounded detailing reminiscent of the "patent furniture" developed by Pullman and others for 19th-century railroad passengers. A pass-through between booth and kitchen facilitates serving food and clearing dishes. Booths, some complain, force evacuation of the whole bench when a person sitting on the inside wishes to leave. Small price to pay, say its advocates, for the special face-to-face eating the setup provides.

The Italian Restaurant

On the side of the room opposite the cooking area is a raised platform with a restaurant ambiance. Low lighting, a floor-to-ceiling wine rack, and a wall mural all contribute to the effect. Even the most hastily prepared antipasto is given authenticity by this environment. The simple device of having two small tables instead of one changes the feel of the room entirely.

151

Children's Places

The activity parts of this chapter are designed for adults and kids to do together, starting with some loosening-up exercises to help get everyone's "child-self" in action. Several fantasies and surveys will bring back memories of favorite childhood spots and help us see our present-day environment from a child's perspective. A section containing practical suggestions for improving children's spaces follows. It identifies environmental changes appropriate to three developmental goals: security, self-expression, and learning. Several pages of suggestions for dealing with indoor exercise and storage of children's possessions come next, followed by description of a "child city" to turn a small apartment into a place where both older and younger inhabitants can live happily.

Made by Kids

Children create an incredible array of environments—real places that promote joyful entertainment, organic insights into the natural world, and profound learning. Unmistakably, these places are the product of children's wisdom and power, not adults'. Most of adult environment-making carefully avoids such inventiveness. More often than not, the places that adults design for work seem to house machines rather than people, and there are elaborate restrictions on the spontaneous use of public open space, parks, and plazas.

The homes where children grow up are often equally unsympathetic to environmental exploration. Space is often an issue. One hundred years ago, 80% of American children grew up on farms, with easy access to a variety of natural environments and a small village of sheds, barns, and outbuildings. How different is contemporary life in a city apartment or suburban house, where space is minimal, voices must not be raised, and outdoor exercises usually require adult supervision.

Even more important than amount of space, however, are the attitudes of adults about how space should be used and shared. The bathroom , for example, can be a world's fair of great environments for kids. There is breath-holding under water, washing doll clothes, spitting like a fountain, doing the Australian crawl, and people undressed, washing their bodies. All this is available to children only if their adult friends are open to such playfulness themselves.

Most frequently, lively children's environments come at some cost in household neatness and order. Most adults don't realize how strongly they feel about these qualities until it's time to negotiate them in detail. The rights of adults to order and privacy need not compromise childhood spontaneity, but the issues involved require dedicated attention.

Until they are six or seven, most children would rather be with their parents than alone. This means that if you're sewing, they want to be doing *their* clothwork nearby; that if you're figuring house bills, they want to be doing *their* paperwork at a nearby desk. The best contracts about use of space by a family are thus worked out on a room-by-room and week-by-week basis.

"the warm one"

once upon a time There was a cold little
squirrel. When Christmas came the
Squirrel asked for a warm cozy house
At the ame time a nice raccon
totd his mother I wish santa would
bring me a real doll. then the squirrel
fell down the chimny. ANd landed
in the racoons hands and they both
loved each other.

the end

Environments serve many purposes for the growing child. It is said that we never learn faster than during our first year. Much of this early learning derives from observing and manipulating the environment. As children develop, the environment provides a scoreboard for personal accomplishment. Here pictures are displayed, ladders climbed, and dreams acted out. Children's fears and wishes are intimately linked to feelings about the environment. Frightening creatures may grow in the heart, but they are *seen* in the dark corners of a room. Happiness is fed by trust and love; but it is acted out first in a nurturing cradle of blankets, pillows, and soft animals.

Adults have much to gain from working at children's environments. Ten years ago, a research psychologist set out to explore the dynamics of creative problem-solving to develop new management techniques for business and service organizations. As a first step he administered a test of creativity to adults of various ages to find out when creativity began to falter. He was able to find the faltering but not the age at which creativity peaked. Younger and younger adults were included in the test. Still no peak. In desperation, he administered the test to children, and finally was able to establish age five as the high point of creative thinking. This insight prompted him to include several free associative techniques, more characteristic of child than adult thought, in his system. The resulting problem-solving process, called Synectics, is now an accepted part of modern "process management" lore.

The modern world has set the child in each of us at bay. Hard-bitten men dominate the movies, cool women set the sexual style, successful manipulators manage the jobs we hold. There is money to be made from conjuring feelings of envy and insufficient possession, but no percentage in the spontaneity and self-sufficiency of childhood. Inevitably, this cultural dynamic takes its toll through the distance it creates in our relationships with people, the natural world and the places we inhabit. Many people are becoming aware of this problem, and have begun to invent ways of dealing with it. But there are no better guides to the child within than children themselves. In helping children create happy environments, adults can renew their own ability to experience the world joyfully.

Childhood Fantasies

These fantasy exercises will help you remember what environments felt like as a child. They can be done by adults alone, or even better, by adults and children together. All you have to do is read one of the stories below, then shut your eyes, relax for a minute, and begin imagining a completion to the story. When you have completed your fantasy, open your eyes and share what you have been thinking.

Hideaway

Think of one of your favorite childhood places. It can be a place that you made—like a blanket house or a snow fort—or a place that you discovered—like a forest or a special room. Remember how it felt to be in this place. Imagine you are going there again to play. What time of day is it? What is the weather like? Whom are you with? How do you get there? What do you do once you arrive? How does the place look and feel?

The Scary Place

Many of our lifelong fears can be traced to the frightening places, real and imagined, of our childhood. Telling a child "Don't go in there" might end a physical danger, but it can begin the kind of thinking which gives inner fears real rooms to live in.

Think of a scary place from your childhood, maybe a recurring setting for a bad dream, a place you were afraid to enter or a place where something bad happened to you. Imagine returning to that place. Approach it slowly, thinking what it will be like.

Go in. Memories like these usually end half-way through. It's natural to avoid thinking—or dreaming—about the bad things that might happen to us. But try to complete the fantasy this time. If you reach a point where your fantasy is ending before the worst happens, try to stay with it and let the story come to an end.

It is very important to share scary fantasies with other people, especially if there are kids involved. Have one of the adults begin by telling the story of his scary place. Avoid interpreting people's stories, and don't rush to reassure anyone, adult or child, that "it's all over now and everything will be all right." Insistent reassurances convey the message that "scary thoughts aren't real, and happy people don't have them." Listen carefully to everybody's stories; then start talking about them.

House-a-rama

While adults often take environments for granted, kids typically have strong feelings about the places they live and play. They remember the corner where the Christmas tree was set up, or the chair where they like to watch for Dad out the window, or the place where someone said something mean to them. The activities that follow can help you regain this child's perspective on environment. Playing these games as a family—and giving everyone a chance to participate—is a good way to start talking about fixing up your home.

One of the best ways to give recognition to a place is to draw it, with all the details, flaws, and idiosyncracies that make it special. This activity results in a series of drawings of interior walls; place them side by side to make a long mural of your house. Drawing the wall of a room is usually easier for kids than adults, who may be ashamed that they "can't draw," but when the finished product is displayed, no one will know the authorship. Each wall drawing should be a square about eight inches by eight inches. If you want to coordinate the effect, have everybody work in the same medium. Stick pastels are a good choice—they are used like crayons, but have dazzling colors. Decide as a group which rooms to include. Each person selects one wall and completes a drawing of it. When a drawing is done, it is placed at the appropriate spot in the house-a-rama, and its author selects another wall. To finish the display, put a thin strip along the bottom of the drawing with titles under each room.

The Tour

This game can be played by toddlers as well as older participants. Each person is given a chair, and a chance to decide which room of the house to visit first. When you've all chosen the room to begin, place the chairs in a circle and have each player do the following things:

1. Pick your favorite object in the room.
2. Choose an unfamiliar place or object in the room to visit and get to know (a closet corner, a little drawer, etc.).
3. Tell what you like about the room.
4. Tell what you don't like about the room.

Make sure that everyone who wants to talk has a chance to speak; at the beginning it is best to go person-to-person around the circle on each topic. When you have finished in one room, move your chairs to another room and start again (don't forget the places between rooms, like hallways and pantries).

Ideal Place

Drawing is a simple activity, but great fun when adults and kids do it together. Everybody should get a favorite medium for drawing—crayons, pencils, watercolors—and some paper. For five minutes everyone draws a subject that all have agreed on. Some subjects that are interesting from an environmental point of view are:

A Room
A House
A Tree
A Yard
A Playground

When everybody has finished, take turns in describing what each person has drawn. Psychologists put a lot of stock in exercises like this: a tree, for example, can be drawn with strong roots or unattached; filled with fruit and animals or empty, as large as the page or huddled in a corner; filled with life or dying. You can make as much or little of your drawings as you like. The final step is the display. Glue everyone's room or yard drawings on a big sheet of paper and outline a house or fence around it.

Goals/Solutions

The next several pages match a variety of developmental goals with some solutions for attaining them. The three goals covered represent key aspects of child development: self-expression, security, and learning.

If your goal is

To encourage a child's self-expression

Feeling that one's creations have value is an important part of fulfilled growth. Adult feelings of inadequacy—that we can't do math, or be attractive, or make friends—can often be traced to a lack of support for personal expression during childhood. Self-expression is fundamentally a problem of human attitudes, not interior design, of course. But many of the most direct ways to reward self-expression work through the environment.

For Ages 0-2

Dance

The self-expression of infants is primarily physical. We can contrive environments that magnify and reward the infant's impulse to expression. In a door jumper, for example, pre-crawling babies can be placed in a secure cloth seat that hangs from a door jamb by elastic cords. The child's smallest effort to move is transformed into a rocking bounce. Most models sell for under $10. (Test the hook with your own weight before entrusting a child to it.)

Rocker House

We have included instructions for a device that will serve as a group rocker, a climbing staircase, and a playhouse (see p.167). Flexible mini-environments like this suggest dozens of ways for infants to invent their own form of expressive play.

Color

Find out your infant's favorite colors—by offering some choices (or perhaps noting which crayons are eaten first). Buy several sheets of colored paper at an art supplies store that match these colors and cut out some shapes to hang over the crib.

Reaching Out

Babies learn through exploration, and we can enhance their development by providing a safe and stimulating environment to explore. For pre-crawling infants, toys and objects hung within batting or kicking distance speed early learning and give the child the experience of having some control over the environment. As the baby begins to move about the house, accident-proofing is in order. Equally important, however, is providing access to the house for the child: removing those valuables that shouldn't be handled, and placing shaped and textured objects at toddler level. (Burton White details the developmental gains of this approach in his book, *The First Three Years of Life* [Avon Books]).

Cruising Bar

When the child holds onto a piece of furniture, or an adult's legs, and moves about carefully on two legs, this is called "cruising"—a pre-walking activity. A child who is encouraged to cruise learns ground rules for safety around the house early. You can foster cruising by placing sturdy low surfaces within the child's reach—coffee tables with rounded corners, shelves with unbreakable objects, open bureau drawers, etc. We built a cruising bar when Robin was six months old by using U-bolts to attach lengths of wood closet pole to wood boxes. The boxes store toys and stabilize the structure. More bars and boxes can be added for more ambitious cruisers.

For ages 3-10

Display

The best way to support self-expression in kids is to honor things they have drawn, made, or collected in special display areas. A friend of mine had a favorite drawing by his four-year-old daughter framed behind glass. When

158

the artist saw this tribute, she was incredulous, and stayed high for a week. A display area for children's art should be big (at least door size) but have clear boundaries so that no one will mistake it for clutter. A sheet of tackboard (or less expensive, less dense, ceiling tile) can be purchased through a lumber supplier and painted. If you're concerned about younger children putting fallen tacks in the mouth, attach artwork with tape. If you have an area for display of pictures of photos at adult eye-level, consider adding a parallel strip underneath, at child's eye-level.

Visible Storage

Children express themselves most directly in the things they collect. Bins in which things are dumped and drawers which hide them away diminish the importance of this expression. Open shelves, boxes, and cubbyholes let the child's personality come through, while putting toys within easy reach for ready use.

Poster Trip

Most cities have at least one store with a huge selection of reasonably priced posters. All kinds of poster themes appeal to kids as well as adults: storybook characters, animal families, famous people, sports . . . take your child on an expedition to buy a poster. Before you go, figure out where in the house to hang it and set ground rules about size and price. Be sure to pick out one for yourself on the same trip.

Outposts

There are non-disruptive ways of incorporating children's creations in adult parts of the house. Have kids spend Saturday afternoon making a fancy table decoration or drawing placemats.

If you have an out-of-the-way spot by the stairs to hang things, make a temporary display of paper fish. Cut out two identical fish shapes from paper. Color or paint them with bright colors. Staple around the edges, leaving an opening to stuff in some tissue paper. Hang by a thread.

Earth-moving Equipment

Young children may not be so good with hammers and saws, but they hold union cards in the sandbox trades. Start with some sand, a pail of water, some small stones and sticks, and soon you've got a whole environment. Old trowels, serving spoons, and refrigerator bowls (or their plastic toy equivalents) help. A good homemade addition is a "sand comb," a 4 x 8-inch rectangle of thin wood (1/4-inch thick) with patterns cut along the long edges with a coping saw (in Japan, raking patterns in the sand of landscaped courtyards is a high art).

If your goal is

To help develop a child's sense of security and trust

All humans have a fundamental need for people who care about their needs and accept them as they are. No amount of attention to the environment can substitute for such relationships, but there are many natural ways an environment can reinforce trust. The ones suggested here relate to a few basic strategies. The first is to populate a child's space with friendly remembrances of trusted people and pleasurable events. The second is to create a cared-for environment. The analogy between cared-for environments and cared-for people is deep. More important than the cost of an improvement is personal involvement in bringing it about. Better than having a room wallpapered is spending an afternoon painting together. Better than buying new pillowcases is to decorate old ones as a family with embroidery or permanent textile paints. The third strategy is to provide enough familiarity in the environment to evoke the larger continuities of life. Trusting that one's inner thoughts and images correspond with outer reality requires consistency in that reality.

For ages 0-2

New Friends
Populate the nursery with friendly presences. Make pillows out of your old T-shirts by sewing the openings shut and filling with cotton or foam. Hang a strip of wallpaper or fabric beside the bed with pictures of animals or imaginary beings that will make good company.

Night-light
Most children feel more secure sleeping with a gentle night-light which familiarizes the room. You can make one using a night-light socket with a small 7-watt bulb. Place the light inside a large "photo cube" (a box with clear plastic sides for displaying snapshots). Choose pieces of cloth or familiar illustrations (blank on the back) and glue them onto the box. You can make printed illustrations translucent by wiping them with vegetable oil.

That's Me
Decorate a child's bedroom with traced body cutouts. Each birthday, have the child lie down on a piece of heavy cardboard or plywood and draw a body outline. Cut it out with a saber saw. Dressing the cutout in outgrown clothes will keep the memory of earlier years alive.

For ages 3-10

Child's House
For young children a normal-sized room feels more like a gymnasium than a cozy hideaway. Having child-scaled places within a room contributes greatly to feeling at ease.

Make a playhouse from a large appliance carton. Cut window and door holes; kids can help if you use a pistol-grip handsaw rather than a matte knife. Decorate as you please. Lace together several boxes and you have a house with rooms. Keep the boxes separate and you have a village, with "telephone lines" between houses made of plastic clothesline. Roofs can be slanted (two sides of a carton), or peaked (four equilateral triangles).

Tube Telephone
Being able to talk from hideaway to hideaway by "secret" communication device is an adventure for children.

Get an old garden hose. Tape up any holes in it and insert a kitchen funnel in each end. Cut off the end fittings, or tape the funnels inside the fittings. The hose can be as long as you want—connect two hoses for going between buildings. With a "Y" hose connector you can rig up three-way conversations. (For more good ideas on environmental adventures, see Stephen Caney's *Toy Book,* Workman Publishing Company).

Flying Carpet
There is no better way to animate a place than to make it the gateway for fantasy travel. A friend of mine purchased a small Oriental rug which he and his daughter sit on to travel to the land of Orb. When not in use, it is reverently rolled up and stored in a special spot.

Puzzle House
Make a big jigsaw puzzle of your house and yard. Draw the plan on paper and let the children participate in coloring it. Next cut the picture into puzzle-sized pieces. Make a bowlful of paste (three parts white glue to one part water). Dip the puzzle pieces in the mixture. Let them drip off, and place them face up on a piece of wax paper. After about one hour, cover them with another piece of wax paper and weight them with books to keep the pieces from curling. The next morning you will have hard, clear pieces of house puzzle which you can put together.

To help children learn about the world and their place in it

The early American home was the primary source of practical action-learning for children and their parents. Here young people learned through experience about producing food, making clothes, building barns, and selling for a fair price. Schools, by contrast, taught book-learning and played a socializing and civilizing role by introducing students to the wider world of culture and current events.

In many ways the situation today is the opposite of this. Schools can't hope to keep up with television as a source of information about the broader culture. At the same time, home life has atrophied as a source of action-learning. Few adults work at home. Activities like homebuilding, supplying heating fuel, and cooking have been truly "domesticated." To keep a proper balance of action and reflection in development, homes must regain their status as places of action-learning. And for younger children, action-learning generally means learning through environmental play. The suggestions that follow are based on the principle that a varied and accessible environment will stimulate the curiosity of the child and encourage exploration and learning. The goal is to fill a child's world with as many engaging objects and places as possible. During infancy, emphasis should be placed on the near world of crib and play spot. As children grow, the focus should widen to include first the child's room, then the full house, and finally, the larger natural and built environment.

For ages 0-2

Travel

The best way to instruct infants is to let them experience the full variety of environments open to adults. Children who are restricted to their cribs can fall years behind in speaking, reading, and walking. Designate a child's place in each room where you spend a signifcant amount of time. For babies, this can be as simple as an overstuffed chair in the living room, a soft throw rug in the study, or kitchen couner space for a portable baby seat secured to prevent falls. For older children, create play areas in each room, with adequate storage and specific boundaries (behind the sofa, on a corner rug, between the dressers), so chaos doesn't dominate the house.

Vacation

Papoose carriers and lightweight folding strollers are inexpensive and make it easy to take an infant on excursions. The baby enjoys the change of scene, and people are invariably friendlier to travelers with a baby. (Some parents find there's nothing like a ride to lull a fussy child to calm, as well.) Once you have learned the local word for disposable diapers, most practical problems disappear.

Texture

Young children learn about the world largely through the sense of touch. You can make a good touch-textbook with pieces of textured material—vinyl, shag rugs, velours, tufted carpets, nylon, etc. Sew a variety of these into patchwork quilts. Drape one across the end of the crib and use the other for a play rug.

Sight

It's thought that babies' vision first focuses on light and movement. What better toys for a newborn than mobiles and prisms hung beside the bed or in a window! Crystal prisms from old chandeliers are common fare at flea markets, and a prism mobile sends light patterns all over the room. Other good materials for a mobile include seashells, pieces of colored cloth and paper, beads, bottle caps. If the mobile also chimes, the baby will get double pleasure.

Music

On the 37th day after conception, the hearing apparatus of the embryo first begins to function. By birth a baby has been listening in for almost eight months. Although the nearest and most constant sounds are mother's heartbeat and the gurgling of digestion, many outside sounds are also clearly transmitted. A cassette of new and familiar sounds will keep an infant company. Include some mother's heartbeat (and some heartbeat rock-and-roll), cuts from your favorite records (the baby already likes them too), some natural sounds, some creature-children noises (kittens, birds, bear cubs), and a reading in familiar voices.

Water

A fluid environment is the infant's natural habitat. In fact, for the first 10 months babies retain a choke-proofing reflex which keeps liquids from being inhaled. Babies can become excellent swimmers. Make water environments accessible to your child. Enroll in a local class of infant swimming, or do the teaching yourself with a book from the Red Cross, YMCA, or library. Emphasize the fun of water play under the close protection of adults, until the baby's coordination and strength are enough to keep it afloat.

For ages 3-10

Learning Floor

Children do most of their playing—and thus learning—on the floor. Tile linoleum is an excellent playroom surface, better for puzzles and toys than a rug, and easy to clean. If you are laying a new tile floor, use a grid pattern, checkerboard or lined, to help suggest structures for games, play villages, and the like. If you are painting the floor, include some learning patterns—a blue "pond," a curving "roadway" for follow-the-trail board games, and a painted yardstick for measuring toys and friends. It is important that a playroom have some carpeted areas as well, for floor play on colder days and active exercise. Polypropylene cord rugs are cheap, easy to clean, and cushiony.

Indoor Nature Learning

There are many indoor growing projects which help kids (and adults) appreciate the cycles of nature. Sprout some seeds, grow a potato, or watch butterfiles emerge from a chrysalis, eggs hatch, and ants burrow.

Barometer

Here's a simple project that allows you to predict the weather. Take a large-mouthed peanut butter or cookie jar. Stretch a piece of balloon across the top and hold it in place with rubber bands. Cut both ends of a paper straw off diagonally and tape one end to the balloon so that it points off in an upward direction. As the barometric pressure goes up and down, the straw will point higher and lower. Draw a scale on the wall to register this movement. Calibrate your barometer by noting where the pointer is on the scale and writing opposite that point what the weather is like outdoors. Be sure to locate the barometer away from windows or radiators where the temperature and humidity will change too radically.

Sundial

Turn your environment into a clock. A homemade sundial is an excellent way to learn about time, astronomy, and sunlight. Find an outdoor area free from trees and other obstructions. Use an existing upright (a tree or a pole), or put a stick in the ground. Calibrate it by placing markers where the shadow is pointing each hour.

Indoor sundials are interesting as well. Use a thin piece of masking tape placed vertically on the window to cast the shadow. End the tape about two thirds of the way up the window. Tape hour markers around the room where the top of the shadow points. Does the sundial change from month to month? Is it accurate in summer and winter? What time does the first beam of the morning come in?

Make a Lamp

Children can make beautiful, Mexican-style tin lanterns. Start with large juice cans. When they have been emptied, rinse and fill with water. Freeze two days until solid. Placing the cans on a towel to prevent rolling, draw a pattern with a crayon and puncture holes in the tin with a hammer and nails of various sizes. Work fast, before the ice melts. Remove the ends of the can with a can opener, remove the ice, and wire the can in place over a lightbulb. If you have a table lamp with a shade holder, attach the tin can directly to the holder, or make a hanging lamp using the can as a shade.

Play/Living Structures

1

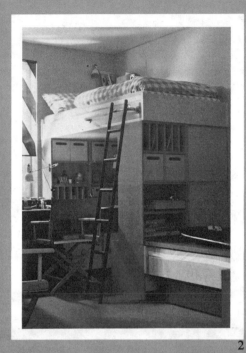

2

3

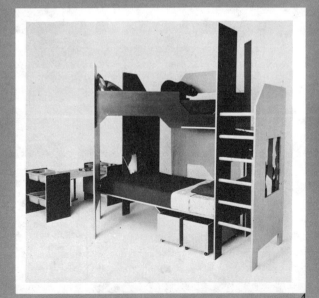

4

Some ingenious play/living structures for kids: **1.** A stack of boxes, one containing a variety of door latching hardware. **2.** A structure which contains areas for sleep, study, and storage. **3.** An outdoor gym. **4.** A bunkbed which has grown to incorporate a puppet theater and exercise ladder.

Made by Kids

try to frown with your eyes
and smile with your mouth.

JENNIFER, JAKE AND TALLY'S FROSTING COOKIES

You need 2 teaspoons of food coloring. Put in 4 teaspoons of
sugar, 6 pounds of grape juice and 10 boxes of butter. Add
3 spoons of powder and 3 spoons of rice. Then you need more
of sugar. Add one pound of soda. Put in 1 cup of onions and
11 cups of alphabits. Just get a spoon and mix it up. You
can put it in a mixer. Then you can bake it. Leave it
65 minutes at 102 degrees. Then it will be cookies.

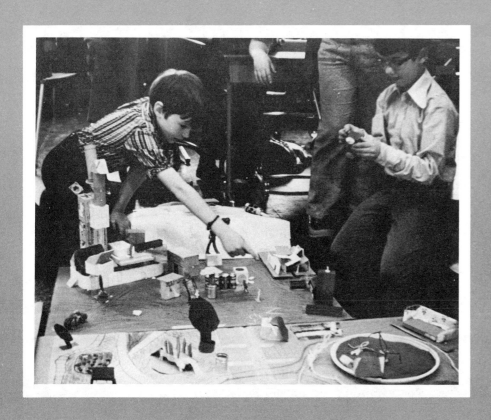

I will tell you what i think about Floying take two pieces of steel and drill 60 hooles in each pieace of steel then tak 12 pieces of string and tie them on you and the steel then go to A High plas and Jump off then Stever with your orms then you are flying.

Indoor Exercise

Small apartments, dangerous playgrounds, and lack of outside areas that can be supervised from inside the house all make indoor exercise an important need for contemporary families. When kids don't get a chance to let off steam physically, pressures build up between people instead. The projects in this section will help you equip an indoor space for more active children's play. There are suggestions here for a variety of ages and needs. Each of the projects describes a different approach to exercise; one of them should help you in solving your particular problem.

There are a number of good books on making children's furniture. (See sources section.) Think a design through carefully if you want it to be really useful for exercise. Some pieces of play equipment are quickly laid aside because they can be used in only one way (teeter-totters, barbells); others are too active for indoor use (swings, tetherball); others are too difficult to be much fun (knotted climbing rope, rope ladder) for younger children.

Play Mats

Start with the floor. Kids can think up a thousand physical activities if there is a safe place for them. Floor mats are an easy way to begin turning a bedroom into a part-time gym. You'll find that a good floor mat helps induce adults to exercise as well. It's a lot easier to wrestle with your kids (or your spouse) if there is a good place for it. (For some good family exercise, try a "muscle circle": Everybody, age 1 and up, gets in a big circle and each person in turn suggests an exercise that everyone has to do.)

MAT NUMBER ONE.
Cheap ($10-$20).
Find a thrift shop with used mattresses and buy a foam or innerspring one in good shape.

MAT NUMBER TWO.
Cheap and beautiful ($20-$30).
Foam rubber comes in a variety of grades, from a thin "regular" foam which crumbles in six or seven years, to a dense "luxury foam" which lasts for 12 to 15 years. Find a foam rubber outlet which sells "skins"; thin, one-inch sheets of foam left over when a large block is cut up into mattresses. Skins are $8 to $10 for a 4 by 6-foot piece and come with a "crust" on one side which can greatly increase the foam's ability to absorb blows. Find two skins, about 4 by 6 feet, cut from dense "luxury" foam, with good thick crusts. Place the two mats on top of each other, crust to crust and test them by sriking down hard with your fist or elbow. If you can feel your fist striking the table beneath the foam, it's not thick enough. If you can't find skins that are dense enough, a piece of regular foam, 5 inches thick (about $30), is your next best bet. From a vinylized fabric, solid or pattern, make a simple pillowcase cover for the mat.

MATS NUMBER THREE AND FOUR.
Any department store will sell you a 48- by 75-inch mattress of 5-inch foam for about $55. Child Life Play Specialties Inc. (55 Whitney St., Holliston Mass. 01746) will ship a 2-inch mat of firm density bonded polyfoam, covered with vinyl-coated nylon fabric, for about the same price.

Rocker House

Here's a design for a versatile piece of children's furniture that will help kids aged 1 to 4 get exercise. With its curved side down, it's a rocker that a child can use alone or with a friend. Upright, it forms a series of simple steps, endlessly challenging to kids learning about standing, crawling, jumping, and negotiating real-life stairs. Cross slats are arranged so that the piece also serves as a table with two benches for kids aged 2 to 4 (the period when adult-sized furniture is most out-of-scale). Finally, there is room under the stairs (through the rainbow door) for a semi-enclosed play space for fantasy games.

To construct the rocker house you will need a 4 x 6-foot piece of 3/4-inch plywood; 18 feet of 10-inch nominal (9-inch actual) pine shelving; two dozen 2-inch wood screws; and lead-free paint. Cut the end pieces out of plywood with a saber saw. Be very careful to cut the outer curve exactly as shown. This curve sets safe limits to forward and backward movement when the device is used as a rocker. Countersink the screws so there is nothing to get caught on, sand splintery edges, and paint.

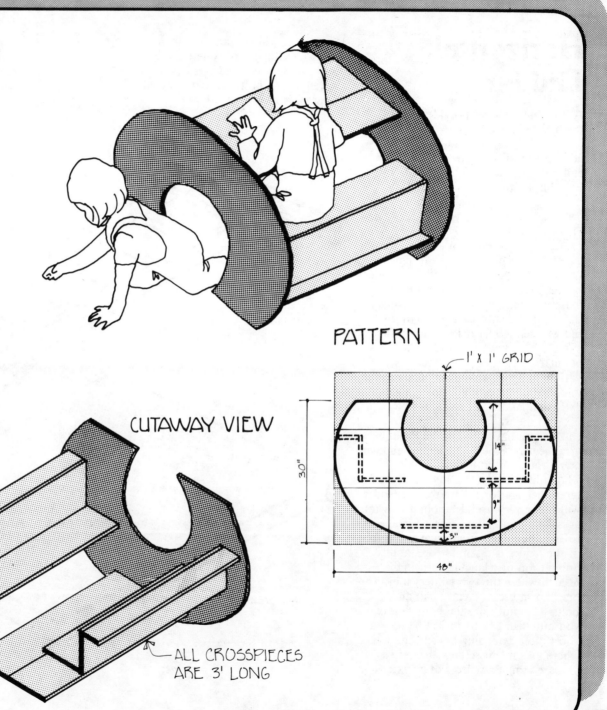

PATTERN

1' X 1' GRID

30"

14"

9"

3"

48"

CUTAWAY VIEW

ALL CROSSPIECES ARE 3' LONG

Horizontal Ladder

A horizontal ladder provides one of the best indoor exercisers for kids aged 3 to 9. Climbing around on it is an adventure trail in itself. For years, children will invent exercise feats just a little harder than the one they just mastered (one-arm hangs, monkey swinging, hanging by your knees. . .). Day care centers like the devices because the chest and arm exercise they give helps keep kids from hitting each other. Placing a mat beneath the ladder makes things safer and opens up a variety of jumping exercises. You can build the one shown here out of an old wooden ladder if it is still quite sturdy. A new wooden ladder will cost about $45 for two 8-foot sections. A variety of arrangements is possible; the one shown can be made from a small extension ladder but requires bolting a 2 x 4 to the wall for a brace on one end. If you have enough ladder, the arrangement shown on the free end can be repeated on both ends, making the whole thing movable. Having two different heights for the horizontal ladder will prove very useful, about 4 feet for ages 3 to 4 and about 6 feet for ages 5 to 10. The 5-foot crossbrace at the foot of the ladder is essential for stability. Some form of triangular bracing is needed where the two ladders join. The one shown uses a metal strap and bolts. Carefully size the bolts before you buy them, so there will be only a short piece extending beyond the wood where kids might scratch themselves. If you are using two pieces of an extension ladder, one will be narrower than the other. Use the narrow one for the horizontal ladder, and add washers to tighten up the bolt where the two different sizes meet.

Cleanup

I have never seen a magazine photograph of a children's room that wasn't as neat as a pin, and I have never seen a children's room that was. For most families, children's cleanup is a constant issue.

Compromise

Children and adults have equal rights to environments which support their lives. Adults should not have to live in a place which offends their sense of order, nor should kids have to suffer constant aggressions into their own world and its standards. A continuously updated agreement between kids and adults is the best answer—different standards for different rooms, flexible chore schedules, etc.

Cleanup as Game

Very young kids are as delighted by ordering as they are by disordering. Their joy at hurling plastic blocks all over the room is only matched by the joy of dropping them all back into a container. Adults, as well, have their secret pleasures in cleanup. Sometimes a little tidying is the only satisfying completion that we can find in a hectic day. Day care centers have devised a variety of ways to emphasize the game quality of cleanup, like special storage places (a long bench for stuffed animals, a sock bag, or a block bin that rolls around the room) and division of cleanup chores to emphasize learning (you clean up red things, I'll clean up blue; you clean up cloth, I'll clean up wood). Games around order should be played at times other than cleanup. Ask kids' advice in arranging things in your own room. Take some objects that need storing on a trip to the discount store to find a good container.

Everybody Plays

Many of the negative feelings people have about cleanup come from the seeming impossibility of the task. An adult peeks in and says, "Clean up your room, *now,* it's a mess," and leaves. What is the child to do? There seems to be lots of anger afoot and no obvious way to get around it. The place doesn't *feel* like a mess. What is wanted? Should these dolls be on the bed, on a shelf, or on the table? Putting a *few* things away is only asking to be angrily told that the job is incomplete. Putting *everything* away is beyond hope. Adults must be willing to work at cleanup with kids—to provide instant appreciation, to insure that tasks are doable, and to prove that there *is* a public interest in getting them done.

Visible Storage

Most children's possessions should be stored in a way that makes them visible —in cutaway trays, on shelves, in open chests. Adults keep their favorite possessions (cars, TVs, food processors . . .) where everyone can see them. Kids should be able to as well. Visible storage has the added benefit of easing cleanup by making it obvious where things are supposed to go. If you want kids to help with cleanup, design storage with them in mind. It must be at a level they can reach, (three quarters of the space in all dressers is inaccessible to small children). It must be easy to open (drawers of all kinds should be avoided). It must be easy to use (portable bins help greatly in picking up small objects). The projects here will help you reorganize children's storage. The wooden boxes are useful for all kinds of storage needs. The "wall of storage" is particularly helpful in cramped quarters.

Wall of Shelves

This storage system is built out of Tri-Wall triple-ply cardboard. It is the cheapest, fastest way to get a wall of cubbyhole shelving. This 6 by 6-foot section will cost about $17 and can be installed in an afternoon of work. The cheapest equivalent in metal shelving, although only about $30, would not provide the compartmentalization which makes pigeonhole storage look and work better. Concrete-block and board shelving is worth considering if you would like low shelving with a solid counter on top. A simiarly sized wall of shelves would cost about $30 in industrial grade block and board, and about $70 in unfinished wood bookshelves.

Three pieces of 4 by 6-foot Tri-Wall triple-ply cardboard are required for the unit described here. Lay out and cut one of the slotted pieces carefully and then use it as a pattern for the rest. The slots should be 1/2 inch wide and 6 inches deep. Be sure to leave two inches on the outer edge of each slotted piece as indicated on the drawing. The unit can be painted with latex or enamel, but paint both sides to avoid warping. Use a saber saw with a knife-edge blade for the cutting. To install

the shelves, carefully push the slotted pieces together on the floor (no glue needed). Place the finished unit against the wall and slip shims under the front to lean the shelves back against the wall. The unit will be more stable with

some protection against sideways movement. Placing it in a corner will help, as will simply tying the top of the unit back to the wall. Four or five "backs," cut to fit individual squares and pushed into random cubbies will greatly increase lateral stability.

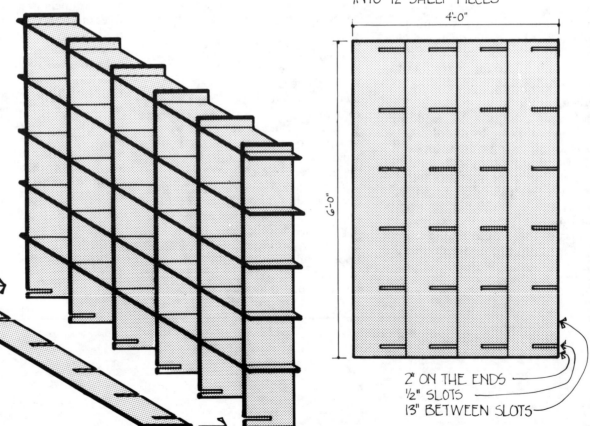

LAYOUT

CUT 3 PIECES OF 4'X 6' TRIWALL INTO 12 SHELF PIECES

4'-0"

6'-0"

2" ON THE ENDS
1/2" SLOTS
13" BETWEEN SLOTS

Storage Boxes

You can never have enough stackable storage boxes. We once bought about 40 of them and they all found a place in our apartment the day the shipment arrived. Boxes are especially good for kids because they can change as activity needs change into toy storage, desks, climbing structures, room dividers, etc. Although they look simple, boxes can be difficult to make, especially if you want to have lots of them . . . and with modular boxes, quantity is everything.

Soda or milk bottle crates make good storage boxes. The new plastic ones come in bright colors and fit well into a children's room. The older version of this crate was wooden with metal strapping.

There are many advantages to modular wooden boxes like the ones described here. The consistent size (two little ones equal one big one) allows rearrangement of boxes to fit your needs. With a few boards you can create an intricate wall arrangement that is elegant as well as functional. Modular boxes can be quickly arranged into a work area, a bedside arrangement, or a reading nook. Because objects being stored are visible, regularity in box size and construction will help unify what might otherwise seem a chaotic storage system. Modular boxes are handy on moving day. A dozen boxes similar to these, packed in the back of a van, were all we needed for a recent six month stay in the Midwest. When we unpacked, this luggage became our furniture.

Two people should be able to build 15 of these boxes in a day at a cost of $60. Buying an equivalent number of boxes in a furniture store (they are hard to find) would cost anywhere from $250 in pine to $700 in walnut.

These boxes are constructed of 1/2-inch plywood finished on one side only. Since plywood will not connect to plywood in a solid way, making the ends of 1 x 12-inch pine boards and detailing them as shown solves this problem. Have your local lumber store cut the plywood into three planks with dimensions as shown in the diagram. Lumberyards always charge a lot to do cutting for you, but these three long cuts will not be expensive and will take care of the toughest part of your sawing (having the lumberyard do the cross-wise, as well as the lengthwise cuts, will add to the cost per box because they typically charge for the number of cuts, not their length). Have the person who

cuts your plywood make four planks, each 11 7/8 inches wide. The odd dimensions are necessary to make maximum use of the wood, establish a useful size box, and account for the width of the saw cuts. Once you have all the pieces cut to the proper size, join the boxes together with nails and glue along all seams. When the glue has set, sand all exposed edges with sheets of fine sandpaper wrapped around wooden blocks. The boxes will be quite handsome with or without finish. If you like, add a coat of linseed oil or varnish to accentuate the natural grain.

BOX CONSTRUCTION

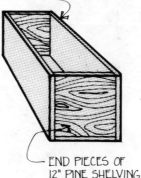

SIDES & BOTTOM OF ½" PLYWOOD

END PIECES OF 12" PINE SHELVING

LAYOUT

LAYOUT ON 4'x8' SHEET OF ½" PLYWOOD TO MAKE 1 SMALL & 3 LARGE BOXES

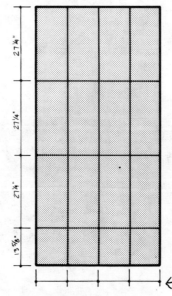

27¼"

27¼"

27¼"

13⅝"

ALL THESE DIMENSIONS ARE THE ACTUAL WIDTH OF YOUR 12" PINE SHELVING PLUS ½ INCH

Child City

The project described here came to life when Stanley, a friend of mine, asked for help in turning his small apartment into a place where he and his daughter could live in harmony. It is more substantial than most of the projects suggested in this book. I spent a couple of days designing it, and a carpenter worked on it for a week. Having something similar built for yourself would cost between $300 and $500. You may or may not be interested in this large a project. It illustrates lots of ideas about children's space, however, so you might adapt parts of it for your own purposes.

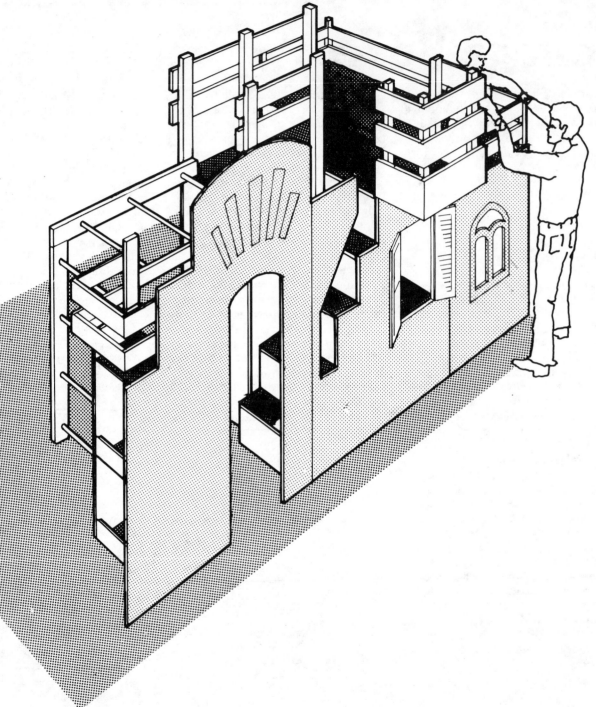

The problem

Stanley lives in a small apartment. Between writing, doctoring, and music, his life is very full. His apartment reflects this fullness with walls of books, racks of keyboard instruments, and a floor covered with records. At five, his daughter Alex has an equally full life. If she isn't putting on a spontaneous operetta, she is drawing up a storm. Most of Alex's days are spent across town with her mother, but weekends she spends with Stanley. Environmentally, things were at a standoff. Maybe because he had more days to get wound up, Stanley's activities and possessions dominated the space. But Alex had the natural child's advantage of respreading her possessions throughout the apartment every couple of hours. Stanley didn't like dominating the space, but he wasn't feeling great about having Alex's possessions everywhere either. All Alex wanted, she said, was somewhere to put up a sign that would read NO ADULTS ALLOWED.

Solutions

Peek-a-boo Space

Children have extreme opinions about how close they want to be to adults. One moment they will tell everyone to get away, and slam the door; the next, they will insist on sleeping in the middle of your bridge party, and nowhere else. The surface issues—whether the bedroom light is left on or the door ajar —only lightly cover the deeper ones of trust, belonging, and loneliness.

Alex was clear about her need to be apart from adults who would be occupying the other half of the room. It seemed important, however, not to make the separation too final. All spaces within the structure were thus given several degrees of isolation from the rest of the room. Closing the shutters on the "office window," for example, lets sound through but completely isolates activities within from adult view. With the shutters open, a person working at the desk can communicate freely with others in the room, but is still enclosed within the walls of the play structure. The bunk bed is placed perpendicular to the adult zone beyond. If Alex wants, she can sleep with her head toward the adult zone and keep one eye on what is happening in the rest of the apartment. She can have real privacy as well, however; the bunk bed is high enough so that its occupant feels protected from prying eyes. It is entered only by a circuitous route through the heart of the play structure. If Alex were to sleep with her feet toward the adult zone, her one open eye would survey only toys, books, and furniture. This peek-a-boo quality is important in children's spaces generally. Rooms close to adult activities are generally better for kids than ones isolated in a distant part of the house. A blanket house has more intrigue in a corner of the living room than in the attic.

Sturdy Portable Components

Stanley and Alex were not sure how long they would remain in their apartment. It thus seemed best to design the play structure so that it could easily be moved if the need arose. As the diagram indicates, the structure breaks down into six pieces. One of these was built around an existing bunk bed with the slats of the lower bed removed to create a lower play area. Each of these pieces has enough structure to keep it sturdy on moving day, but not enough to keep it from fitting through a door. Joints in each of the six pieces were secured with screws (nails would loosen with the constant jumping and rocking which the structure had to sustain). The six pieces, however, were joined to each other with bolts, to make it clear how to disassemble the structure on moving day. The structure survived its first test even before it was set up for use. The carpenter built it in his own basement and had to carry the pieces across town for assembly.

Exercise

Stanley's three-room apartment contained little space for active play. The structure helped solve this problem with an exercise ladder that spans the walkway behind the main entrance. When the mattress from the lower bunk is placed at the foot of this ladder, the entire zone behind the ladder becomes an exercise area.

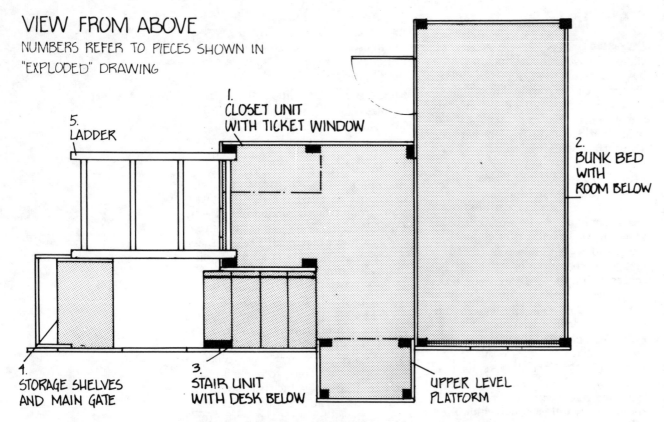

VIEW FROM ABOVE
NUMBERS REFER TO PIECES SHOWN IN "EXPLODED" DRAWING

5. LADDER

1. CLOSET UNIT WITH TICKET WINDOW

2. BUNK BED WITH ROOM BELOW

1. STORAGE SHELVES AND MAIN GATE

3. STAIR UNIT WITH DESK BELOW

UPPER LEVEL PLATFORM

One of your own

The diagrams on these pages would be enough to direct someone with some carpentry experience to build this particular structure. Surfaces are 3/4-inch plywood, except around the bed where they are 1/2-inch; uprights are 2 x 4's; stairs, shelves and railings are 1″ pine shelving. This was designed for a particular child and a particular room. If you want to design one of your own, study the ideas here and in other books devoted to children's furniture, make a list of the functions and primal spaces you wish to accommodate. Sketch up a plan. If you want to get an architect or interior designer involved, now is the time.

If you want to keep going on your own, build a small 1-inch to one-foot model using foam core and balsa wood (available at art supply stores). Alex's structure had a Mediterranean theme, but yours can be any style you wish—perhaps a medieval castle or Swiss chalet.

If you want to do the carpentry, dive in. If not, find a freelance carpenter who will do the work for you. Get a couple of estimates. An experienced carpenter could finish a project this size in four to six days.

Primal spaces

One reason Stanley's apartment seemed small was that it contained only one "kind" of place—a multipurpose adult room. Adding a variety of primal spaces, symbolizing different kinds of emotional experience, helped make the apartment more complex and rewarding. Although it is instructive to think of such spaces from a child's point of view, the conclusions reached have meaning for adults as well as children. The special pleasures of being "on stage" or "hidden away" or "at work in the studio" are not for children alone. You can get these pleasures into your own space too. The best architects can achieve these qualities in newly designed houses, or renovations, but they haven't got much experience in doing so because people don't insist on getting homes that "feel" right. If you like the idea of getting primal spaces into your house, come up with a lot of your own ideas before getting any professionals involved. *The Place of Houses* (Holt, Rinehart and Winston) is a book by several architects sensitive to this problem which might help you with your thinking.

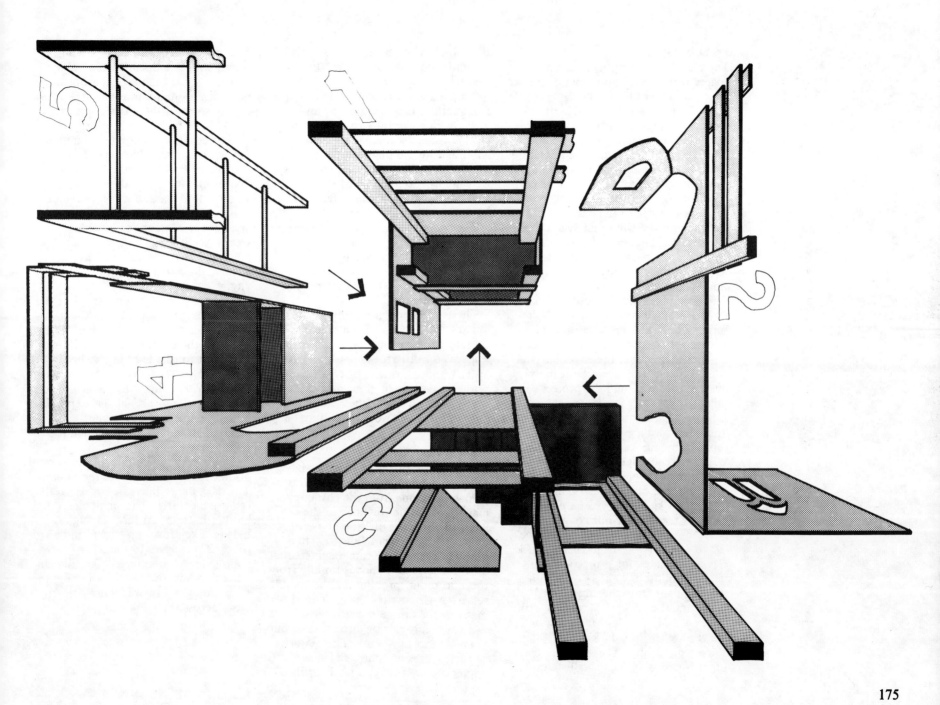

175

From Nature

The world of nature suggests many spaces with special emotional qualities, the nest is one of these. Swinging lightly in the breeze, a fragile jumble of twigs and grass clinging mysteriously to a branch. And to be *in* a nest . . . peering over the edge, examining the miniature world below. Does anyone see us? How could they, high up here in the leaves? A soft swirl of feathers and grass makes a bed within the nest and protects against the wind that sways the treetops. Curling up and closing our eyes we can almost forget that we are waving in the sky, closer to sun and clouds than earth.

Several places have a nestlike feeling in Alex's play structure. A small platform rides at the top, accessible only by steep stairs or a ladder. A corner of this nest hangs over the edge, into the adults' realm (which can be secretly observed from behind the protective railing).

Caves suggest quite different emotions. Now we are underground, surrounded by masses of stone and earth. Will the great weight collapse the walls? We think not, but can't begin to safeguard our delicate bodies against such a threat. A small fire creates enough light for recognizing our comrades, but later on it will go out, and we will be left to feel our way from rock to rock. Caves are places for protection and retreat. Philosophy enters only with a shaft of light from the entrance.

Around the back of Alex's play structure, entered by a door (and a secret crawlspace) is the "dark chapel," an aboveground cave. The walls are black. Light is cast only by a small stained-glass window at one end. It is a place for initiations and whispered skulduggery.

Ledges are yet another primal space from nature. Here we are tiny and helpless, clinging carefully to a small outcropping against the danger below. Although we are thankful for the momentary safety the ledge provides, we cannot relax. A gust of wind, a sudden rainfall, and our safety evaporates.

The stairs in Alex's play structure are pitched steeply. They are safe for climbing, but dangerous for sitting. From the top, they form a series of precarious ledges which one does not descend casually.

There are many more primal spaces in nature, of course. Sunny meadows conjure up memories for some, turbulent seas for others. Some people dream of dark forests, others of arid deserts. With a little imagination, memories of such places can make their way into the environments we inhabit on a daily basis.

From Home

It is not by accident that houses have come to symbolize whole literatures of human emotion, from the cliffside manors of gothic romance to the haunted corridors of "the house of blood." Whose heart fails to skip a beat when the movie camera enters that dreaded house and moves timidly from room to room, probing for the terrible secret? As filmwriters have divined, many of the primal spaces that move us most deeply emerge directly from our remembrances of home. The majority of such spaces are ones we use and appreciate every day: a kitchen filled with good smells, a friendly living room, windows opening to a balmy breeze. . . . If Stanley's apartment had been a one-room efficiency, establishing some of these basic spaces would have been a high priority.

Houses contain many less familiar spaces, however, which are equally capable of evoking primal emotions. Spaces like the attic, all unfinished wood, cobwebs, and garret hideaways. It is in the attic that we carefully arrange the museum of our past treasures. But who will ever visit this museum? Perhaps only an adventuresome child who sneaks up on a rainy day.

And, of course, the cellar. Here the air is thick, the floor damp, the heavy walls braced against the task of holding back the earth beyond. In its endless quest to cast light everywhere, civilization has carried electricity even to the cellar. "But," as Bachelard, our faithful guide to primal space, points out, "the unconscious cannot be civilized. It takes a candle when it goes to the cellar. . . ."

Alex's play structure contains several primal spaces drawn from the house. The dark area under the bed suggests cellar adventures. The small closet around back is just large enough to hide in, like grown-up closets and wardrobes. The shelves to the left of the main gateway are placed high, like an attic, and best reached by climbing the steep stairs and then inching precariously across the front wall.

From City

Another set of primal spaces derives from the ways that people interact in public. Children love such places and constantly invent new ways of playing at adult roles in them. The ticket window is one such place. A bit specific, yet how much of our contact with others rests on this paradigm—a person with something to offer *behind* the counter, another, with needs to satisfy, *in front*. In such places the primal exchange can be negotiated in the timeless ritual of questioning: Is what we need available? Must we choose between two of this and three of that, or perhaps face a harder reality that nothing is affordable? Is our credit trusted? Should it be? Are we participating in an honest exchange, or is someone trying to parlay our innocence into profit?

Alex's mini-city contains a small ticket window, along the side street through the main gateway. A lower slot allows for transfer of money and goods. An upper window, protected from sun and rain by a little awning, allows participants to maintain that eye contact essential for in-depth bargaining.

City streets form another primordial public space. Along them are ranged the places we have invented to serve our needs through commerce. We are free to walk along such streets, free to look at the signs and displays which beckon us, free to wander inside and enter a universe dedicated to pies and cakes or beautification or electric stoves.

There are two "streets" in Alex's play city. A stately one, along which are found a stained-glass window, a shuttered opening to the office space within, and the main gateway. This "main street," painted in quiet earth colors, was designed as an appropriate termination of the adult zone beyond. The second street, painted in bright reds and greens, is much livelier. Opening off the main gateway, it includes the stairway to the upper level, an exercise ladder, a storage wall, and the ticket window.

There is no provision within the structure for a stage, another primal public space for children. If you want to make one of your own, find an appropriate nook you can close off with a pole and curtains hung on big rings. Make sure there is room to place four or five chairs in front, and a place to store the family's supply of costumes behind.

The gateway in Alex's structure provides a clear entrance to the world that is hers. The door is cut to child, not adult, size. To read Alex a goodnight story, one must duck through the main gateway, climb the stairs, cross the upper platform, and climb into the upper bunk. With her front gateway, Alex finally has a place to hang her NO ADULTS ALLOWED sign.

There are many other primal spaces with meaning for children and adults. Alex's play structure includes a bridge and an office, for example. Perhaps you would be more intrigued by a gallery, a bus, or a captain's quarters. Whichever spaces are dear to you and your child can be built into a play environment. The one illustrated here is constructed of hardware and wood, but there is nothing to keep you from guerilla actions like turning your front hall into an art gallery, making a bus out of a refrigerator carton, or constructing a captain's quarters in the tree out back.

7 Lighting

You are guaranteed satisfaction for the time you spend improving your lighting. Two thirds of present home lighting is OK, but without spirit. Much of the rest is negative. Everywhere people flinch at their kitchen fluorescents, strain their eyes while reading, and squint to see their friends during evening conversation.

Fortunately, lighting is very easy to change. You really can turn the lighting in your home around in a weekend. For many reasons, it's a great area for home design and puttering. First, almost any skill you already have can be turned to account in lighting. You can macrame or sew a lampshade. You can make lamps out of things you have collected. You can build lights from plumbing pipe or car parts. And you can save money.

Lighting is also an area where you can pick up some useful skills. Basic wiring is very simple (although those who admire your work won't believe it). Knowing it opens the way to a hundred new projects, from making light sculptures to installing burglar alarms. Finally, lighting is the great facilitator. While it should be beautiful in itself, lighting is most fulfilled when it helps you appreciate other things—a meal with friends, a favorite object-turned-lamp, an evening with an airplane model.

The following pages offer some guidance in improving and appreciating your lighting. First, several light fantasies illuminate some feelings about light. A relatively technical section on task lighting is followed by a chart which matches your purposes with a variety of suggestive lighting designs. The chapter concludes with a variety of how-to projects—home wiring, lamp making, and light sculpture.

Light as Drug

Most frequently, we think of lighting only as it affects our eyes. In important ways, however, our bodies feast on light as avidly as our eyes. Researchers have recently begun to understand a number of light-as-drug phenomena, most involving the barely visible light at either end of the visible light spectrum. Their work highlights the pathologies of the modern light diet, with its near total reliance on processed light, punctuated by occasional roastings in the sun.

Overdose

The most familiar use of light-as-drug is on the beach, where we notice very much how light changes the outermost cells of our bodies. Three effects are involved: tanning, burning, and skin cancer. Tanning results from the activation of the enzyme tyrosinese by sunlight. This enzyme in turn stimulates melanin production within the pigment cells of the skin. The wavelengths of light which produce tanning are unfortunately the same as those which produce burning. So far, no one has been able to develop a light source that promotes one without the other. (window glass, for example, eliminates both effects). The damaging rays fall in the mid-ultraviolet range. Slightly shorter wavelengths would be even more damaging, but are prevented from entering the earth's atmosphere by a layer of ozone, hence concern for depletion of atmospheric ozone by the mighty spray can and the humble jumbo-jet. Large amounts of sunlight, over many years, increase the incidence of skin cancer. Some people—the Celts of Ireland, for example—are particularly susceptible to this effect, although no one seems to know why.

Cold Turkey

For many, however, the problem is not too much ultraviolet light, but too little. Exposure to UV is critical to the synthesis of Vitamin D. At one point in the process by which this vitamin is synthesized, a precursor substance is carried by the blood to a point near the body's surface where it can "see" through the skin. If there is no light in sight, or only light without UV rays, the process ends. If it sees sunlight through the skin, the substance is activated and carried to the liver and kidneys where synthesis is completed. It is Vitamin D which facilitates the absorption and use of calcium by the body. Children who grow up without adequate sunlight develop rickets, a common ailment among kids in early 20th-century tenements. About 25,000 babies a year receive a critical light-as-drug treatment. When red blood cells die, after 120 days of life, they produce a substance called bilirubin, normally destroyed within the liver. In adults with liver dysfunctions, and among premature babies whose organs are not yet fully developed, bilirubin can accumulate to toxic levels. If there is an Rh incompatibility between the parents of a premature child, the problem can be acute. The old treatment for the disease was to change the baby's blood, an understandably difficult business. The new, and even more effective, treatment is to put the child near a window for three or four days. Although there is some argument about whether blue or white light does the trick, there is no doubt that a few natural rays solve the problem.

Light and Sex

Light affects sexual development. Girls blind from birth have an accelerated sexual development. The effect is proportional to the years of blindness and seems to involve the pineal gland. In lower vertebrates, like the frog, the pineal gland itself is photosensitive, constituting a true eye in the back of the head. Humans accomplish the same effect by more devious (and evolved?) means—our eyes register the amount of light around us and tell the brain about it; the brain then sends an internal memo to the pineal gland which adjusts hormonal output, and thus sexual development, accordingly. Similarly, a message goes out to the parotid gland, which decelerates saliva production to a minimum when it hears that it's nighttime "out there."

Seeing and Health

Our response to light is more than visual. If lighting is improper, or if we misuse our eyes, our body lets us know. Getting in touch with our own particular physical response to light is an important step in understanding the role of lighting in the environments we create. Eyes are a focal point for the cumulation of tension and stress. Poor lighting contributes greatly to the problem, although it is only one factor among many.

Many people spend hour after hour each day in concentrated attention to visual detail. Eye stress is inevitable: squinting, redness, tearing, burning. Throw in some air pollution and you have a major modern discomfort.

Light Fantasies

The fantasy excursions on this page can touch some of your deeper feelings about light and its evocative power. They are easy to complete. Just read the descriptions, shut your eyes, relax, and let your mind complete the fantasy for as long as it takes. Exchange descriptions if you are with a friend.

Historical Illumination

Choose an intriguing era from the past. Imagine what kind of a person you might have been in that era. . . . See the country and town you might have lived in, and your home. There is going to be an important event in your home this evening. Imagine what kind of an event it is—who is coming, what people will be doing. Imagine how you would light each part of the house in preparation for the event.

Light on Your Past

Choose one of your homes from the past. Walk through it slowly during an evening, noting in detail how the light feels, and where it comes from in each room. Don't worry about the acuracy of your memories of the place, just let the thoughts flow. What are the darkest and lightest spots in the house?

Task Lighting

Places where you do tasks which require good light deserve careful attention. The information here can help you make such places pleasant and efficient.

For most people, the most critical task lighting is at work rather than at home. If you use your eyes a lot at work, use these pages to evaluate the quality of light there. If you feel changes should be made, take steps to bring lighting standards up to the quality you need.

There are many household activities which require good task lighting as well, however: cooking, reading, hobby work, ironing, shaving, doing jigsaw puzzles. . . . It is up to you to create adequate lighting for all of these activities.

Brightness

The first quality of good task lighting is adequate brightness—enough quantity of light. But how much light is enough? Studies show that we reach 85% of highest visibility at rather low levels of lighting—10 footcandles. This is the level I recommend for kitchen counters, casual reading, shaving, etc. This much light would be achieved by: two 75-watt bulbs directed toward nearby walls; one 75-watt bulb shining directly on the work surface from under the shade of a table or floor lamp three feet away; or a 75-watt bulb with a reflector shining directly on a work surface from five feet away.

For more intense visual tasks (studying, carpentry, sewing), a higher level (20 footcandles) is preferable. This could be achieved by: two 100-watt bulbs directed at nearby walls; two 75-watt bulbs shining directly on your work surface from under the shades of lamps three feet away; or a 75-watt bulb with a reflector shining directly on your work surface from three feet away, plus a 60-watt bulb directed toward a nearby wall.

The psychological dimension of brightness is as important as the visual. Light levels can go very low if you want to create a meditative atmosphere for conversation or dining. They can also be very high if you want an especially lively work place or are doing precise tasks, like model-making or drafting. A friend of mine is a photographer. His workspace is flooded with light (ten times the amount of light recommended above). Bottles of subtly colored chemicals glow along the wall; shiny beakers with delicately embossed markings line the shelves. All of this makes the space alive and responsive for his work. He has tried using less light but doesn't like the uphill struggle which occurs when *he* is more excited than his space.

Technically, brightness is a quality of surfaces *reflecting* light, not light sources themselves. It takes much more light to make a room with dark walls feel bright. In such rooms it is often best to keep to an essentially dark feeling—spotlighting a few places where light is needed for tasks or will create a pleasant focal point. If one of the places where you do visual tasks is in a room with dark walls, be especially careful to get enough light directly on your work surface. In such instances, reflected light doesn't contribute much.

Contrasts in brightness level should be valued in most lighting. The fluorescent wash of contemporary office buildings creates a sterile environment. Places which reflect the many interests of their users naturally generate a great variety of lighting effects. The 10 light sources in the two rooms near me now generate seven distinct light qualities. The place is fuller for them.

Contrast

Contrast is very useful in distinguishing three-dimensional objects. If light is completely uniform, there are no shadows to bring out an object's shape. The best arrangement for work lighting, then, is two lights, one a little brighter than the other, aiming down on your work surface from just over each shoulder. One light alone is usually too harsh, and if you get in the wrong position, your shadow cuts off the light altogether. Having one light a little brighter than the other will cast a gentle shadow on one side of an object and thus help define its shape. It is best if the brightest light is opposite your writing hand so it will not cast a shadow on your work.

Our eyes need some contrast to function, then, but *not too much*. It would be impossible to sort black checkers by designs embossed on their surface on a very bright table. To protect against overexposure our eyes adjust to the *brightest* spot in the field of vision. When the pupil closes down to keep out brightness, it can't let in enough light to let us see the detail in darker areas.

Because the eye has trouble adjusting to extremes in contrast, keep them to a minimum. It is wrong, for example, to have a work area brightly lit if the rest of a room is dark because it forces the eyes to juggle between two extremes of brightness. Doing paper work on a dark desktop is inadvisable for similar reasons.

Direct Glare

When there are extremes of contrast in the field of vision, it causes what is called "direct glare." The most common cause of direct glare is visible light bulbs. A bare 40-watt frosted bulb is 10 times as bright as a candle flame, half again as bright as snow in sunlight. Reckoning with this much light is physically painful and leaves you unable to see other things. The problem is particularly important in conversation areas, where you want to have a relaxed feeling, but still want to see facial expressions clearly.

There are several ways to correct direct glare. You can spread light out so it won't be intense at any one point: Use a larger bulb, or put the bulb behind a glass cover or shade that will diffuse the light.

A simple test for direct glare is to get a 15-watt, full-size, inner-frosted light bulb and compare it to the brightest spot in your environment. If there is something brighter than the 15-watt bulb (outdoor sky, a bright wall, another bulb . . .), it will be causing direct glare and you should take some action to reduce its brightness.

Reflected Glare

Reflected glare comes not from looking at a light source directly, but from looking at its reflections in a work surface. It's more difficult to spot reflected glare, but it is equally debilitating. Reflected glare is particularly bad when you are looking at something which has a glossy finish. Some shiny objects, like photographs, reflect so much light it is often hard to find a good position from which to view them. Many other objects reflect a lot of light as well: the pages of a book, shiny cloth, the keys of a typewriter, a kitchen countertop. The graphite used in pencils is very shiny. A page of pencil writing can easily be rendered illegible by glare.

There is a simple way to test for reflected glare. Take a piece of cardboard and wrap aluminum foil around it, shiny side out. Place it on your work surface. If you see strong reflections, it is quite likely that reflected glare will be causing problems with the tasks you perform there.

Sometimes reflected glare is called "veiling glare" because it seems to "veil" information in a kind of haze. Working in a condition with too much reflected glare leads to eyestrain, squinting, and headaches.

There are several ways to correct reflected glare. Most important, light sources should be placed where they won't reflect back into your eyes. This is why the over-the-shoulder position for work lighting was suggested earlier.

Light from sources in this position reflects out in front of you, not back into your eyes. Decreasing the intensity of a light source helps also. Aiming a light against a wall spreads its intensity out, as do most glass diffusers and lamp shades. In an office setting, reflected glare is often reduced by increasing the number of light sources (sometimes the whole ceiling is designed to be luminous). Finally, it helps if you make the surfaces where you are working less reflective. If your desk top is shiny, cover it with a matte surface that reflects less light.

 # Task Lighting Survey

The form included here will help you evaluate those specific places in your environment where you have to count on good task lighting. Most of the lighting in your home need not be evaluated this rigorously; in most places the *feeling* that lighting conveys will be more important than its efficiency. Where task lighting is important, however, this survey can help insure that it is up to the job.

Specific places in your environment where task lighting is important

List several places where good lighting is important to you across the top of the survey form—a reading chair, a desk or hobby area, your office, a kitchen counter. . .

Put a "yes" in the box for each test the place you have listed passes, and a "no" for each one that it fails.

Is there enough light?

First decide whether this is a place where you do casual tasks, like light reading, kitchen preparation, and shaving which require less light, or detailed tasks, like studying or sewing which require more light. Then look at the light levels recommended for these kinds of tasks and see if you have enough light.

Is the light high quality?

Put a "no" in this box if there are disruptive shadows on the task surface, if the light ever flickers, or if it is an unpleasant color.

Is contrast within an acceptable range?

Answer "no" here if your task and the surface you are working on are quite different in brightness, or if your task is illuminated by one light source only, or if the rest of the room you are working in is relatively dark.

Is all direct glare eliminated?

Answer "yes" here if you have removed from your field of vision all light sources that make you squint when you look at them—visible light bulbs, sun on clouds, etc.

Is reflected glare kept to a minimum?

Are light sources arranged in such a way that none of their light is reflected off your work surface and into your eyes?

Task Lighting Survey Form

Specific Places in Your Environment Where Task Lighting Is Important

Qualities of Good Task Lighting	Place 1	Place 2	Place 3	Place 4	Place 5
Is There Enough Light?	YES ☐ NO ☐	YES ☐ NO ☐	YES ☐ NO ☐	YES ☐ NO ☐	YES ☐ NO ☐
Is the Light Quality High?	YES ☐ NO ☐	YES ☐ NO ☐	YES ☐ NO ☐	YES ☐ NO ☐	YES ☐ NO ☐
Is Contrast Within an Acceptable Range?	YES ☐ NO ☐	YES ☐ NO ☐	YES ☐ NO ☐	YES ☐ NO ☐	YES ☐ NO ☐
Is All Direct Glare Eliminated?	YES ☐ NO ☐	YES ☐ NO ☐	YES ☐ NO ☐	YES ☐ NO ☐	YES ☐ NO ☐
Is Reflected Glare Kept to a Minimum?	YES ☐ NO ☐	YES ☐ NO ☐	YES ☐ NO ☐	YES ☐ NO ☐	YES ☐ NO ☐

Goals/Solutions

On these pages are listed some purposes you might hope to achieve through lighting. If you find one that is relevant for you, read the concrete suggestions which accompany it to find one that makes sense for you.

If your goal is

To zone space

It is often useful to transform a room into a series of "zones," each appropriate for a particular activity or feeling. The problem is acute for those who live in cramped quarters and thus have to cook, entertain, exercise, etc. in the same room. Even if you have enough space, however, it is good to enhance the personalities of zones within your environment. Lighting is a greatly underutilized tool for zoning space. Most of us experience our homes most intensely during the evening hours and night, precisely when lighting can have the strongest impact on how we perceive the space around us.

Zoning space with lighting is relatively easy. The main principle is simply to give each zone a different light spirit. Kind of fixture, amount of light, and light color can all be varied to fit the needs of a particular zone. It is very useful to arrange lighting controls so all the lighting in a zone can be turned on and off with one switch. The most carefully planned lighting is of little value if you never get around to using it.

Character

The more you know about how you will use a zone, the easier it is to find the right lighting spirit. List the activities you will be doing in a particular zone and some of the qualities you want it to have (cozy, bright, efficient . . .) in preparation for determining how it should be lighted.

Contrast

Try to establish strongly contrasting light identities for different zones—especially important when one room contains overlapping zones or becomes different zones at different times of the day. Make one zone very dim and another very bright. Light one by casting lights on plants and another by washing the walls with light. Light one zone by spotlighting the tools you use there and another by low-key table lamps.

Light color

Changing the color of light can help establish different zones of activity. Blue-white fluorescent is often associated with kitchens and work space; warm-colored light—like that from a yellow bulb or a dimmed incandescent —can establish a mood of quiet and relaxation.

Focus

Establish a focus for each zone and give it all the light you've got. Some spots or objects are particularly good for capturing the spirit of a place: a spice rack or shelf of cookbooks, a warm rug or coffee table, a tackboard or bookshelf. Make one of these take the spotlight when a zone is in use.

Control

Get as much of a zone's light on one switch as you can. Wire a number of lights from a single ceiling fixture. Screw a double socket into a regular lamp to get an additional lamp to go on and off with the same switch.

To make a room seem larger

Lighting can be used to make a space seem larger than it is. The first principle is to get light to the *outside* of a space. Having a single bulb in the middle of a room leaves no secrets, no depth. Lighting the walls of a room opens a space. The second way to enlarge a room is to light it in a *variety* of ways. Having only one kind of light trivializes a space. A single table lamp makes a space feel neglected and small. Having only a bright ceiling light makes the rest of the room shrink from exposure.

Wall lighting

Buy or make two "wall washers"—lights designed to cast light on a wall without creating any glare. There are many of these for sale in lighting stores now. Many are adjustable, so you can aim the light up toward the ceiling, down on plants, or at a picture mounted on the wall. Some have several attachment plates so you can move them around as you please.

Enlargement sculpture

Design a light sculpture whose theme is making your room seem larger. Mount three 30″-square pieces of smoky plexiglass on top of each other, 1″ apart, and put Italian lights behind each layer. Find a dollhouse and display it with rooms lit from inside.

Ceiling lighting

Lighting the ceiling of a room can help open it up. Keeping the light source hidden will add depth to the effect. If you have a ceiling light with a flat or curved glass cover that screws into the center peg, spray the cover inside with reflective silver paint to light the ceiling from an invisible source. Be sure there is enough light on the ceiling to make a difference (at least two 100-watt bulbs in a typical room). A ceiling can be lighted by clamp-ons or uplights mounted on the wall, or from a strategically placed floor lamp with a large 200-watt bulb.

Variety

Get as much variety into room lighting as you can. An ordinary medium-sized room can easily accept two or three kinds of lights. To make a room seem larger, get five or six different kinds of light in it. Add a light on some plants, a spotlight on a wall-hanging, a floor lamp by a favorite chair, a picture with a frame light. . . .

To create a meditative atmosphere

Bad lighting can destroy the relaxed, meditative quality of a space. The right lighting, even without other design features, can go a long way toward creating this feeling. Using dim warm-toned light is the best way to give a place a meditative atmosphere.

 ### Tranquilized daylight

It is difficult to achieve a meditative feeling in a room flooded with sunlight. Unfortunately, drawing heavy curtains in the daytime makes a place feel barricaded against the sun—not the best for meditation. Desert cultures face the problem in extreme—a shaft of desert sun falling into a shady interior can render a room uninhabitable. They solve the problem with screens: woven palm fronds in Oman, elaborate constructions of small lathed pieces in

Egypt. Having rounded pieces in the screen eases the transition from light to dark by molding shadows on each piece. The more intricate and layered a screen is, the more meditative will be its effect. Easily available for screen construction in this country are straw mats, bamboo roll-up screens, hanging bead curtains, baskets and lattice-woven cloth.

Dimmers

The most meditative light of all is candlelight, but deeply dimmed light runs a close second. Install a few

rheostats in the controls for lights over the dining table, by the bedside, in a meditation room, or in a conversation area.

Meditative focus

For a room to have a meditative feel, it should have a meditative focus. A particularly meaningful picture or wall hanging can be spotlighted with a reflector flood on a dimmer. Altars and special display shelves can be illuminated with candles, Italian Christmas tree lights, or hidden display-case fluorescent fixtures.

To make a place more hospitable

It doesn't take much bad lighting to compromise whatever friendly feelings a place might have. Nor, however, is it difficult to make a place seem especially warm and gracious. The keys to hospitable lighting are gently glowing faces (be ruthless with glare where you and your friends gather), warm light tones, and human scale.

 ### Light tone

Warm colors in lighting (yellows, golds, reds) are more hospitable than cool (blues, whites). Fluorescent fixtures are cold; replace the ones you have to make a space seem friendlier. Put a yellow insect lightbulb in a fixture and shade or block view of the

bulb for a warm glow. Try a red or orange bulb, too, although these will give off much less light. Putting several lamps on a dimmer is best of all. As the light dims, it changes dramatically in color toward the candle-flame tones. With adjustable lights you can also create much gentler lighting about people's faces.

Scale

Ceiling fixtures, spiky shades, 8-foot chromium lamp arms, fixed fluorescent tubes, and pretentious chandeliers can dwarf the people and activities in a room. Much better are quiet table lamps, spotlights which set pictures on the wall glowing, stained glass (or plastic) lampshades, plant lights, glowing spheres of lights, and candles. The general rule is to use smaller or more intricate fixtures to make a place cozier.

The welcoming beacon

Light your place so that it feels more hospitable from the *outside*. (If you wonder what kinds of changes might be appropriate, do a quick fantasy of the weary night horseman approaching the inn where he will find food, friends, and a bed.) Are any light bulbs visible from outside your house? If so, get them covered. Can you arrange to have some gently illuminated natural textures like plants or wood visible from outside? If you live on the 34th floor of an apartment building, make the changes anyway; the higher you are, the further your hospitality travels.

Variety

Place pools of light around a room in ways that inhabit it at a human scale. Have one pool emphasize the pleasures of music, another the presence of good things to read, another the colors of an appreciated painting or the structure of a favorite piece of apparatus.

If your goal is

To make a place more lively

Lighting is the most important factor in making a place feel lively at night. To create a lively atmosphere, add *more* light (too little makes a space feel subdued), introduce *sparkle* light, and focus light on *lively places* within a room.

Sparkle

As a general rule, light sources should not be directly visible. Properly done, however, there is no more lively effect than the visible presence of sparkling lightbulb filaments. Strings of Italian lights—tiny, clear, Christmas tree lights—are a great source of sparkle. In the off-season, pick them up at a theatrical display house. Put a small weight on a double or triple string of lights and hang them ceiling-to-floor. Line the frame of a mirror with them, or scatter them among the branches of a potted plant. Many other clear filament bulbs will give a sparkle effect, although you'll probably find anything above 15 watts is too bright to look at. You can create reflected sparkle as well. Shine a bright spot on a sparkly surface such as a collage of tiny mirrors, kitchen utensils, a candy-apple painting, glassware, or a collection of rhinestones.

Brightness

Increasing the light level in a space will make it seem more lively, but only if it is done purposively. Begin by throwing lots of light on lively places: flood a bookcase, a record collection, or a photographic display with light. Then add more general lighting (indirect lighting of walls or ceiling). If you want some spot to be especially lively—a desk area, a workplace, a display of memorabilia—throw 250- or 300-watts of light on it, but do it without direct or indirect glare.

Sunshine

Make a place lively during the day by bringing in the sun. Strings of chandelier cut glass hung in a window will send spectrum rainbows darting around a room all day. A mirror (especially a convex one) placed in the right position will fill your ceiling with sunlight. Light is swallowed by dark objects. Get some light things (a yellow chair, white curtains, a silver lamé rug) into parts of your house where the sun falls.

Sculpture

A light sculpture will invariably liven up a space. Make one, or buy an ever-emanating light box or an illuminated tourist memento. Set up a couple of display places (one a wall, one a pedestal) where the lighting is always intense, but the subject changes depending on what you want to admire at the time.

189

Lamp Family Survey

A family of lights lives with every household of persons. This page will help you make the acquaintance of this family. It already exists, mind you, welcoming newcomers, casting light from member to member, mourning those who leave or short out. Although we have life-and-death control over who belongs to this family, few of us have ever taken stock of it.

Make a Tour

Make a tour of your house with this in hand. List each kind of light source you have.

Write

Write the names of lights that live in your place. Make the descriptions as specific as you can: "built-in bathroom wall lamps," "cut-glass living room chandelier," and "chrome desk lamp." Note quantities of each kind of lamp.

Draw

Draw small pictures of all your lamps. Simple outlines are fine, just enough to remember the light being named. Color any colorful parts.

When you have completed the survey, look over the family. Is it a happy group? A funeral? Are there any surprise members? Any superstars? Are there any members that could strike up a deeper acquaintance? It's not hard to move two lamps so they can be together for a while.

Future Members

Light families, like human families, can often stand a little improvement. Some are plain dull, filled with inherited and built-in stuff. What these families need is something unexpected: a new perspective, color, a decorative outline.

Many families are too homogenous, with everyone dressing and thinking alike. What these families need is a strong new presence.

Some families are too respectable. A little generation gap generally helps here. Add a lamp that will outrage the other lamps in a room.

Light Sculpture

Light is a wonderful medium for home-made sculpture. It is inexpensive, easy to put together, and the results can be as showy or subtle as you please. You don't have to know much about lighting to begin. Learn more as you go along.

Themes

Each light sculpture should have its own "spirit"—a guiding theme which suggests which objects to use, what kind of light the piece should emit, where it should be located, etc.

A particular store can provide a theme: Discount stores are great sources of light sculpture materials—cut glass salad bowls, shiny kitchen apparatus, aquariums, cakestands, mirrors.

Stores that specialize in materials for display windows are natural sources of light sculpture themes. They have rack after rack of showy items: sheets of reflective balls, elaborate plaques and doilies, Italian lights, fake rain. . . .

Flea markets have a spirit of their own which can be the basis of a light sculpture. Because things are cheap, it's easy to get multiple items. In one trip I found five second-hand spotlights to make into a light sculpture.

Lumberyards, hardware stores, theater and costume shops, restaurant supply stores, cake decorating shops, all can produce materials and themes for light sculptures.

You can base the theme of a light sculpture on an art style. Art Deco geometrics are easy to work with. Small, circular and straight fluorescent bulbs are good "deco" shapes to start with.

Activities can be used as themes for light sculptures. The section on making lamps, p.202. describes a musical lamp made from a clarinet. Appreciation of things automotive can be turned into a sculpture: a camshaft light tree or a thirties teardrop headlight on a table stand.

Light sculpture can cohere around a *purpose*. You can build a multilayered illuminated construction that will help make a space seem larger, or prepare an illuminated box for the display of family mementos, or construct back-lit shelves for your liquor bottles.

191

Elements

You will have to make decisions about the following elements of a light sculpture. The more you can relate your choices to the theme you are pursuing, the stronger your sculpture will be:

- light color
- light quality: sparkle, indirect, direct
- bulbs: incandescent, fluorescent, high intensity; tiny, medium, or large
- cord: white or black, thick or thin
- bulb sockets: porcelain, chrome, brass
- form (see below)
- materials

Forms

There are a number of basic light sculpture forms. Floor-to-ceiling columns are striking (try Japanese paper globes, weighted strings of Italian lights or translucent papier-mâché tubes). Light sculptures can hang on the wall like pictures, coil like snakes, sit on the table, stand on the floor, or hang by one arm from the ceiling.

Proud traditions

Light sculptures have historical traditions. Some evoke plug-in religious art or the endless variety of turn-on tourist pieces sold all over the world. Many follow in the footsteps of psychedelia, celebrating the heyday of rock and roll light shows. During Christmas holidays, nearly everyone trucks some piece of light sculpture out of the basement—rotating color disks, illuminated bubble candles, colored lights. The tradition has its "serious artists" as well, with neon and lasers being the most popular contemporary media.

With the correct equipment, laser beams of light can be shot for miles to envelop an entire city in a visible web of light.

Materials

There are many sources, and few rules, in finding light sculpture materials. Often getting to the right place will suggest the right materials.

A simple way to make a light sculpture is to go to an electrical parts counter and start plugging together an assemblage that will hold a dozen bulbs. Push plug-in sockets into three outlets of a three-way plug, push this into another, etc. Insert low wattage, clear filament display case bulbs in the sockets and you have a chandelier. Finish it off with disk-type nightlights and you have a tabletop sculpture.

Many light sculptures use chrome and steel. Elements that can contribute to this effect are: clear filament light bulbs, hollow plexi rods, shiny adhesive-backed paper, aluminum spray paint, Christmas tree tinsel, glass building block, chromed flexible gooseneck, and tile-size mirrors.

Light Sculpture

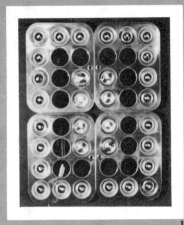

1

2

1. A wall-mounted light sculpture constructed of display store goods (Italian lights, formed Mylar spheres, and round mirrors) mounted in four muffin tins. 2. A ceiling globe. 3. Clusters of large bulbs rise like bubbles from a 2 by 4 frame with a side-mounted rheostat and cord peg. 4. Light salad. Recipe: In a large cut glass plastic punch bowl mix 2 strings of Italian lights and 3 cups clippings from imitation Christmas tree branches. Serve with clear plastic salad forks.

4

3

Home Wiring

Once you get the hang of it, many home wiring jobs are simple. Anyone can learn to wire a lamp, install a dimmer and more. Start with an extension cord or lamp first—they're easiest. It also helps if you can get someone who knows more about wiring to look over your shoulder—but don't let your advisor do the actual work. Don't do any wiring you are confused about. Stop and ask advice until someone who knows can answer your question.

First Rules of Wiring

It takes two wires to make electricity. That is why there are two prongs on a plug, and two wires on a cord, each of which must attach to a separate terminal.

The first rule of electricity is never to connect these two wires directly to each other. There must be something between them—a light bulb, a radio, an appliance—to "tame" the current. If you connect these two wires directly, they will make a big spark and short out the circuit. You will have to put a new fuse in at the circuit breaker box to get the current flowing again.

When you connect something between these two wires, it turns on. If *you* get connected between these two wires—by touching both terminals at the same time, or by cutting through a live wire—*you* get turned on. Thus the second rule of electrical wiring: Do not

work around live wires. If you are working on a lamp or other appliance, it *must* be unplugged. If you are working on a wall or ceiling outlet, wall switch, etc.,you must unplug the entire house by shutting off the power at the fuse box. You can turn the power off in a particular part of the house by testing which one of the fuses controls which part of the house. Sometimes, however, there are wires from several fuses in the outlet box, so it's safer to turn off electricity to the whole house when you are working on house wiring. There are several ways that house power is switched off. Sometimes the fuse box contains a "main switch" which can be turned to "off"; sometimes this is accomplished by simply opening the door of the fuse box; sometimes there are "plug blocks" that pull out with a little handle. Test to see if the electricity is off to the place where you are working by making sure that you can't turn anything on there. Remember to reset all the clocks in a house after you turn the electricity off, and not to leave the refrigerator without electricity for too long.

Wiring Dimmers

Dimmers adjust the amount of electricity flowing through a wire so you can get lights to shine at various intensities. Using dimmers will save electricity—if a light is dimmed by half it reduces its power use by about one quarter. Savings are much greater in bulb life. Every five per cent reduction in power *doubles* a bulb's life expectancy. There

is a tiny high-pitched whine associated with most household dimmers—light bulb filaments complain when operated at less-than-full power. Dimmers that eliminate this whine are a bit more expensive. Dimmers cannot be used on fluorescent bulbs, appliances or electric motors. For this reason it is best not to wire a wall outlet so that whatever is plugged into it is automatically dimmed. General Electric makes a rheostat that will dim up to 600 watts for $6.25. Switch dimmers can be purchased with capacities up to 1000 watts. To install one of these, make sure the power in the entire house is turned off. Remove the cover plate from the wall switch (see illustration), unscrew the switch assembly and remove it from the box. Unscrew the wires from either side of the switch assembly, and reconnect them on the terminals of the new dimmer switch. If the switch is two- or three-way (with a number of switches controlling one fixture), you must buy a special three-pole dimmer and carefully match the new wiring pattern to the old. Place the dimmer switch back in the box and screw it in place. Replace the cover plate and push the knob on the end of the projecting shaft.

Rewiring a Ceiling Outlet

If you have a lamp fixture already at the ceiling outlet, you can get power for other purposes easily by screwing a plug-in adapter into the light bulb socket and plugging other things directly into it.

If you want to wire a lamp directly into a ceiling outlet, or change a fluorescent fixture to an incandescent, you have to take off the ceiling cap plate and tackle the house wiring directly. You must first turn off the electricity to the entire house. Remove the cap plate and let the lamp fixture down slowly (if you let it hang by the wiring it may pull the connections off). Examine the wiring in the box carefully. Wires will probably be attached to each other by colored screw-on plastic caps.

The wiring of a ceiling outlet gets more complicated when there is more than one switch or outlet at different points along the run. The trick, then, is to look carefully at the wiring and make sure that when you replace the lamp fixtures, the connections are exactly the way you found them, with your two new wires taking the place of the two wires you removed. If the lamp you are wiring has a third, green wire (a mechanical ground), this should be attached by a screw to the outlet box itself.

To replace the wires, unscrew the plastic caps from the appropriate bundle of wires, remove the old wire, insert the new one, and screw the plastic cap back on. Before you are through, recheck the box to see that there are no wires showing. Thread your new cord through the ceiling plate and wire a lamp socket to the free end of the cord before turning the power back on.

Getting More Than One Fixture on a Single Switch

Light fixtures in the center of the ceiling are often a problem. If you put enough bulbs in them to make a difference, they make a place seem cold and empty. The light they give doesn't help much in task lighting because they often force you to cast a shadow on your work surface. Ceiling fixtures can easily be capped, however, and used to attach a hanging lamp that floats over a dining room or game table.

The best feature of ceiling lights is that they go on and off with a wall switch. If you put care into your lighting, you are bound to have three or four lights in a room, all of which could be turned on at once to set the space up. Some rooms have baseboard outlets that work off a wall switch. If you have one, plug all your room lights into it by long extension cords and consider yourself lucky. If you don't, you have a problem. The simplest solution is to screw plug adapters into the ceiling fixture and run extension cords from there to other fixtures in the room, although some people find this unacceptably untidy.

(The problem isn't so bad in an old, high-ceilinged house with molding where you can hide the cord as in a modern apartment with low, bare ceilings.)

Another solution is to use one lamp as a control point for one or two other fixtures. You can buy a double light bulb socket, use one side for a bulb and screw a simple adapter into the other which allows you to plug in other lamps. If this double socket is then screwed into your existing lamp socket, the switch on the lamp will control the other fixtures you have plugged into it.

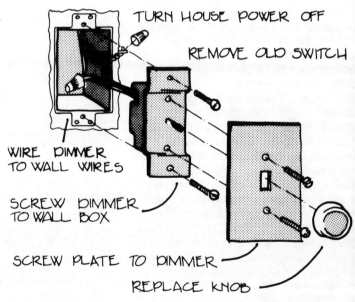

WALL DIMMER

TURN HOUSE POWER OFF

REMOVE OLD SWITCH

WIRE DIMMER TO WALL WIRES

SCREW DIMMER TO WALL BOX

SCREW PLATE TO DIMMER

REPLACE KNOB

Making Lamps

Lamp Wiring

If you are going to wire a lamp, read the introductory section to "home wiring" before you begin to follow the instructions here.

We have included a diagram indicating the main parts of a lamp socket. To wire a lamp, first make certain the cord is unplugged, or if the cord is directly attached to a ceiling or wall outlet, turn off the electricity to the whole house. Separate the socket parts by pressing where it says "press" and pulling the parts apart (a little prying with a sharp tool might be required). Cut the cord to the appropriate length, separate the two wires for about two inches, and strip 1/2 inch of insulation from each wire. Twist the strands of each of the two wires into its own tight bunch. Run the lamp cord through the cap and slide the cap up the cord and out of the way while you wire the rest of the socket. A small knot in each wire will keep pressure on the lamp cord from pulling the wires off the terminals. Bend each of the wires into a small loop; wrap each loop clockwise around one of the terminal screws in the socket assembly and tighten the screws down to hold it in place. Make sure all strands of wire are either

securely fastened under the screw or trimmed off. Slide the cardboard liner over the socket assembly so that it covers the electrical connections (never leave out the cardboard liner). Slide the metal barrel over the cardboard liner and push it over the cap until it fits together with a click.

Wiring a Plug

Make sure the electric cord you are working on is *not plugged in*. To install a male plug on the end of a cord, cut off the old plug plus an inch of cord to remove any weakened portion; split the insulation on the cord to create two inches of separated wires; strip 1/2 inch of insulation from each of the two wires. If the wires are multistranded, twist each bunch of strands into a tight unit. Push the cord through the plug. Form a loop on each wire so it will curl clockwise around each terminal screw (tightening the screws will then wrap the loop even tighter around the screw); tighten the terminal screws to hold the wires down securely.

For light appliances—radios, lamps—you can use a self-connecting plug like the one shown in the sketch. To install these, separate the insulated wires for a quarter of an inch, push the cord into the plug, and clamp the lever shut.

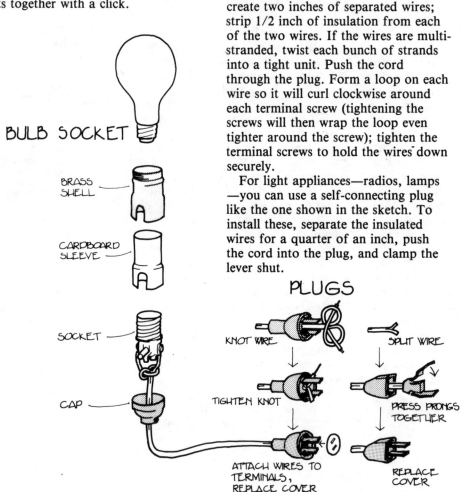

BULB SOCKET

BRASS SHELL

CARDBOARD SLEEVE

SOCKET

CAP

PLUGS

KNOT WIRE

SPLIT WIRE

TIGHTEN KNOT

PRESS PRONGS TOGETHER

ATTACH WIRES TO TERMINALS, REPLACE COVER

REPLACE COVER

Shades

One of the best things to do with shades is to do without them. You can buy lots of beautifully shaped light bulbs now that don't need shades if you can keep them dim enough. I find a dimmer is necessary with any bare bulb over 25 watts. Don't try to construct a standard shade holder out of wire; it's nearly impossible to get it right. Inexpensive stiff wire shade holders, ''harps,'' are available in lamp, hardware, dime, and department stores.

Shutter Shade

A very interesting shade idea from Harvey the Wizard (my private source of mystico-practical concepts) is to make a lamp box out of movable window shutters. The shutters allow you to let just the right amount of light out in each direction. The light filtering through the wooden slats creates a gentle, natural-wood effect. Put shutters on four sides for a hanging lamp. Attach the shutters to the top piece as shown in the diagram and line each corner with a piece of inside molding strip. If you leave the bottom open, it will emit enough light for reading or dining.

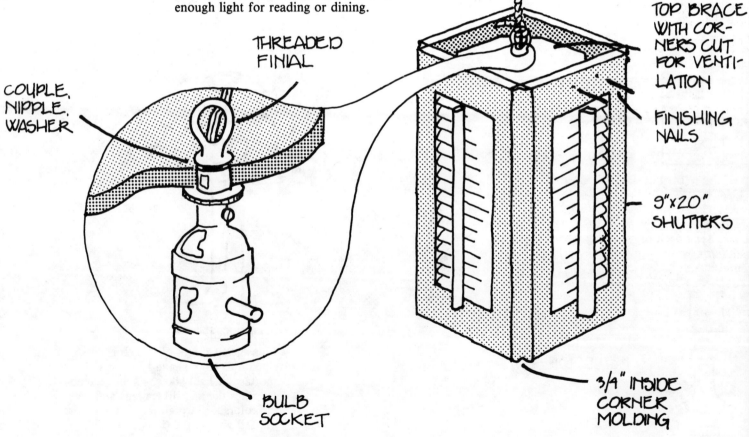

THREADED FINIAL

COUPLE. NIPPLE. WASHER

BULB SOCKET

TOP BRACE WITH CORNERS CUT FOR VENTILATION

FINISHING NAILS

9"x20" SHUTTERS

3/4" INSIDE CORNER MOLDING

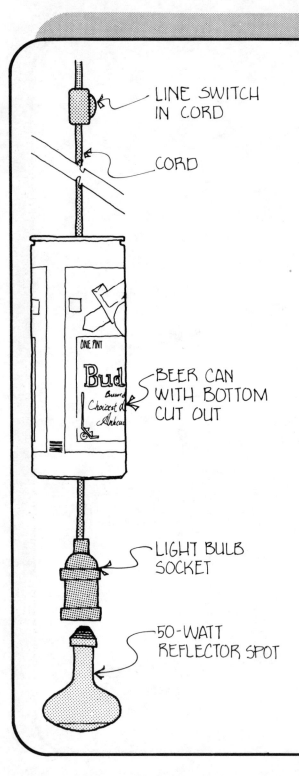

LINE SWITCH IN CORD

CORD

BEER CAN WITH BOTTOM CUT OUT

ONE PINT

Bud

Budweiser
Choicest
Anheuser

LIGHT BULB SOCKET

50-WATT REFLECTOR SPOT

Pop-top Downspot

As elegant a downlight as you could want. Wire a small, heavy-duty socket on the end of a white cord. Place a beer can with the bottom cut out over the socket (the center of the flip-top keyhole will let the cord out just right). Cut the can off to a length where the bulb is fully shielded. Insert a 50-watt reflector spot. Paint the can white, black, silver, or leave it Bud. Hang.

Pebble Shade

Translucent pieces of stone or glass, glued into lamp shade form, make a spectacular light show. Each piece concentrates the light like a lens and gives the colors a sharp glow. A crafts store will sell you all the parts you need.

Kitchen Shades

You can often get elegant shades from kitchen apparatus. A large funnel (shiny metal or translucent plastic) works fine, as does a deep mixing bowl. Light sparkling through the patterned holes of a colander is very pleasant. If you like kitchen things, go to two or three of your favorite kitchen stores—including at least one restaurant supply house—and look for things you can turn into lamps. Baskets make beautiful shades. A large dome-like basket from Korea costs only $4.

Traditional bamboo screen, the kind people use as awnings on their porches, makes good shade material. Cut two ends in any shape out of wood and wrap the bamboo around them. A section of bamboo screen, 6 by 2 feet, enough for two large shades, costs about $8.

BAMBOO SCREEN GLUED
TO PLYWOOD OR TRI-WALL-
CARDBOARD BRACES

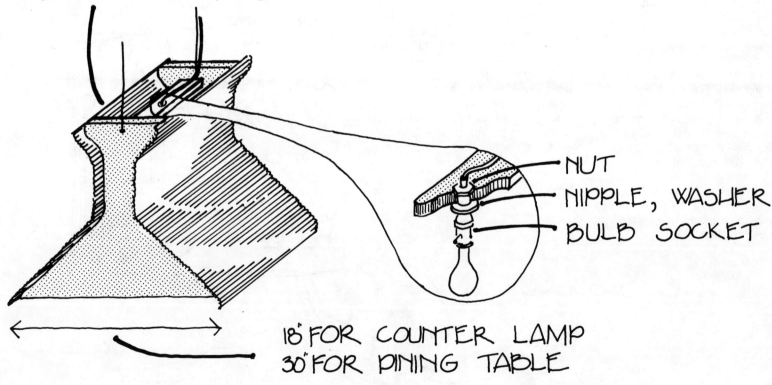

NUT

NIPPLE, WASHER

BULB SOCKET

18" FOR COUNTER LAMP
30" FOR DINING TABLE

Electrics

There are lots of good electrical parts on the market. Safety standards are high; just insist on Underwriters' Laboratory approved status for things you buy. Some hardware and variety stores have large selections of electrical parts. Visit a couple of them and look over their supplies—plugs, sockets, bulbs, etc.—to see what kinds of things are available. An electrical supply store is by far the best place to go once you have a purpose, however. Sketch up your contraption and ask the salesperson to help you get the parts right. A *lighting* supply store is useful for buying standard kinds of lamps at a discount—track lighting, industrial fixtures, etc. These are the stores that architects and interior decorators buy from, and many of them will give anyone off the street 25% off on anything in the store. They are not, however, very interested in helping you *find* the parts to build your own lamp, even though they have the fixings to make one for you in the back room, so know what you want before you go. One final note: When you are making a lamp, always put 10 feet of extension cord on it. The extra cost, 50¢, will be reimbursed a thousand times over in hassle-free locating.

Highlight

Would you believe a light to get you high . . . not by how it shines but by what it does to the air (more wizardry from Harvey). It uses a bulb which produces ozone (oxygen with an extra molecule) and makes the atmosphere like it is just before a storm, which makes the cilia of your lungs move faster, which is like a touch of hyperventilation on the sly. The bulb puts out ultraviolet rays and so should be shielded from direct view. The device sketched here hides the ozone-producing bulb behind a tin can. Use GE bulb #G4s11, sold over the counter as a germicidal (GE salesman are innocent of the bulb's hidden powers). Do not use more than three of these bulbs in an average-sized room, and you must wire a 40-watt appliance bulb *in series* with it to act as a ballast (see diagram). In the new, improved design shown here, the 40-watt bulb also acts as a vent to get more air circulating by the UV lamp. All the parts are standard and can be purchased at your local electrical supply store.

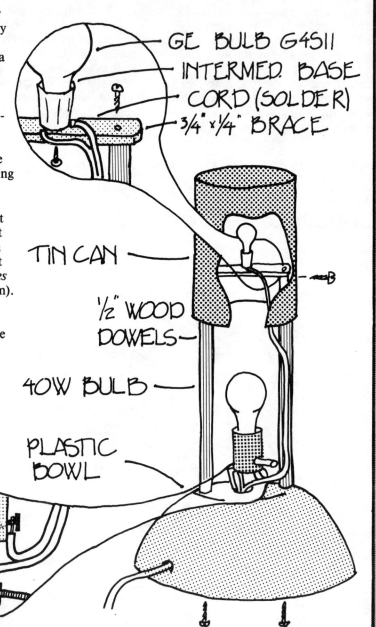

GE BULB G4S11
INTERMED. BASE
CORD (SOLDER)
3/4" x 1/4" BRACE

TIN CAN

1/2" WOOD DOWELS

40W BULB

PLASTIC BOWL

BULB SOCKET

BOWL

NUT

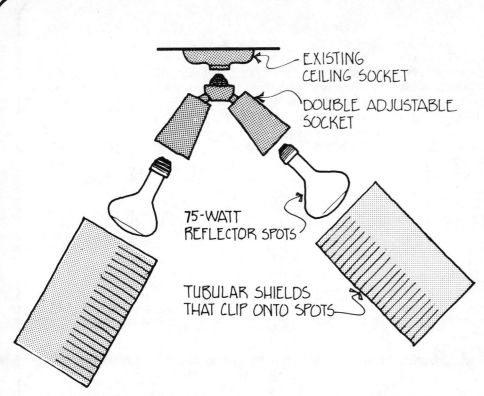

EXISTING CEILING SOCKET

DOUBLE ADJUSTABLE SOCKET

75-WATT REFLECTOR SPOTS

TUBULAR SHIELDS THAT CLIP ONTO SPOTS

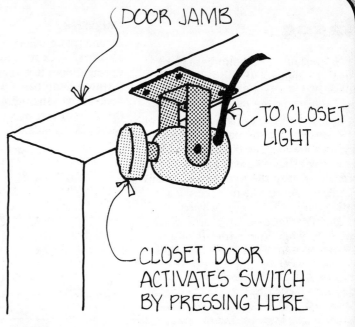

DOOR JAMB

TO CLOSET LIGHT

CLOSET DOOR ACTIVATES SWITCH BY PRESSING HERE

Instant Spots

Two simple electrical fittings will turn any ceiling fixture into instant adjustable spotlights. The first is a swivel socket that screws into the existing light socket (Swivelier makes the best one). Screw a reflector flood into the new socket and mount the second fitting on it—a black tubular shield that blocks extraneous light and gives the whole thing a mean, modern appearance ($4.50 per shield).

Closet Light

Here's a device you can buy at any electrical supply store. Properly installed, it turns the light bulb in your closet on when the door is open and off when the door is shut.

Bulbs

There are lots of bulbs to choose from these days. A long, thin bulb called the "display case bulb" is often useful in constructing your own lamps. Bulbs come in a variety of colors. Although some colors (green, blue, red) will radically reduce the amount of light you get, others (yellow and pink) are quite bright. Reflector floods will concentrate light for a spotlight effect. They come in sizes from 50 to 150 watts, and in growlights for your plants as well. Decorator bulbs come in candle flame and other shapes, with any quality flicker you could want. There is an entire line of small-base bulbs that use the same current as regular bulbs but are easier to wire in small configurations. Large, 5″-diameter bulbs are good for lamps without shades and come in clear filaments or white.

Bases

It is important for a lamp base to be properly weighted. If you have a choice, pick the heavier of two alternate bases (a frying pan instead of a pie tin). If you are using a container of some sort for a lamp base, fill it partway with gravel. The biggest problem in making a lamp base is getting the cord out of it in the right place. In this regard, an old candle-dripped wine bottle couldn't be worse. Always try to get the cord out of a lamp base down low, right where the lamp sits on the table. Jostling the cord will then pull the lamp sideways, not tip it over.

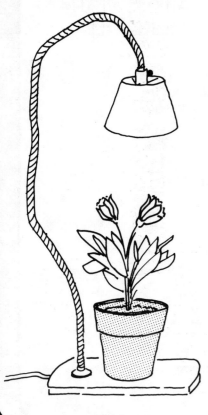

Cork Tree

A large piece of cork tree section, sold as a basket, costs only $6. Turned upside-down, it makes a beautifully textured lamp base. Another one, suspended over the bulb on a lamp harp ($1 at hardware and variety stores), serves as a shade.

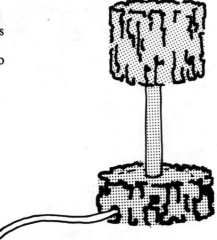

Plant Base

This base uses a potted plant to weigh it down. Anchor a 4-foot section of flexible gooseneck in a 6 by 10-inch piece of wood, curved at both ends. You can get gooseneck from old lamps at a flea market or an electrical supply store (call first, it's an unusual item). Get a porcelain socket fitted to the end of the gooseneck at the store. Put a plant light bulb in the socket and add a shade. Put an extra length of extension cord on it so you can move it where your plants want to be. You will always have one plant that is sufficiently starved for light, or the limelight, to be begging for the next turn.

Musical Light

If you are a music fan, make a lamp from a retired clarinet. You can get one that will polish up to a beautiful silver at a pawn shop for about $15. Glue or solder it to an overturned pewter plate; thread the cord through the instrument, and add a shade of translucent sheet music.

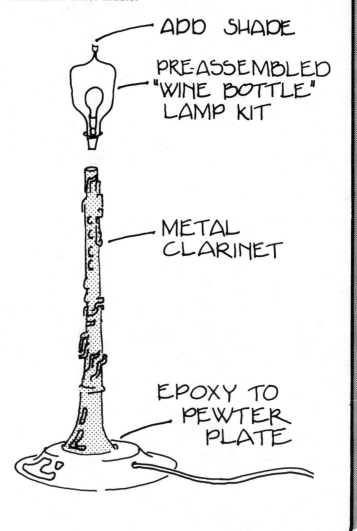

ADD SHADE

PRE-ASSEMBLED "WINE BOTTLE" LAMP KIT

METAL CLARINET

EPOXY TO PEWTER PLATE

Sewer Pipe

I have made lamps made of cast-iron sewer pipe junctions. The pieces are all about 6 inches in diameter, and come in a variety of evocative forms, as the sketches included here indicate. They are extremely heavy—good for lamp bases—but can get tippy if set in the wrong position. The only way to get a cord out the base is to mount the junction on a thin disk of wood drilled to let the cord out. Many states now allow plastic pipe fittings. If yours does, a local hardware or plumbing supply store will have a full line of these shapes—much easier to cut and drill for installation of electrical fittings.

CUTAWAY VIEW OF SEWER PIPE LIGHT

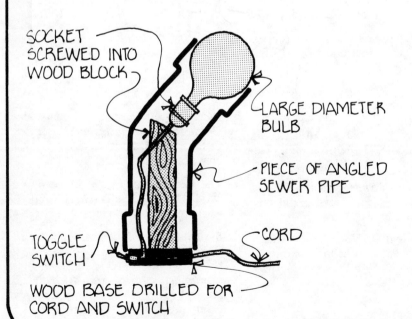

SOCKET SCREWED INTO WOOD BLOCK

LARGE DIAMETER BULB

PIECE OF ANGLED SEWER PIPE

CORD

TOGGLE SWITCH

WOOD BASE DRILLED FOR CORD AND SWITCH

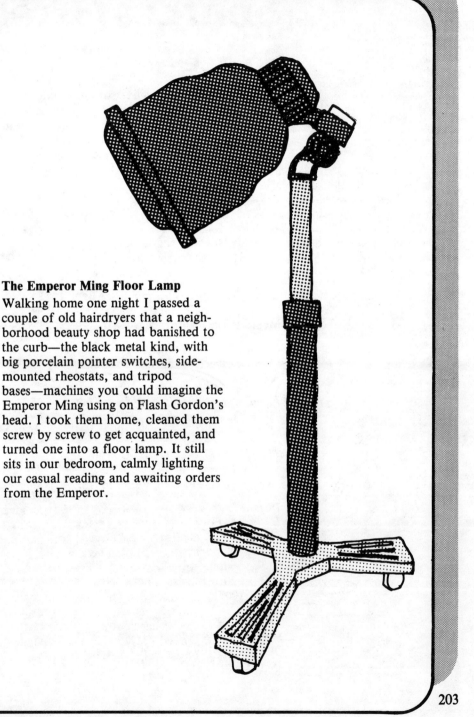

The Emperor Ming Floor Lamp

Walking home one night I passed a couple of old hairdryers that a neighborhood beauty shop had banished to the curb—the black metal kind, with big porcelain pointer switches, side-mounted rheostats, and tripod bases—machines you could imagine the Emperor Ming using on Flash Gordon's head. I took them home, cleaned them screw by screw to get acquainted, and turned one into a floor lamp. It still sits in our bedroom, calmly lighting our casual reading and awaiting orders from the Emperor.

Sources/Credits/Index

Sources

There are many good sources of information on understanding your living space and fixing it up. On this page are listed details concerning some of the best of these so you can find them at a bookstore or send away for them yourself. Prices are included, although these tend to change frequently. The fastest way to get a book, if your local bookstore doesn't have it in stock, is to write the publisher at the address listed here and enclose a check written for "no more than" the price listed plus two dollars (to cover postage and price increases). The publishing company can then fill in the precise amount on the check and mail the book without having to bill you first.

General

A Design Guide for Home Safety, U.S. Dept. of Housing and Urban Development, $1.50, U.S. Government Printing Office, Washington, D.C., 20402.

Easy to Make Furniture, Sunset Books, $2.95, Lane Publishing Company, Menlo Park, California, 94025.

Furniture in 24 Hours, Spiros Zakas, $6.95, Collier/MacMillan, 866 3rd Ave., New York, New York, 10022.

Handicapped at Home, Sydney Foott, $5.95, Quick Fox Books, 33 W. 60th St. New York, New York, 10023.

The House Book, Terence Conran, $30.00, Crown Publishers, 1 Park Ave., New York, New York, 10016.

Instant Furniture: Low-Cost, Well-Designed, Easy-To-Assembly Tables, Chairs, Couches, Beds, Desks and Storage Systems, Peter S. Stamberg, $7.95, Van Nostrand Reinhold Co., 450 W. 33rd St., New York, New York, 10001.

Lifespace: A New Approach to Home Design, Spiros Zakas, $15.00, Macmillan Publishing Co., 866 3rd Ave., New York, New York, 10022.

Exploring Your Awareness of Living Space

Body, Memory and Architecture, Kent C. Bloomer and Charles W. Moore, $6.95, Yale University Press, 302 Temple St., New Haven, Connecticut, 06520.

Experiences in Visual Thinking, Robert H. McKim, $9.95, Wadsworth Publishing Co., Belmont, California, 94002.

Fantasy Encounter Games, Herbert A. Otto, $1.95, Harper and Row, 10 E. 53rd St. New York, New York, 10022.

The Place of Houses: Three Architects Suggest Ways to Build and Inhabit Houses, Charles Moore, Gerald Allen, Donlyn Lyndon, $17.95, Holt Rinehart and Winston, 383 Madison Ave., New York, New York, 10017.

The Poetics of Space, Gaston Bachelard, $4.95, Beacon Press, 25 Beacon St., Boston, Mass. 02108.

The Sociology of Housework, Ann Oakley, $3.95, Pantheon/Random House, 201 E. 50th St., New York, New York, 10022.

Synectics, The Practice of Creativity, George Prince, $1.95, Macmillan Publishing Co., 866 3rd Ave., New York, New York, 10022.

Taking Part: A Workshop Approach to Collective Creativity, Lawrence Halprin and Jim Burns, The MIT Press, 28 Carleton St., Cambridge, Mass., 02142.

Living In One Room, Jon Naar and Molly Siple, $5.95, Vintage Books/Random House, 201 E. 50th St., New York, New York, 10022.

Nomadic Furniture, $4.95, and *Nomadic Furniture 2,* $4.95, James Hennesey and Victor Papanek, Pantheon Books/Random House, 201 E. 50th St., New York, New York, 10022.

Putting it All Together: A Consumer Guide to Home Furnishings, Peggie Collins, $6.95, Scribners, 597 5th Ave., New York, New York, 10017.

The Responsive House, Edited by Edward Allen, $9.95, The MIT Press, 28 Carleton St., Cambridge, Mass. 02142.

Systems of Living Space: A Guide to Building Nests for People, Desk Lofts, Swing Set Bookshelves and Other Components for Liberated Living, James Provey, $6.95, Henry Regnery Company, 180 N. Michigan Ave., Chicago, Illinois, 60601.

Materials and Techniques

The Apartment Carpenter, Howard Fink, $3.95, Quick Fox Books, 33 W. 60th St., New York, New York, 10023.

Basic Home Repairs, Sunset Books, $2.95, Lane Publishing W., Menlo Park, California, 94025.

Calico Corners Guide to Do-It-Yourself Decorating With Fabrics, Jan Jessup, Calico Corners Inc., Bancroft Mills, Drawer 670, Wilmington Delaware, 19899.

The Catalogue of American Catalogues: How To Buy Practically Everything By Mail in the United States. Maria Elena De La Iglesia, $4.95, Random House, 201 E. 50th St., New York, New York, 10022.

Country Floors Tile Catalogue, $2.00, Country Floors Inc., 300 E. 61st St., New York, New York, 10021.

Fieldcrest Decorating Digest, Judy Lindahl, $3.00 from Judy Lindahl, 6705 N. Commercial St., Portland, Oregon, 97217.

The Further Adventures of Cardboard Carpentry, How To Build Furniture with Tri-Wall Cardboard, George Cope and Phyllis Morrison, Workshop For Learning Things, 5 Bridge St., Watertown, Massachusetts, 02172.

Historic Textiles Reproduced for Today, Brunchwig and Fils, Inc., $1.00, 410 62nd St., New York, New York.

Making Your Place a Home, Kevin Ruedisueli, $6.95, Quick Fox Books, 33 W. 60th St. New York, New York, 10023.

Preventive Maintenance For Your House or Apartment: A Money-Saving Guide on How to Spot Trouble and Get It Cured Before It Happens, Hubbard Cobb, $4.95, Random House/Pequot Press, 201 E. 50th St., New York, New York, 10022.

A Reverence for Wood, Eric Sloane, $7.95, Harper and Row Publishers, Scranton, Pennsylvania, 18512.

The Sensuous Gadgeteer: Bringing Tools and Materials to Life, Bill Abler, $3.95, Running Press, 38 South 19th St., Philadelphia, Pennsylvania, 19103.

Inspirations

About the House, W.H. Auden, Random House, 201 E. 50th St., New York, New York, 10011.

All Color Book of Art Deco, Dan Klein, $2.95, Crescent Books, 419 Park Avenue South, New York, New York, 10016.

All Color Book of Art Nouveau, Geoffrey Warren, $2.95, Crescent Books, 419 Park Ave. South, New York, New York, 10016.

All Their Own: People and the Places They Build, Jan Wampler, $9.95, Halsted/John Wiley, 605 3rd Ave., New York, New York, 10016.

American Album: Rare Photographs Collected by the Editors of American Heritage, $5.95, Ballantine Books, 201 E. 50th St., New York, New York, 10011.

Behind the Picture Window, Bernard Rudovsky, available in libraries only.

Carl Larsson's Home, Karl-Erik Granath, $6.95, Addison-Wesley Publishers, Jacob Way, Reading Massachusetts, 01867.

Chairs: A Pictorial History of the Chair Representing Every Style and Period. Hart Picture Archives, $5.95, Hart Publishing Co., 15 W. 4th St., New York, New York, 10012.

Converted Into Houses: 33 Uniquely Imaginative Homes Created From Unconventional Structures, Charles A. Fracchia and Jeremiah O. Bragstad, $6.95, Penguin Books, 625 Madison Ave., New York, New York, 10022.

Handmade Houses: A Guide to the Woodbutcher's Art, Art Boericke and Barry Shapiro, $6.95, Addison-Wesley Publishers, Jacob Way, Reading Massachusetts, 01867.

Living Places, Herbert H. Wise, Jeffrey Friedman-Weiss, $6.95, Quick Fox Books, 33 W. 60th St. New York, New York, 10023.

Mechanization Takes Command: A Study of the Evolution of Mechanization in the Last Century and a Half, Its Effects on Modern Civilization, and Its Historical and Philosophical Implications, Siegfried Giedion, $4.95, W.W. Norton and Co., 500 5th Ave., New York, New York, 10036.

Old House Plans: Two Centuries of American Domestic Architecture, Compiled by Lawrence Grow, $4.95, Universe Books, 381 Park Avenue South, New York, New York, 10016.

Shelter I ($6.00) and *Shelter II* ($9.50), two books from Shelter Publications, a nonprofit educational corporation formed for the purposes of providing research, design and education in the fields of housing and the building crafts; cataloging and preserving traditional as well as innovative construction techniques; maintaining a network of contributors; and disseminating information. P.O.B. 279, Bolinas, California, 94924.

The Streamlined Decade, Donald J. Bush, $7.95, George Brazilier, 1 Park Ave., New York, New York, 10016.

Talk to Me of Windows: An Informal History, F. Palmer Cook, $6.95, A.S. Barnes and Company, Box 421, Cranbury, New Jersey, 08512.

The Tasteful Interlude, American Interiors Through the Camera's Eye, 1860-1917, William Seale, $20.00, Praeger Publishers, 111 4th Ave., New York, New York, 10003.

Victorian Houses: A Treasury of Lesser-Known Examples, Edmund V. Gillon Jr. and Clay Lancaster, $4.00, Dover Publications Inc., 180 Varick St. New York, New York, 10014.

Bedrooms

The Bed and Bath Book, Terence Conran, $30.00, Crown Publishers, 1 Park Ave., New York, New York, 10016.

Dream Power, Ann Faraday, $6.95, Coward McCann and Geoghegan, 200 Madison Ave., New York, New York, 10016.

The Dream Collector, Arthur Tress, $3.95, Avon Books, 959 8th Ave., New York, New York, 10019.

Gramp: A Man Ages and Dies. The Extraordinary Record of One Family's Encounter with the Reality of Dying, Mark Jury and Dan Jury, Grossman/Viking Publishers, 625 Madison Ave., New York, New York, 10022.

Life After Life, Raymond Moody, $1.95, Bantam Books, 666 5th Ave., New York, New York, 10019.

Naturebirth, Danae Brook, $3.95, Pantheon Books, 201 E. 50th St., New York, New York, 10022.

Pamphlets on rebirthing from The Institute of Natal Therapy, 3 East 80th St., New York, New York, 10021.

The Sleep Book: Current Research, Dream Interpretation, Folklore, Fantasy and Myth, Relating to the Mystery of Sleep, Shirley Motter Linde and Louis M. Savary, $5.95, Harper and Row, 10 E. 53rd St., New York, New York, 10022.

Spiritual Midwifery, Ina May Gaskin, $8.50, The Book Publishing Company, The Farm, Summertown, Tennessee, 38483.

Bathrooms

The Bathroom, Alexander Kira, $7.95, Viking Press, 625 Madison Ave., New York, New York, 10022.

Bathroom Ideas, Hudson Home Improvement Staff, $4.95, Bantam Books, 666 5th Ave., New York, New York, 10019.

Clean and Decent, Lawrence Wright, available in libraries only.

How To Build, Maintain and Enjoy Your Own Hot Tubs, Leon Elder, $4.95, Vintage Books/Random House, 201 E. 50th St., New York, New York, 10022.

Planning Your Bathrooms, Anthony Snow and Graham Hopewell, $4.95, Quick Fox Books, 33 W. 60th St., New York, New York, 10023.

The Sauna Book, Tom Johnson and Tim Miller, $7.95, Harper and Row, 10 E. 53rd St., New York, New York, 10022.

Watteau: A Lady at Her Toilet: Art in Context, Donald Posner, $7.95, Viking Press, 625 Madison Ave., New York, New York, 10022.

The Well Body Book, Mike Samuels and Hal Bennet, $5.95, Random House, 201 E. 50th St., New York, New York, 10022.

Living Rooms

Sunset Ideas for Leisure Rooms, A Sunset Book, $2.45, Lane Publishing Co., Menlo Park, California, 94025.

Super Living Rooms, Emily Malino, $4.95, Random House, 201 E. 50th St., New York, New York, 10022.

Kitchens

The Kitchen Book, Terence Conran, $30.00, Crown Publishers Inc., 1 Park Ave., New York, New York, 10016.

One Bowl, Don Gerrard, $1.45, Random House/Bookworks, 201 E. 50th St., New York, New York, 10022.

Planning and Remodeling Kitchens, A Sunset Book, $2.45, Lane Publishing Co., Menlo Park, California, 94025.

Credits

The Psychologist's Eat Anything Diet, Leonard Pearson and Lillian R. Pearson, $1.75, Popular Library, 1515 Broadway, New York, New York, 10036.

Children's Places

Catalogue, Child Life Play Specialties Inc., 55 Whitney St., Holliston, Massachusetts, 01756.

Children's Rooms and Play Yards, A Sunset Book, $2.95, Lane Publishing Co., Menlo Park California, 94025.

Housebuilding for Children: Six Different Houses That Children Can Build by Themselves, Les Walker, $10.00, The Overlook Press, Lewis Hollow Rd., Woodstock, New York, 12498.

How to Make Children's Furniture and Play Equipment, Mario Dal Fabbro, $7.95, McGraw Hill, 121 Avenue of the Americas, New York, New York, 10036.

The First Three Years of Life, Burton L. White, $4.95, Avon Books, 959 Eighth Ave., New York, New York, 10019.

Making Children's Furniture and Play Structures, Bruce Palmer, $3.95, Workman Pub. Co., 231 E. 51st St., New York, New York, 10022.

Toy Book, Stephen Caney, $3.95, Workman Pub. Co., 231 E. 51st St., New York, New York, 10022.

Cover photo and p. 8: Sam Sweezy; p. 11: *Window Gardening,* Henry T. Williams; p. 13: 1. *The Decorator and Furnisher,* 2. Professor Ernst Lichtblau, Vienna, 3. Plumber's advertisement, Boston, 1850, 4. Piano-bed, 1866; p. 14: 1. *Old English Cottages,* Charles Holme, The Studio, London, 1906, 2. *Ville Casetti,* Alessandro Lissoni, 1949, 3. *Historie de l'habitation,* Violette-le-Duc; p. 15: 1. *The Wilderness Cabin,* Calvin Rutstrum, 1961. 2. *Examples of American Domestic Architecture,* J.C. Stevens, 1889 ; p. 17: A home on the Tennessee, *The Homes of America;* pp. 20-21: A.T. Andreas, *Illustrated Historical Atlas of the State of Iowa, 1875;* p. 27: author's drawing; p. 28: Arthur Rackham, "When night was come and the shop shut up," from *Tales of Hans Christian Anderson,* reprinted in *Arthur Rackham,* David Larkin ed., Peacock Press; p. 30: photo, Jim Harrison; p. 32: The Ring Biscuit, engraving by Bertony, 1783, after Jean Honoré Fragonard, courtesy Bibliothèque Nationale; p. 33: Sleep photography, copyright Theodore Spagna; p. 35: "Seein' Things," Maxfield Parrish; p. 37: Photo copyright Mark and Daniel Jury, from *Gramp,* Grossman Publishers; p. 39: Lady Barker, "The Bedroom and Boudoir," 1878; p. 40: Paul Woodroffe, *Humpty Dumpty and Other Songs;* p. 41: Camera Press Limited; p. 46: 1. Sheraton Bed, 1791-94, 2. the Andrews' Improved Parlour Folding Bed, 1885, 4. American matrimonial bed, 1850; p. 47: 1. Van Ravestyn, from The New Interior Decoration, Dorothy Todd and Raymond Mortimer, Charles Scribner, 1929; 2. A French *lit clos;* Museum für sächsische Volkskunst, Dresden; 4. *Japanese Homes and Their Surrounds,* Edmund S. Morse, Ticknor and Co., 1886; p. 58: 1. Joseph Nash, *The Mansions of England in the Olden Time,* The Studio, 1906, 2. Francesco Colonna, "Hyperotomachia," Venice, 1499, 3. Byron Collection, Museum of the City of New York; p. 59: 1. Professor Ernst Lichtblau, Vienna, 2. Mamhead House, Mamhead, South Devon; 3. Atelier Martine, prior to

1925, Walker Publishing Co. Inc.; p. 64: copyright John Pearson, from his book *Magic Doors* published by Addison-Wesley Publishing Co.; p. 66: 1. A radiant heat bath patented in 1900, 2. Shower for the treatment of abdominal maladies, 1860, 3. Luca Pulci, *Driadeo d'Amore,* 1506; p. 67: Sweat tent of the Mandan tribe, George Catlin; p. 68: Le Soir, P.A. Boudouin, courtesy Bibliothèque Nationale, Paris; p. 69: Bathroom in Boughton House, Northamptonshire; p. 70: late 15th century illustration; p. 79: 1. Kohler Company Catalogue, 2. Medical Rain Bath for Medical Purposes, France, 1860, 3. from *Gems of American Architecture,* 1935, the L.A. Vitorie Co., 4. Edmund S. Morse, *Japanese Homes and Their Surrounds,* Ticknor and Co., 1886; p. 80: 1. Photograph by Richard Einzig, 2. American Standard; p. 90: Chevrolet backing through a bookcase, Philip Garner, Ant Farm, 1976; p. 93: Joseph Nash, *The Mansions of England in the Olden Time,* The Studio, 1906, 2. Fat Fau's House, *American Architect and Building News,* Feb., 1876; p. 94: 1. Vardagsrum, i förmöget 80-talshem, 2. Mies van der Rohe, The Tugendhat House, 3. Henry Edward Creiger, Architect, *Architectural Record,* October, 1904; p. 97: Humoristisk deklamation, oljemålning av Knut Ekwall; p. 99: 1. One-Piece Duchesse, Mathieu Liard, *Recueil des Petits Meubles,* Paris, 1762, 2. American Kangaroo Sofa, Virginia, 1830's, 3. French borne, early 1880's, Havard, *Dictionnaire de L'Ameublement,* 4. German Chair, *L'Art Pour Tous,* Vol. 39; p. 100: 1. Advertisement for one of a series of "pulsating health chairs," courtesy Bella C. Landauer Collection, New York Historical Society, 2. One of the winners of a chair design competition sponsored by the San Diego Chapter of the AIA, a "wearable walking chair" of aluminum with nylon webbing by Ralph Henniger of Scottsdale, Arizona, 3. A mechanized hammock, patent number 495,532,18, April 1893, 4. A patented dentist's chair from 1879, 5. An inflatable chair, Design Council, London;

Index

p. 101: 1. Peter Stamberg, *Instant Furniture,* Van Nostrand Reinhold, 2. Huddle-furniture by H.U.D.D.L.E., 3416 Wesley St., Culver City, California, 90230, 3. Edmund S. Morse, *Japanese Homes and Their Surrounds,* Ticknor and Co., 1886, 4. Chair occupied by the chairman of the Republican National Convention, 1860, *Harper's;* p. 120: Freedom From Want, Norman Rockwell; Queen Victoria's Larder, Windsor Castle, The Mansell Collection, 42 Linden Gardens, London, W 2; p. 123: from "The Christmas Book," a Peacock Press/Bantam Book, copyright 1975, Bantam Books Inc.; p. 124: Carl Larsson, Breakfast Under the Big Birch, The National Swedish Art Museum; p. 127: Joseph Nash, *The Mansions of England in the Olden Time,* The Studio, 1906; p. 128: photo, Erwin Smith Collection, The Library of Congress; p. 129: 1. The Hoosier Kitchen Cabinet, 2. Sears Roebuck Catalogue, 1911; p. 133: *L'Année Industrielle,* Paris, 1887; p. 146: Illustration courtesy of Carl W. Drepperd; p. 147: 1. Professor Josef Hoffman, 2. Kitchen in the basement of the James Henry Smith residence, McKim, Mead and White architects; p. 152: photo, Randolph Trabold; p. 155: photo, author; p. 156: drawing by Alex Sagov; p. 163: 1. Photo, author, 2. *The House Book,* Terence Conran, 3. Child Life Play Specialties Inc., Holliston, Mass., 4. Placewares, 13 Walden St., Concord, Massachusetts, 01742; p. 178: photo, author; p. 181: engraving, Gustav Doré; *New Light on Old Lamps,* Dr. Larry Freeman, Century House, Watkins Glen; p. 191: photo, author; p. 192: *New Light on Old Lamps,* Dr. Larry Freeman, Century House, Watkins Glen; p. 193: 1. photo, author, reproduction, Peter Lorenz, 2. photo, author, 3. Lamp designed by Ron Alex, photo, Sam Sweezy, 4. photo, author; Back Cover: photo, Nick Wheeler; Drawing, Kay Nielsen, *East of the Sun and West of the Moon,* Hodder and Stoughton.